SPADEWORK
IN ARCHÆOLOGY

The jewelled head-dress of a court lady from the Royal Cemetery at Ur

3560

SPADEWORK
IN ARCHÆOLOGY

by

SIR LEONARD WOOLLEY

PHILOSOPHICAL LIBRARY
NEW YORK

Published 1953 by the Philosophical Library, Inc.,
15 East 40th Street, New York 16, N.Y.
All Rights Reserved

Printed in Great Britain for the Philosophical Library, Inc.
by Latimer, Trend & Co. Ltd., Plymouth

CONTENTS

LIST OF ILLUSTRATIONS

To

Hamoudi—Mohammed ibn Sheikh Ibrahim,
Sheikh of the Damalka tribe—a life-long
helper and friend

I have to express my thanks to the Trustees of the British Museum for the use of the Carchemish photographs, Plates 7, 8 and 9; to the Trustees of the University Museum, Philadelphia, for that of the Karanòg photographs, Plates 2 and 3; and to the joint Trustees for that of the Ur photographs, the frontispiece and Plate 10.

INTRODUCTION

I HAVE seldom been more surprised than I was
when—it is nearly fifty years ago now—the Warden
of New College told me that he had decided that I
should be an archæologist. It is true that I had taken
a course in Greek sculpture for my degree, but so had
lots of other undergraduates. Because of their bearing
on Homer I had read Schliemann's romantic account
of his discoveries, the Treasure of Priam at Troy and
the Tomb of Agamemnon at Mycenae, and like everyone else I was rather vaguely aware that Flinders
Petrie was, year after year, making history in Egypt
and that Arthur Evans was unearthing the Palace of
Minos in Crete; but all this was at best only background knowledge and the idea of making a life study
of it had never occurred to me. And I must confess
that when the prospect did present itself, not as a mere
idea to be played with (for one did not lightly play
with the Warden's decisions) but as something definite
and settled, I was not altogether happy about it. For
me, and I think for the Warden too, archæology meant
a life spent inside a museum, whereas I preferred the
open air and was more interested in my fellow men
than in dead-and-gone things; I could never have
guessed that after a short—and invaluable—apprenticeship in the Ashmolean Museum at Oxford, all my
work was to be out of doors and, for the most part, out

of England; and I had yet to learn that the real end of archæology is, through the dead-and-gone things, to get at the history and the minds of dead-and-gone men.

Although in this book I deal with my own experiences, and that in the order of their happening, I am not writing an autobiography, nor even giving an

Map of Syria and the Eastern Mediterranean

account of archæological discoveries, although such do of course play their part in it; what I want to do is to show how very alive the science of archæology is. As in all science there is in it a vast amount of laborious detail which is of interest only to the worker; there are any number of false trails that have to be followed and dropped when they are proved false, conclusions that at first seem absolute are later found to be but partially true; the dull routine, the mistakes and the disappointments are part of the day's work, and there is no need to talk about them. Spreading mortar and laying on it brick after brick would be a dull job if it were an end in itself, but it is the essential process of building, and it results in what may be a great work of art; so out of our broken pots and pans we hope to build up a vision of a vanished world. To that vision everything contributes, the pots and pans themselves, their position in the ground, their association, all that, but also the country with all its natural features and the men who to-day live in it and work for you; one can neglect none of these if the past is really to be recalled to life, and it is the all-roundness of field archæology that makes it the fascinating study which I have found it to be.

Chapter One

FIRST EXPERIENCES

England, Nubia and Egypt

MY first experience of digging was at Corbridge in Northumberland, and I know only too well that the work there would have scandalized, and rightly scandalized, any British archæologist of to-day. It was however typical of what was done forty-five years ago, when field archæology was, comparatively speaking, in its infancy and few diggers in this country thought it necessary to follow the example of that great pioneer, Pitt Rivers. *The Northumberland County History* was being written and the writers wanted to know more about the Roman station at Corbridge, so proposed a small-scale dig to settle the character of the site. The committee naturally appealed to Professor Haverfield as the leading authority on Roman Britain and he, as he had intended to take a holiday on the Roman Wall, agreed to supervise the excavations. Somebody, of course, had to be put in charge of the work and because I was an Assistant Keeper in the Ashmolean Museum my qualifications were, in the eyes of an Oxford professor, *ipso facto* satisfactory. Haverfield arranged with Sir Arthur Evans, the Keeper, that I should go to Corbridge. In point of fact I had never so much as

14

seen an excavation, I had never studied archæological methods even from books (there were none
at that time dealing with the subject), and I had not
any idea of how to make a survey or a ground-plan;
apart from being used to handling antiquities in a
museum, and that only for a few months, I had no
qualifications at all. I was very anxious to learn, and
it was a disappointment to me that Haverfield only
looked in at the excavations one day in the week and
then was concerned only to know what had been
found—I don't think that he ever criticized or corrected anything. Fortunately it had been arranged
that the plans should be done by W. H. Knowles, an
architect with very wide archæological experience,
and he not only relieved me of an impossible responsibility but gave me practical lessons in planning and
surveying, the only lessons on the subject that I have
ever had, and I am proportionately grateful to him.

My other helpers were amateurs like myself. Admit-
tedly the first season was but experimental; it lasted
for no more than five weeks and at no time did we
employ more than nine labourers; but it was so far
successful that a committee was formed to carry on
the excavations with a view to the complete uncover-
ing of the site. In 1907, therefore, I found myself in
charge of a really important dig, being still, of course,
quite unfitted for the task, and again my helpers, apart
from Mr. Knowles, were as inexperienced as I. But
the work went very merrily, I had beginner's luck,
which pleased everyone, and we were all, I think,
happily unconscious of the low standard of our performance, nor did anyone from outside suggest that
it might have been better; actually, of course, it did

improve with time, as both we and our workmen
learned our job.

The most dramatic discovery was that of the Corbridge Lion. We had found a stone cistern attached to
a large Roman building and in the course of the morning had cleared about half of the earth filling. It happened to be a Saturday and after my lunch I went to the
bank to draw money for the men's wages, and as I was
kept waiting for some while, the interval was over and
work had started again before I got back to the site.
As I came near I saw all the men crowded closely together by the side of the cistern, and wondered what
had happened; only when I was close up did they
separate this way and that, and between the two groups
of them I saw the stone lion grinning over the fallen
stag. They had lifted it out of the cistern (which of
course was wrong of them) and had deliberately staged
a surprise for me, and a fine surprise it was, but what
struck me at once was that the men were even more
excited than I was. The actual finder, who was not
Tyneside but a "foreigner", an East Anglian curiously unlike his fellow miners, a big fellow with a
round fair face and a fair round belly, was shaking as
if with an ague and quite incoherent; when he recovered enough to speak at all in answer to my question "Did *you* find that?" he could only stammer "Yes,
sir, and you'll never believe me, but it's God's own
truth, when I first saw that there lion he had a blooming orange in 'is mouth!". I gave him a cigarette and
told him to sit down and smoke it, and afterwards he
didn't seem to remember what he had said. For the
other men, after the first excitement of discovery, the
main interest was based on local pride; was the lion

Terra-cotta relief from
Corbridge nicknamed
"The Roman Harry
Lauder"

The Corbridge Lion

better than the Hexham horseman? Hexham Abbey
boasted a famous Roman tombstone (looted originally
from Corbridge) on which is represented a Roman
cavalryman, and for Corbridge that was a thorn in
the flesh. I pointed out that the horseman was only in
low relief whereas the lion was a free-standing sculpture in the round, so everybody agreed that it must be
the better of the two, and that evening we drank the
lion's health in the Corbridge inn.

It was this incident that taught me how essential it
is to get the men personally interested in the work.
Our men, mostly coalminers, had taken on the job
simply for want of a better and, at the start, did not
disguise the fact that they thought it rather silly and
certainly not one that called for hard work; gradually,
by dint of explaining and discussing things, we got
them to understand what we were after, and in proportion as they became keen their work got better and
better, and before the season ended we had a really
fine gang.

Archæological digging requires a lot of skill, and
skill directed by intelligence. That does not mean that
the labourers supply the skill and the director the intelligence—which simply would not work—but that
the two qualities should be shared by all alike. The
men are not just "hands", they are fellow-workers.
The director ought to have a more than theoretical
knowledge of the manual technique of digging; ideally
he should be as clever with his tools and his fingers as
any of his men, he ought to be able to show them how
a thing should be done (and convince them that his is
the right way) though he then leaves them to carry on.
And the men ought to have not only the pride of the

expert in doing a job well but also a personal interest
in the object which the job is to achieve; if they can
take a scientific interest in it, so much the better, but
if they can't do that they must take a personal interest
of some sort or other. That is why in the Middle East
one gives *baksheesh*. The Arab or Egyptian peasant is
generally illiterate and has no historical background
whatsoever—you might say less than none, for with
most of them human history begins with the Prophet,
whenever that may be, and if a thing is said to be
older it belongs to "the times of ignorance" and ought
to be destroyed in the interests of piety. An antiquity
therefore gives him no pleasure at all, but obviously it
pleases you. Now you engaged him to dig, and you pay
him for digging, but the finding of objects is a matter
of luck, quite outside the contract, and if he finds
something he ought, he considers, to share in the luck;
so you can keep the object and, since there's nothing
better than money, it's only decent that you should
equalize matters with a cash payment. In Egypt the
failure to give *baksheesh* meant that the bulk of the
small antiquities found in the course of the work never
came into your possession at all but were hidden by
the workmen and sold to the ubiquitous dealers. The
Arab is more intelligent and less mercenary than the
Egyptian, but with him too the reward system is essential. In the first week's work that I did at Ur we began
to find graves containing, among other things, necklaces with beads of various materials including gold.
It was very noticeable that if one of the two foremen
or myself saw the signs of a grave appearing and got
down and cleared it ourselves there would generally
be three or four gold beads in a necklace, but if a

workman kept quiet and finished the grave withou
our interference there would be no gold beads at all.
The gold was being stolen. I had told the men that
there would be *baksheesh* for all finds, but they didn't
really believe it, and the sight of the precious metal
was too much for them. We said nothing, but made a
great show of noting against a worker's name the gold
beads which we (not he) had unearthed in his patch
of ground, and on Saturday, the first pay day, he received for each bead so recorded between two and
three times what I calculated would be paid by a local
goldsmith. On the Sunday, as my scouts informed me,
there was an unusual influx of my men to the market
town of Nasiriyeh to which their women-folk had been
making visits during the week, and on Monday there
turned up in the dig an astonishing number of gold
beads, redeemed from the goldsmiths. Again we made
no comment but duly paid the *baksheesh* for them, and
then shifted the whole gang to another part of the site
where temptation was not so likely to arise. A few
weeks later Hamoudi, my foreman, explained the
whole thing to the men with due emphasis on the
moral, that honesty is the best policy; he further insisted that our treatment of them was a proof of real
friendship and however meritorious it might be to steal
from an enemy, tribal morality forbade stealing from
a friend, therefore in future there would be no thefts
from the dig. To this all the men agreed, and though
in the course of the excavations we unearthed thousands of pounds' worth of gold nothing was stolen, nor
did we have to take any special precautions for its safe
keeping. At Carchemish, where conditions were more
lawless and the first rule we had to make was that no

weapons might be carried on the dig, we supplemented the money *baksheesh* by a salute of revolver shots (fired by the foreman Hamoudi) corresponding to the value of the discovery; it was the natural vent for excitement and it conferred honour on the finder of the object, so much so that a pick-man would boast of the number of shots that he had had in a season long after he had forgotten the amount of cash that he had received. Of course in England no such system is possible, the question of theft need not be considered and a cash payment for finds might even be regarded by the men as invidious, but there are times when an extra incentive is not without its value for the work. I was once digging a Late Celtic cemetery in a gravel-pit at Swarling near Canterbury; the weather was very hot, the gravel was as hard as concrete and the graves were few and far between; there was a natural tendency to slack, and slackness means the waste of one's small funds. So if I could detect in the soil any sign implying that there might be a grave close by I would bet the workman a shilling or so to nothing that he wouldn't find anything within the next hour; or, if there were no signs, start a sweepstake (to which I was the only contributor) for the benefit of the first man to find anything at all; the element of sport was quite enough to counteract the dullness of the job and to add 50 per cent to the output.

In the actual finds the British workman is prepared to be quite as interested as is the professional archæologist, and the more one can encourage that the better. Sometimes one's sense of superiority gets a rude jolt. At Swarling we had turned up a fragment of a millstone and I seized the opportunity to explain the character of the primitive circular quern, with a draw-

ing to illustrate my description. "Ah yes," remarked
one of the men, "the sort of thing they use in south
Palestine. Of course, further north they've got a different sort, a bit saddle-shaped, but in Greece it's the
round kind again," and I was abashed to learn that
during his service in the Middle East in the first war
he had made a study of peasant crafts—"I've got a
fine collection of picture postcards of them all," he
added.

Besides the Corbridge Lion, Corstopitum gave us
that season some inscriptions, including a fine one of
the emperor Hadrian, remains of the great granaries
in which were stored the rations for the troops manning the wall, a fountain unlike anything else known
in Roman Britain, and a fourth-century potter's shop
with the different sorts of pots grouped according to
type, and a number of coins, all close together, representing the shopkeeper's till. This last discovery was
rather a controversial one, for some of the pottery, red-
glazed Roman *terra sigillata* manufactured for the most
part in southern Gaul or on the Rhine, was supposed
to be about a hundred and fifty years older than the
date given by the coins. Altogether it was a great success and I was very pleased with myself and with the
prospects that an excavator's life seemed to hold out.
I said something in this vein to H. E. Craster (afterwards Bodley's Librarian at Oxford) who was helping
me with the coins, and I well recall his answer, which
restored my sense of proportion; he said, "Yes, a very
successful dig. I don't think that anyone would now
write a really detailed history of Roman Britain without putting in a footnote to the effect that 'there was
also a Roman station at Corbridge'." It was a salutary

lesson. And almost at the same time I had another of the same sort. Among other work in the Ashmolean Museum I had had to arrange and catalogue a small collection of tapestries from Egypt, patterned pieces woven in the Coptic and early Moslem periods. At that time hardly anything had been written on the subject and the cataloguing involved a good deal of original research which I found so interesting that I pursued it beyond what was needed for the immediate purpose, until what was to have been a simple guide to the Ashmolean collection assumed the proportions of a book; greatly daring, I submitted this to the Delegates of the Oxford University Press and to my astonishment they agreed to publish it at the University's expense. Feeling very triumphant I wrote to Charles Bell, the Senior Assistant Keeper, who was away on leave, and told him all about it. In reply he wrote congratulating me most sincerely, and then added, "If you had asked my advice, which you didn't, and would not have accepted if you had, I should have said 'get your manuscript back from the Press and burn it'. It is your first book, so naturally you are proud of it, but it's bound to be immature and later on you will regret having published it." The letter was like a douche of cold water and I didn't like the shock at all, but in the end I did recover my manuscript and although I had not the heart to burn it, it never went back to the Press.

To see one's work in its true proportion, to be critical of it and to make sure that it is up to standard is a good rule for anyone and not least for the archæologist, for in archæology it is only too easy to gloss over second-rate work and get it to pass muster. I have always been grateful to Craster and Bell for their lessons.

David Randall-MacIver, head of the Eckley B. Coxe Jnr. Expedition to Nubia, had asked me to join his staff, so in 1907 I left the Ashmolean Museum and went to Egypt. MacIver, who had worked under Flinders Petrie, was a first-class archæologist and I felt that now for the first time I could learn the technique of field work under a competent instructor. We began by rounding off the excavation of a little cemetery, the greater part of which had been cleared by MacIver the year before, and then he went up the Nile by boat to look for a new site while I—so as not to waste time— was to clear what seemed to be another little cemetery of the same sort at a place called Karanòg; this looked like a small job which I could be trusted to do un- aided. So I was left alone with an Italian servant (I knew no Italian) and a hundred Egyptian workmen; (I had only been in Egypt three weeks and knew that much of Arabic.) The cemetery turned out to be a very large one, containing nearly 800 graves, and very important because it was, with the exception of the little Areika graveyard we had just been excavating, the first Meroitic cemetery ever dug. I did my best, of course, but it was hard work, running the dig, taking all the notes, doing my own plans and drawings, and taking and developing the photographs; I remember how difficult it was to keep the expedition accounts in the unfamiliar Egyptian currency, and the household accounts were a comic nightmare, for they had to be done with Venturi, the Italian, who spoke no language but his own, but who was an excellent mimic; he would consult his day-book, give an admirable representation of a hen laying an egg or of a pigeon first flying and then having its neck wrung, hold up so many fingers

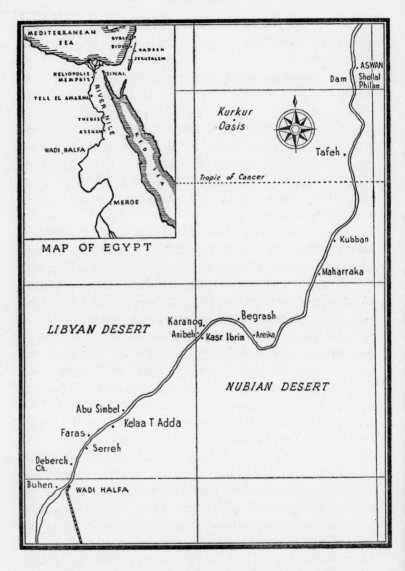

Map of the River Nile between the first and second Cataracts

to give the number of eggs or pigeons bought and then from a pile of mixed coins count out the proper number of piastres paid. That was simple; but when it was a question of lentils or charcoal and the pantomime became more abstruse and there would be a deadlock until it occurred to him to go off and fetch some of the actual commodity (which I could not tell him to do because I could not make myself understood), it was difficult to preserve one's patience. I longed for Mac-Iver's return. When he did come he went very carefully over all that I had done, made a few suggestions and said that as everything was going all right he would leave me to finish the dig while he himself started work on the new site at Buhen which he had chosen. So I finished the cemetery alone.

MacIver was fully justified in this. During the fortnight's work together at Areika he had put me on the right lines, and with that modicum of experience and with the hard work and ordinary care which he knew I should not shirk, there was no likelihood of the dig being improperly done. The fact is, as I learnt afterwards, Egypt is a very easy country for the archæologist. Not only are objects, for the most part, preserved in good condition by the dryness of the soil, but in most cases they are buried in clean sand. Sand has buried the walls of buildings, sand has filled the tombs; with his broad-bladed adze-shaped tool the Egyptian workman pulls away the sand and there is the wall, of stone if it be a temple, of grey mud brick if it be a house, or, if a grave be dug, the sand and grey dust trickles between the fingers and leaves coffin or vase or what-not clean and unmistakeable. It is quite good training for the beginner, if only because it gives him confidence and, of course, experience in handling objects; but I very much doubt whether a man who has dug only in Egypt can rightly be called a good field archæologist, because he has never been up against the real difficulties of excavation. The Germans who dug at Tell el Amarna were capable men with plenty of local experience, and when they were excavating the houses, which lie well back in the dry desert and are buried in sand, they did admirable work; but when they attacked a mound close to the river where a temple built of mud brick was buried in the damp debris of its own bricks, they failed completely—they cut away all the walls and could not produce even the groundplan of what had been a building standing six or seven feet high. Similarly I have found well-trained Egyptian foremen completely at a loss and quite useless when brought face to face with the conditions of excavation in Syria. Karanòg and Buhen taught me a great deal, but I was lucky in that I moved on to Syria before I had become hidebound by the traditions of work in Egypt.

What made the work at Karanòg most interesting was that it was the first cemetery of the sort to be dug; everything about it was new (and here again I was lucky, for I had not that knowledge of Egyptian antiquities that a digger on a normal Egyptian site ought to possess, whereas no one could be criticized for not knowing about Meroitic art and culture), and every object found was by way of being a historic document. It was a curious hybrid civilization that we were bringing to light. The people were of a pure African stock having no more in common with the dwellers in the Lower Nile Valley than have the Sudanese of the

Meroitic grave with chapel and offering table

Left
Alexandrian bronze jug from a Meroitic grave

Right
Roman cut-glass bottle from a Meroitic grave

present day. Some centuries before the date of our graves they had raided Egypt, and their kings had for a time assumed the throne and the dignities of the Pharaohs, and when they were driven back into their own land they had taken with them something of the religious beliefs and fashions in art that they had adopted during their sojourn in a country so much more civilized than their own. Later, through their contacts with Egypt, trading and raiding, they learnt something of the Greek culture introduced by the Ptolemies, and later still the Roman occupation of Egypt brought to them more models of classical art—they resisted the Roman arms, so that not even Augustus had been able to overthrow the kingdom of Candace, but they appreciated Roman inventions. By the third century A.D., which was about the date of our cemetery, these various influences had combined to produce a mixed culture of a very queer type. A well-to-do citizen of Karanòg might have in his tomb a cut-glass unguent-bottle of Roman manufacture, an example of a type so standardized by Rome that a duplicate of the Karanòg bottle might be found at Cologne or in Northumberland, and with this a bronze jug in the Hellenistic fashion made, undoubtedly, at Alexandria; the pottery would be local, mostly wheel-made and painted, but occasionally among these sophisticated wares we would find a hand-made vessel of black clay with punctured decoration whose origin must be sought in the far-off days when the people of Meroe were pure African savages. To this extent the culture of third-century Karanòg would seem to have been just a mixture of undigested elements, but there was more to it than that. The body of our citizen lay in a tomb chamber, burrowed cave-like in the hard mud which is the subsoil of the river valley; above the chamber and the sloped approach leading to it, there was built of mud bricks a memorial in the form of a solid flat-topped square from one side of which there projected what was really a tiny chapel—two low walls with bricks laid across to make a roof—and in front of that again a few bricks making a square altar on which was laid a stone "table of offerings" inscribed in the Meroitic script with the name of the dead man.

The square superstructure of the tomb with its little chapel had precisely the same shape as the stone offering-table in front of it, and that was the shape of the Egyptian offering-table; here was a religious idea borrowed from Egypt. Inside the chapel there might be cups of offering or a painted stela derived from an Egyptian prototype, but above this, on the chapel roof, there was set a stone figure of a human-headed bird which is the *Ba*, one of the forms in which the ancient Egyptian represented the soul of a man; again we have a clear case of borrowing from Egypt but, and this is the remarkable point, you do not find any such figure associated with tombs in Egypt itself. The Meroitic people did not simply ape the ideas of the more advanced race which for a while they ruled; they took over from the complex Nilotic religion only what harmonized with their own beliefs, or they harmonized with those beliefs something which appealed to them on its own merits, setting their own peculiar stamp on all their borrowings.

This is most evident in the case of the painted pottery. The shapes of many of the vases are derived from classical or Egyptian origins, and the same is true of quite a number of the painted designs, but nobody could possibly mistake any one of them for imports from Egypt, Greece or Rome. The range is astonishing. In our publication of the cemetery we figured about 370 complete vases and no two are duplicates. Some have purely abstract patterns, some the Egyptian *ankh* or the Eye of Horus, many have plant motives, perhaps the Egyptian lotus, perhaps the Alexandrian garland, or there may be scorpions or frogs, guinea-fowl or ostriches, and even naturalistic scenes such as a hunter with his dogs. I know of no country whose painted pottery shows a more exuberant fancy than we see displayed in this Meroitic ware; the most commonplace subject as treated by the Meroitic artist becomes an original creation. But it remains a barbarous art. That truth is brought home to us by the most curious object that the cemetery produced, a bronze bowl on which is engraved a picture of native life, and here the treatment is reversed. Outside a reed-built wigwam sits a grossly fat woman with her attendants; in front of her, cows are brought up to be milked and a husbandman with a wickerwork pail fills with milk the bowls set ready for her drinking; like some of the Negro ladies of modern times the queen is being dieted to produce the fatness which passes as beauty. The drawing in its style and technique belongs to the civilized world but the subject is taken straight from "darkest Africa".

Karanòg was a fascinating dig because of its novelty, and the unravelling of the complex fabric of its culture, the tracing of its different strands, was fascinating too; but when all was done and the work published it was a relief to think that it was off our hands. Here was an unusually good illustration of what may happen when a primitive race is brought into contact with alien and higher cultures, and the reaction of the human mind to its surroundings is always of interest. But though Meroitic art flourished up to a point, it led to nothing; it was sterile, and it died without having any effect upon the after world. The value of any ancient culture,

Design on a Meroitic bronze bowl

as against its intrinsic merit, lies in the contribution it has made to human progress, in the part it has played in building up the world of to-day, and the art of this negroid backwater cut off from the stream of history played no such part and can rank only as a curiosity.

Later on, in 1910, I dug in the town of Karanòg, clearing a few houses and the three-story castle whose ruins still dominate that reach of the Nile. Two curious things happened there. MacIver, who had walked over the site, told me that he had noticed at its southern end what seemed to be an enclosing wall, and he suggested that I should start work on that so as to get the general outline of the town. I had no difficulty in recognizing the wall. From the river bank there ran inland a double line of large flat slabs of stone with a packing of smaller stones between; it was flush with the surface of the sand, ran dead straight to where the low shelf of rock marked the rise of the upper desert and then with a slight change of angle ran inland again to disappear over the gentle down-slope beyond. I decided to clear the outer face and so began to dig in the sand close to the river, and was dismayed to find that the stones were only one course deep with clean sand below them; I could only suppose that they were the foundation of a wall of mud brick totally denuded by the weather. I tried again on the stony ground above, with the same result; at last in desperation I went inland over the bluff—and then I could only sit down and laugh. In the hollow in front of me was a British army camp, the rows of tents marked by the circles of big stones to which the guy-ropes had been made fast, neat lines of pebbles bordering the paths, the built horse-lines, everything in order as if it had been deserted but the day before—one could even distinguish the doctor's tent by the empty medicine bottles—and my "town wall" was simply the causeway joining the camp to the river where the gunboats had lain when in 1889 Colonel Wodehouse was warding off from the waters of the Nile the Dervish army that had set out to conquer Egypt and was to meet its end at the battle of Toski. It was a good illustration of the way in which things may be preserved by the Egyptian climate, and of the wisdom of the precept "Look before you . . . dig".

31

The second incident was this. We were clearing the castle and in one of the rooms, under less than two feet of fallen rubble, found two fragments of gazelle skin inscribed in Coptic which must have dated to the last years of the building in the sixth century A.D. In the next room, under seven feet of rubbish, we found an unused United States postage-stamp and a fragment of a Yorkshire newspaper of 1878. At first sight the two discoveries seemed irreconcilable, upsetting all the rules of archæological stratification. But those "rules" are not merely mechanical, and measurements of depths are not final; they have to be combined with common sense. In the present case we were dealing with a mud-brick building which still stands to a height of more than thirty feet, and the simple explanation of our conundrum was that a big lump of wall had fallen just after the year 1878 when newspaper and stamp were dropped in an almost empty room.

To go from Karanòg to Buhen (which is Wadi Halfa) was a great change, for Buhen was a real Egyptian site whose temples, tombs and houses were of more or less normal type and had to be interpreted by comparison with those already recorded further north; instead of regarding each object found as something throwing new light on an unknown civilization one had to check up the number of times a similar object had been found in Egypt so as to work out the relation in which this outpost of the Empire stood to the home country. The outlines of Egyptian history are by now familiar, and the task of archæology is, for the most part, to fill in the details which may complete the picture; it is generally a question of adding not a new chapter but a footnote to history. One must not under-rate the im-

Examples of Meroitic painted pottery

portance of that, for it is the details that give life to the
bare record of kings and wars.

Buhen, lying just below the Second Cataract, was
the natural southern frontier of Egypt, and by 2000
B.C. had been fortified and garrisoned by the Pharaohs
of the XIIth Dynasty, and in the time of the XVIIIth
Dynasty (fifteenth century B.C.) that remarkable lady,
Queen Hatshepsut, built there a temple only less splendid than her own famous mortuary temple at Deir el
Bahari by the Valley of the Kings. Later on her name,
wherever it occurred, was erased by her stepson,
Thothmes III, and his own substituted for that of the
stepmother whom he so loathed. Immediately outside
the fortress wall of the XIIth Dynasty we found the
rock-cut chamber tombs of the higher Egyptian
officials, many of them very large and elaborate. They
had all been plundered in antiquity, as is indeed the
rule in Egypt, but in three cases a fortunate accident
had anticipated the robbers—the stone roof of a chamber had collapsed and, since the debris was more than
anyone could remove without drawing attention to
himself, it had preserved the contents intact. Here we
found splendid jewellery of gold and amethyst which
witnessed to the wealth and rank of the dead, a very
fine little statuette of "the gardener Merer, born of the
lady of the house Neferu", an iron spear-head, a vase
of obsidian—black volcanic glass—bound with gold,
and vessels of bronze and alabaster. It was clear that
the colonists of remote Buhen were just as luxurious
and art-loving as their kinsmen in Egypt proper, but
the different conditions in which they had to live were
suggested by the fact that inscribed monuments such
as would have been common in an Egyptian cemetery

as rich as this were here sadly lacking; when once the royal craftsmen who carved the inscriptions in the temple had gone back home there was no one in Buhen who could compose and inscribe in stone the biographical texts that a tomb in Egypt would boast. These were of course the early days of the colony; in the time of the XVIIIth Dynasty more skilled labour was available and it was quite a usual thing for officials or private persons to put inscribed memorials of themselves in the temples and to have inscribed *stelae* in their tombs, but even then the carving of the reliefs in the coarse local sandstone is very rough and the language and style of the texts is barbarous to the verge of illiteracy; life at Buhen must always have seemed to the Egyptians a dreadful exile in a savage land.

The most remarkable object that we found on the site was the iron spear-head which I mentioned above. It was in the side chamber of an undisturbed but not rich grave—the man's face was covered with a plaster mask plated with gold leaf and there was a bronze mirror by his head—and the blade, leaf-shaped and just a foot long, lay by his left shoulder; in the other chambers there were twelve more bodies with which were small objects of gold and amethyst, ivory and bronze, but nothing in any way unusual. There could be no question as to the date of the tomb, which was one of the XIIth Dynasty series, and all the objects were characteristic of their time; but to find a weapon of worked iron in a 2000 B.C. setting was revolutionary; the spear-head is the oldest iron implement yet discovered in any country. We are accustomed to think of iron-working as the invention of people in the Caucasus area of eastern Anatolia, but it was only later, in the XVIIIth Dynasty, that any was exported to Egypt, and then only in very small quantities and by special favour of the Hittite kings; under the XIIth Dynasty none was coming in and if any had come it would hardly have found its way into the possession of a none-too-rich citizen of Buhen. Can then the fact be explained otherwise? We do know that, quite independently of Anatolia, iron was worked in Central Africa at an early date, though how early we have no means of knowing. If the technique had already been mastered by 2000 B.C. it is possible that an isolated example of it should be carried northwards, and a citizen of Buhen would be far better placed than Pharaoh himself to get hold of it either in the way of trade or as a gift from a native friend. This theory has no evidence to support it, but it does less violence to probability than would the assumption that the weapon came from the Caucasus and that our humble exile possessed something which Pharaoh would have thought worth a king's ransom; if a negro brought it from the barbarous south its owner would have had no suspicion of its value.

When the Eckley B. Coxe Jnr. Expedition came to an end in 1912 I thought that I had worked in Egypt for the last time, for I was already looking forward to Carchemish, but in this I was mistaken; I was to do one season's work under F. Ll. Griffith for the Oxford Expedition to Nubia and, in 1922, one at Tell el Amarna for the Egypt Exploration Society. The Oxford Expedition certainly gave one plenty of variety. We dug a cemetery of the Protodynastic type, dating back to the fourth millennium B.C., a XIIth Dynasty fort, a temple built by Hatshepsut and another built

by Tutankhamen, and a lot more Meroitic graves; and
I ended the season by copying fresco paintings in early
Christian churches; a very mixed bag. This last job
interested me particularly because I had never had to
do anything of the kind before, so it was a new experience; one of the joys of archæology is that so often one
is obliged to turn one's hand to something hitherto
untried, and so often has to invent the way to do it,
and though I cannot claim that my coloured tracings
of the frescoes were in any way artistic, they do represent fairly faithfully the far from artistic originals. The
churches were decorated by men whose painting was
not equal to their piety: there was a relatively small
range of traditional subjects and the manner of treating those was also traditional—the formal Byzantine
treatment approved by the Coptic church, so that there
was no call for imagination or originality; but though
the painters were always working on familiar lines their
powers of execution were less than mediocre, and the
pictures which they produced tend to be little more
than caricatures. Nubia was a Christian country from
the time of the Emperor Justinian—about 543 A.D.—
when it was converted by missionaries sent from Con-
stantinople, and its art was always more Byzantine
than Coptic, but how far it is from the glorious mosaics
of St. Sophia! The frescoes, which date perhaps from
the tenth century, illustrate the decadence of a poor
and isolated community soon to be extinguished by
the more virile forces of Islam.

In sharp contrast to the Nubian site where we found
remains, not generally of a very high order, ranging
over a space of nearly five thousand years, was Tell el
Amarna, a royal capital which was built and aban-

"The Three Children in the burning fiery furnace".
Wall painting from twelfth-century church near
Second Cataract

doned within a generation. A good deal of its interest is due to the fact that it was so short-lived, for from it we can get a picture of a definite period, free from all possibility of anachronism, and the period, that of Akhenaten, 'the Heretic King', is peculiarly fascinating. A vast amount of systematic work had been done on the site, and I had merely to carry on what others had begun, the clearing of this sand-buried city founded "on clean ground" as a refuge for the Pharaoh and his luxurious court from the old capital at Thebes overshadowed by the gods whom he had rejected. Much of our work was on the great houses of the nobles; the general type of these was already familiar, but there was a lot to be learnt about the details of architecture and decoration, and often the building would be so well preserved that a complete restoration of it could be drawn out on paper. There had been here no catastrophe, no wilful destruction. When the royal heretic died and the old order was revived under Tutankhamen the nobles, with a convenient change of heart, returned to Thebes and to the worship of Amon-rê; but because you never know what may happen it was just as well to keep the big house at Tell el Amarna ready for re-occupation in the event of the Aten-worship being brought again into favour, so you merely walled up the front door and left it at that. Nobody did come back. Probably in the course of time someone stole the precious roof-timbers; at any rate the tops of the walls crumbled and fell, and powdered brick and wind-blown sand buried the "impious" city. We would find the walled-up door, and behind it the ground-floor rooms very much as they were when the owners moved their furniture to Thebes.

37

The task of restoration was of course one for an architect, and my architect, F. G. Newton, thoroughly enjoyed himself. Personally I was more interested in the excavation of the "model village" in which were housed the labourers employed in making the rock-cut tombs in the high desert behind the town. The village lay in a barren valley, far from water but close to the cliffs where the tombs were to be dug, a square enclosure surrounded by a high wall and entered by a single gateway; inside were five narrow streets running parallel, north by south, between rows of little tenement houses all planned exactly alike—only in the south-east corner near the door there was a larger and more elaborate building which must have been the house of the overseer. The ordinary workman's dwelling consisted of a front hall which served also as kitchen or as workshop, or might be shared with the domestic animals, for a manger was a common feature and occasionally we found a tethering-stone; the animals would be goats and donkeys, but in one case a man seems to have kept a horse. Behind this was a living-room with a low mud-brick divan along one or two of its sides, and close to it a hearth; there might be a low three-legged stool carved out of stone or of wood with a cane or string seat, a flat stone for a table and a big earthenware jar for the day's water supply. At the back of the house were two small rooms, one or both of which might be bedrooms, but one was normally the kitchen and would be partly taken up by a tiny flight of stairs going up to the flat roof; the beds had a wooden frame and a mattress of twisted rushes.

Clearly the inhabitants of this walled enclosure were not free workmen but were kept strictly under dis-

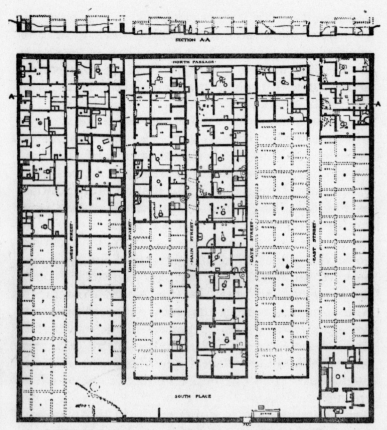

Plan of the Workmen's Village at Tell el Amarna

cipline—there were even patrol roads round it and guardhouses on the main road to the city—and their monotonously ordered quarters out in the desert were very unlike the normal Egyptian village straggling along at the edge of the cultivation; but as an example of ancient town-planning this was a really interesting discovery. Moreover the uniformity of the buildings

39

was set off by the variety of their contents. Since the men were employed on the tombs, which were to be adorned with paintings, they naturally kept back some of the paint, and we find the walls of the living-rooms decorated with roughly drawn designs very much in the tomb fashion.

Although they were employed by Akhenaten on what was really religious work they were themselves no strict followers of his new religion, and the amulets dropped in the houses represented the old gods, Hathor and Horus, Taurt and Bes, all now disowned by Pharaoh. The women-folk spun thread and wove cloth—we found evidence of the looms in the front rooms—and some of the men seem to have carried on minor trades in their spare time, for we found tools of all sorts, clay crucibles, limestone moulds for jewellery and part of a stone-cutter's equipment with stone finger-rings the work on which was only half done. The walled-up palaces of the courtiers in the city seemed very lifeless and inhuman compared with this humble village from which the workmen might have gone out but yesterday; it required no effort of the imagination to re-people its lanes, and our own Egyptian diggers, sitting on the brick divans and warming their hands at a fire lit on the ancient hearth with charcoal found in a store beneath the stairs, vividly brought back the past.

Beyond the southern outskirts of the main town we made a curious discovery, that of the King's pleasure park. This consisted of two walled gardens, side by side. The smaller contained a temple and a tank, the larger, which measured about 220 yards by 110, had in the middle a shallow boating-lake 125 yards long;

at the east end of this there was a group of extremely gay little stone temples, three of them enclosed by a moat with ornamental bridges, and a very curious little building that one can only call a roofed water-garden, a sort of maze of tanks and columns all of which, together with the floors, were elaborately painted with vines, flowers and bushes. On either side of the lake was a mud-brick building, one perhaps a summer-house, the other a bijou palace, and at its west end, behind a screen wall, buildings of a more domestic sort; among them the stalls in which the milking cows were kept and a stable for the royal greyhounds. The whole of the rest of the space was planted with trees or laid out in flowerbeds; wherever we dug we found just below the modern surface the straight mud ridges which divide vegetable-beds and flower-beds, making compartments for irrigation, or else the roots of trees surrounded by low mud walls like tubs filled with imported earth such as are still used in Egyptian gardens. This was a novel and exciting discovery and all the more interesting because owing to the ruinous condition of the buildings it was very difficult to make anything of them. Soon after Akhenaten's death the stone buildings had been pulled down and all the stones carried off for use elsewhere, the inscriptions and reliefs of the hated heretic having been first chipped away; for hundreds of years the local peasants have been digging away the mud-brick walls to manure their fields; very often every brick has disappeared and the wall is represented only by a sand-filled trench running along the broken edge of a mud floor.

When we walked over to look at the site we could distinguish by the alternate mounds and hollows the lines of the enclosure walls, the low-lying rectangle of absolutely level soil in the centre looked like a lake, though now it was cut up into little modern garden-squares; two low mounds showed where mud-brick buildings had stood, but of the stone buildings all that we could see was a litter of carved chips and fragments spread over a flat expanse of cement, the foundation which Akhenaten's builders had laid over the desert sand, and, in the north-east corner, scraps of painted cement pavement. One of my staff disconsolately remarked that there was nothing there to dig. In my heart of hearts I was inclined to agree with him but thought that we ought to test the place properly so, more or less in bravado, rejoined "No, but we'll start digging to-morrow". This was too much for Battiscombe Gunn, who was the epigraphist and the pessimist of the party, and he asked rather scornfully where I proposed to begin. I said "On the temple site", the place where the stone chippings were, "and over there", the little mound north of the lake. "And what is it that's 'over there'?" inquired Gunn. Of course I couldn't have any idea, so for want of anything better I said "Why, the *harîm*, of course!" and the obvious frivolity of the answer was met with a gloomy silence. The stone site *was* that of the temples, and although not a stone was left in position, nor indeed did we find a single unbroken build-block, yet thanks to marks on the cement foundation we could make out the ground-plan, and by measuring all the fragments of carving Newton was even able to draw a restoration of the complete building with all its details of ornament correct. Of the northern mud-brick buildings little more than the cellars remained, cellars full of broken wine jars whose clay stoppers were stamped with seals "Wine of the house of Akhenaten", "Wine of the Western River", "Wine of the Southern Pool", while written on the jars would be the name of the vineyard superintendent, the vintage date, or "very good wine". Gunn had been studying these inscriptions and one day came to me looking very serious. "What made you call that building a *harîm?*" he demanded. "Oh well," I said, "if you've got a pleasure park you are surely going to bring the ladies along, aren't you? Why do you ask?" "Because," challengingly, "as far as I can make out from the texts, it was a *harîm.*" I

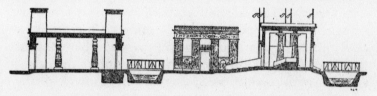

Restoration of the Garden Temple at Tell el Amarna

was as much taken aback as he had been but was not going to show it, so merely murmured "The old story Gunn, wine, women and song"; but when soon afterwards we found one of the cellars with its door walled up and in it the body of a woman I maintained that this was the final proof needed, the inevitable *harîm* scandal.

Much has been written about Akhenaten, his religious reforms, his monotheism, his idealism and his enthusiasm for truth, and I think that a good deal more has been read into his words than the Egyptian language warrants. "By their fruits ye shall know them", and the archæologist who works at Akhenaten's capital, Tell el Amarna, gets a very different

43

impression of the Heretic King. That through sheer neglect of his duties he let the Egyptian Empire go to pieces is a matter of common knowledge, but at Tell el Amarna we can see how the Empire's wealth was frittered away in fantastic extravagance of which our pleasure park is only one example the more. He loved luxury and indulged in it to the full, but it was more a matter of show than anything else.

Most of the work in the capital is shoddy. Everything was gay and highly coloured, but it was with the gaiety of paint; even the stonework was too often executed in poor-quality sandstone disguised by paint, and the decoration resolves itself for the most part into a lifeless repetition of identical subjects. Now that the old gods had been suppressed, the sculptor had lost most of his repertory; the only subject regarded with favour was that of the king and the royal family, and these appear with wearisome regularity on every wall and every column-shaft; in Akhenaten's view the aim and object of art was the glorification of himself. The detailed restoration of the pleasure park temple was only possible because the splinters of carved stone could in every case be identified as coming from scenes only too familiar; they were examples of mass production as mechanical as the laudatory inscriptions which the illiterate workers carved from models which were nothing but plaster-casts from the same inscriptions in other buildings—we found the models which they had thrown away after their job was done. This self-indulgent and superficial ostentation is scarcely consistent with idealism and a passion for truth, and in one further respect our discoveries seem to challenge the reputation in which the king has been held. In all his paintings and sculptures Akhenaten, unlike the Pharaohs before him, makes a great parade of his domestic life and is seldom represented except in the company—sometimes the very intimate company—of his beautiful queen Nefertiti and perhaps also of their two daughters, and his family affection has been considered one of the most pleasing traits of the king's character. In the buildings of the pleasure garden the same stereotyped domestic scenes all reappear, but here, at a later time within the reign of Akhenaten, Nefertiti's name has in nearly every case been carefully erased and that of her eldest daughter substituted, her distinctive attributes have been blotted out with cement and her features recut to resemble those of the Princess Royal. This was a public affront if she were still alive, and if she had died the devoted husband would not have taken the opportunity to obliterate her memorials; we are driven to assume that even the family affection of the royal household was superficial and that a quarrel so serious as to lose Nefertiti her position had ended the idyll which had hitherto been the standing theme of the court artists.

I might be told that all this is a fuss about nothing and that to us to-day it does not matter in the least whether a king of Egypt who died about 1,350 years before Christ was really a high-minded idealist or not, whether he was a self-centred pleasure-loving heretic or, as Professor Breasted has said, "the most remarkable of all the Pharaohs, the first *individual* in human history . . . strong and fearless", in whose hymns to the Aten "the universalism of the empire finds full expression" so that we "must be moved with involun-

45

tary admiration for the young king who in such an age found such thoughts in his heart." This language used by Professor Breasted is in itself enough to show that it does matter. We are all of us agreed that history has value for us to-day, and for that reason it must be true history. If the facts be distorted the lessons drawn from them will be wrong, and the experience of the last thirty years has proved that the distortion of history may have disastrous results on the minds and morals of a people so deceived. If, from what we found at Tell el Amarna, we can avoid the exaggeration which would make Akhenaten a saint and a prophet and see him in a truer perspective, the work done was worth while; nothing can alter the fact that he was an important figure in history and a very interesting character, but had he been all that some have claimed for him it would be hard indeed to explain why everything for which he stood perished with him. At his death his gaudy capital was deserted, like a theatre stage after the last curtain falls; but long before its mud walls had crumbled his teaching had passed out of men's minds or was remembered only to be cursed.

Chapter Two

SOUTH ITALY

Among the many things for which I am grateful to MacIver, not the least important is this. Digging in Egypt ended in March of every year and it was not until early autumn that I was required to go to Philadelphia for work in the University Museum; the spring therefore was for me a free time, and MacIver arranged that I should spend it in Italy and, so far as might be possible, should dig there. Nothing could have been more delightful. In my first spring I started by putting in a month's hard work in Florence, learning the language. I was so lucky as to be lodged with my tutor, a dear old Professore Zaccardi, professor of rhetoric in the University of Florence, who carried on during meals and half-way through the night the formal lessons of the morning, with the result that at the month's end I could talk fluently and think naturally in Italian. After that I went south, with Venturi, my major-domo in Egypt, as companion and general factotum, and from then on my headquarters were in Naples. At Naples I had a friend, Lamont Young, an English architect and engineer born and bred there, who made everything easy for me; his flat was the whole of the upper story of the municipal restaurant in the middle of the Villa Nazionale, the public park on the water-front of the lovely bay, and there I always stopped when in the city; it was an ideal centre.

It was impossible for a foreigner to get a permit in his own name for making excavations in Italy, but an Italian landowner could excavate on his own land at his own expense provided that he obtained proper authority, worked under supervision on scientific lines, and handed over to the Government a due share of the objects discovered. It was therefore quite easy to arrange that such a landowner should employ me as scientific supervisor, and nobody would inquire from where the money came for the dig; without any technical breach of the law I could really do just as I liked. For anything in the nature of a survey no authority was required, and one was legally allowed in the course of a survey to make soundings or experimental digs, again without authority or supervision; this was a convenient loophole, for the most expert archæologist would be hard put to it to define the precise stage at which "soundings" ceases to be the correct term and "excavation" properly speaking begins; more than once I found that my definitions and those of the government inspector were very far from agreeing.

One of these surveys was in the valley of the Sabato where was a walled enclosure on a little hill which had been by some writers identified as a fortress of the ancient Sabines. It was a very lonely spot—apart from the forest-rangers' two-roomed cabin in which we lived there was not a building within five miles—and the valley with its tumbling stream below and its wooded slopes rising up to towering stone cliffs beyond which one could see only snow-clad peaks, seemed indeed re-

Roman baths near Teano, Italy

mote and sheltered enough to have been the cradle of
a primitive folk. But a very little work dispelled that
idea. The walls of rubble and concrete proved to be of
Christian date and the enclosure was undoubtedly a
place of refuge to which shepherds and herdsmen
could betake themselves and their beasts when danger
threatened; here was rich pasturage, but it was too far
from home for any help against raiders to come quickly
and only behind a stout wall could they find safety. I
remember how one day at Teano, an Italian and myself were looking at the glorious view, and I made some
comment on the fact that all the Roman ruins lay in
the fertile lowlands of the valley, whereas the medieval
castles were all perched high up on the barren hills.
"Yes," said my companion, "to the age of the eagles
succeeded the age of the vultures." It was a very good
description, and to the state of anarchy and violence
that followed on the downfall of imperial Rome the
cattle-shelter in the Sabato valley bears eloquent witness.

One small job that I did in those days was interesting, not so much for its results as for the methods employed. There had been some talk of a dig at Herculaneum (this was before the Italian Government took
that great work in hand) and the obvious objection
had been raised that as the Roman town was buried
beneath a mass of solidified lava its excavation would
be terribly expensive and almost physically impossible.
I felt quite sure that this was not strictly true. The
theatre had been excavated in the eighteenth century
and it *was* buried in lava so that the excavators had to
tunnel their way along the walls, through what was
almost as hard as the stone walls themselves. But the

theatre was built in the side of the ravine of a torrent-bed, and the molten lava from Vesuvius poured down that ravine and filled it to the brim; but the greater part of the town had been buried, like Pompeii, in ashes falling from the air. That would be the normal thing in a volcanic eruption, and that it had so happened was proved by the fact that the suburban villa of Herculaneum from which came the finest bronzes in the Naples Museum was buried in ashes; it was discovered under King Bomba's palace at the back of the modern town and evidently lay clear of the course of the lava stream. But the problem was complicated by the fact that since the disaster which in 79 A.D. overwhelmed the classical town there have been other eruptions of Vesuvius each of which sent fresh streams of lava across the site and each time following a different course, while at the same time fresh layers of ashes were deposited broadcast. A digger therefore might find near the surface a crust of hard lava and thereunder nothing but soft ash or dried mud masking the ruins; or below a stratum of ash he might come on solid lava, or again the strata might alternate like the layers in a fancy cake, and in any of these cases his work would be difficult and very costly. There might well be areas where nothing but mud or ash had ever come, and only on such an area would excavation on a relatively small scale be worth while. I therefore proposed for archæological purposes to make a map of all the lava streams resulting from the eruptions of the last two thousand years.

A certain amount, but not a great deal, of information could be got from written sources, more or less contemporary records of the various eruptions, but

those, of course, gave only a few main lines and did
not go into detail. They did however help one to
identify some of the tail-ends of the lava streams which
one could distinguish along the sea beach below the
town, and therefore to date them. But what one wanted
to know was not merely where each stream reached the
sea but what course it had followed inland, and there
nothing was visible on the surface.

The back of the ancient Herculaneum lay beneath
the modern town of Resina, where digging was impossible, but the greater part of it, between Resina and
the sea, was open garden land dotted with little farms
or cottages. The volcanic soil is very fertile, but it requires irrigation, so every plot was provided with its
own well; in that fact I saw my opportunity for scientific research; all I had to do was to examine each well
and see through what kind of soil each was sunk. There
was a difficulty there. I could not ask for the help of the
Department of Antiquities, for they would have sus-
pected me of every kind of unlawful purpose; if on the
other hand I, in my private capacity, had asked the
individual landowners for permission to examine their
wells they would have been equally suspicious, for
other reasons, and would promptly have sent me about
my business. So Lamont Young and I posed as a Commission vaguely connected with the Ministry of the
Interior and went round making elaborate notes about
estate boundaries, crops and house property; in every
case we suggested an inspection of the well, explaining
that we had no express authority for that but that it
facilitated our real work—the owner was at liberty to
refuse, but it was in his interest to give us all the help
possible; and there were murmurs of a possible in-

crease in the land-tax which full knowledge on our part might avert. Nobody refused. It was a very harmless imposture on our part, and as a result of it we were able to draw up a remarkably detailed map of the underground lava-flows of the successive eruptions. The map was never used, for soon after it was made the first Great War broke out and after that war the Italian Government took in hand the systematic excavation of Herculaneum, for which nothing of the sort was required; but the making of it was great fun and an excellent piece of training for me.

I did one piece of regular excavation, working on the Roman baths close to Teano. It was an historic site, for the trouble that arose between the local authorities and the Roman consul when the latter's wife first insisted on having the bath reserved for her on the men's day, and then complained that the water was dirty (for which the consul had the authorities flogged) led to the outbreak of the Social War. But it was not a good site for the archæologist; the building was in terraces stepped down the thirty-foot bank of a little stream; the façade, on the high ground where ran the Roman road, had disappeared entirely; the bathrooms lay at the bottom of the valley, close to the water, and here I hoped to find such statues, etc., as had adorned the baths proper and also anything that might have fallen here from the upper rooms. There was deep and apparently undisturbed soil, littered with fragments of decorative marble and the *tesserae* of wall mosaics, which promised well, but unfortunately the water which had made the reputation of the ancient baths was possessed of mineral qualities which may have been excellent for the human body but were fatal to marble. The statues

were there, as I had expected, and those that lay high
up in the soil were tolerably preserved, but from a level
of four feet downwards they were in a lamentable state;
in some cases the softer parts of the stone had been
eaten away so that the figures looked like fantastic
skeletons, in others the whole thing had been reduced
to white sticky mud. When the first two, a Venus and
a rather charming Cupid, were found I was delighted;
but only too soon I had to recognize that from the
point of view of objects there was no justification for
continuing the dig; we did enough to obtain a fairly
complete plan of at least the major part of the bath
building, and with that we had to be content. Again,
it was valuable experience. Conditions in Italy were so
different from anything in Egypt that one had to re-
orient oneself altogether, and that not only in methods
of excavation but also in one's mental outlook.

To a very large extent the present of each country is
rooted in its past and the best way of understanding the
past is to appreciate the present. I am quite sure that
an archæologist who is insensitive to his surroundings,
to the spirit of the land in which he is working, can
never make a real success of his job. The truth of this
was particularly obvious in the little towns and villages
of southern Italy, for there past and present were very
close together. It was not merely that I could walk to
my work down a country lane still paved with the
great polygonal blocks of stone laid by the Romans—
their *via strata* from which our word "street" is derived
—with every fifty paces marked by a round-topped
stone set upright by the roadside; it was not merely
that I worked at night by the light of a lamp identical
with those in use a thousand years before our era—a

clay saucer pinched on one side to support the wick floating in the olive oil; the people were themselves a survival. Their religion was a veneer of the orthodox faith of Rome laid over a core of ancient paganism; their saints were the old gods under different names, and at the spring festival they flogged the image in the church with nettles precisely as their forefathers had flogged the statue of the garden god Priapus, seeking for a good harvest. Their morals were those of a primitive and lawless world; their manners were the exquisite manners of a free and self-reliant race. In contrast with the Egyptian peasants, whose thoughts never rose above money, these open-handed and open-hearted people were delightful companions, but the more one entered into that companionship the more clearly one could understand the human side of the ancient world, whose material remains it is the duty of the archæologist to interpret.

Surrounded as most of us are to-day by machines which, taking the place of the slaves of yesterday, do our work for us, we are enslaved to them and have lost the ability to do things for ourselves. We are obliged to recognize the fact that ancient man, lacking our means, could do very remarkable things, but we are contemptuous of his simple tools and cannot understand how he succeeded where we, left to our own resources, would be impotent. The scholar has been hard put to it to explain how the Egyptians built a pyramid or set upright an obelisk, a stone shaft cut in a single piece ninety-seven feet high. At Ba'albek, in Syria, one of the stones in the wall of the acropolis is just over 64 feet long—about the length of a cricket pitch—and 13 feet high and 10 feet thick, a finely cut block laid flush

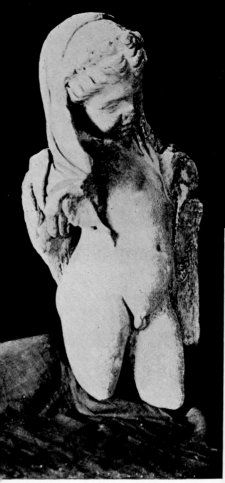

A Cupid and . . . .

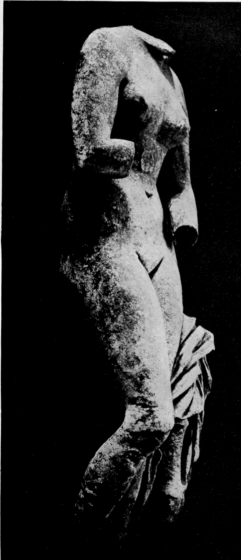

. . . . a Venus found in the
Roman baths near Teano

with the wall face not at ground level but 23 feet up. No machinery that we have to-day could lift that stone and lay it at that height in the wall; ancient man could do it because he had no machines.

I learnt my first very simple lesson at Teano. My expedition was not lavishly equipped but I did possess light Décauville trucks for shifting the soil, and a certain amount of line. But very soon my railway was too short to reach the dump-head and since there was no possibility of procuring any more steel rails I began to feel most unhappy. Not so Venturi. He went round the Teano shops buying or begging the metal binding from old packing-cases; then, on the spot, he felled a number of young poplar saplings, laid them carefully and made them fast with pegs driven into the earth on either side, and nailed the metal binding along the top. In the space of two hours or so we had a railway track which worked perfectly during the short time for which it was required—and of course it could always be mended in the event of a breakdown. That was mere improvization, but it was instructive.

Soon after I began work at Carchemish I was walking back one evening across the site, which was used as the village grazing ground, and saw the boy shepherd sitting with a sheep between his knees shearing it with a flint knife! While I watched he neatly cut off the last of the fleece, released the animal and threw away his "knife"; then picking up two large flints, with a few blows knapped out a fresh knife and pulling down another sheep proceeded to shear it. I asked the boy if he hadn't got any other tool, but he said "no; we used to have iron scissors, but the flint is so much better."

55

In my early days at Carchemish I had as foreman Gregori, of Cyprus, a veteran with fifty years of experience in archæology, who had worked under Cesnola, Arthur Evans and Hogarth; he could neither read nor write but he was a past master of his craft. What he did not know about handling stones (Cyprus is a stony country) was not worth knowing. I had agreed with the German engineers who were building the Baghdad Railway that they could carry off for their work the big Roman stones which cumbered the site of Carchemish and made excavation difficult; they laid down a light railway and one morning three Germans with ten or a dozen Arab workmen started operations. A particularly big block was selected for removal, but it was of an awkward shape and lay rather low down, and at the end of two hours of strenuous effort the stone had scarcely budged. Gregori lost patience and asked if he might be allowed to do the job. The Germans obviously resented his impudence in suggesting that he could do what they with all their tackle had failed to do, but I urged them to let him try. Gregori took two men armed like himself with crowbars and gradually tilted the block, putting small stones beneath it; then he arranged carefully selected pebbles and small boulders on a line leading from the block to the flat truck of the light railway. Measuring things by eye and shifting the stones an inch this way or that until he was satisfied that each was in exactly the right place, the three of them then went behind the block and with their crowbars gave it a further tilt. Perched as it had been on small stones it now slipped and rolled over; one of Gregori's boulders caught it just short of the centre of gravity and it rolled over again; the same thing happened, and by the time the initial impetus was exhausted the stone was half-way to the light railway. Once and twice the operation was repeated, and there was the great block sitting quietly on the truck. My workmen shouted applause and the engineers went away without a word.

Hamoudi, my Arab foreman, learnt his trade from Gregori. When we excavated the south gate of the city we found that the facing-stone at the end of one of the piers had fallen down and lay in the gateway; it was a block of hard and heavy limestone measuring rather more than nine feet by five, and the base on which it had stood rose eighteen inches above the pavement of the entry. For the sake of appearances I wanted to set it up again in its place and for that I had, I thought, the right machine, a tripod with heavy tubular steel legs and a stout chain working on a differential pulley. So we set this up and made the stone fast and pulled on the chain—and the steel legs bent into graceful curves and the stone never moved. So that was that. Then Hamoudi asked if he might try. I said, did he think that he could do it? and he said "Yes, if God will, but not if you are there; if you were about I should be nervous and kill someone." So I left him to his own devices and watched unseen. He had eight men to help him, and they used crowbars, a long and very stout rope and two strong poles, and with that simple equipment it took them but a short time to get the block up on its foundation, exactly aligned and precisely centred. Many years later I showed Hamoudi the huge stone in the wall at Ba'albek; he sat in silence, looking at it, for perhaps twenty minutes, and then rose to his feet. "I must go away," he said, "my head aches"; and as he went I heard him murmur "By Allah, *what* a foreman!"

One's own workmen, because they are simple folk, may teach one a lot about how men did things in a simpler age, and also (which is more important) how they thought about things. It is not so much *what* they think—though that is sometimes illuminating—as their way of approaching a problem or an idea; at least it is not our way, and we can only understand it by shaking ourselves free of our normal and traditional modes of thought, and by virtue of that freedom becoming to some extent mere human beings instead of civilized creatures of the twentieth century. In so far as we can do that we may be able rightly to interpret the works of primitive man that have come down to us. There are plenty of books in which modern writers analyse the art, the religious and the social ideas of the ancient world, with the most delicate instruments of psychological science and in the most abstruse philosophical language; a study of that sort may be very valuable for us, but—and this is the point on which I would insist—it is an analysis, and it does not in the least represent the way in which the ancient world actually thought. A Latin grammar gives us an elaborate analysis of the language spoken by the ancient Romans, putting it in the form of definite grammatical laws which are most useful; but the ancient Roman who spoke or wrote Latin as his native tongue was sublimely unconscious that any such laws existed—he merely wanted to say something and said it in the only way that expressed his thought. He did not speak according to rule, but we deduce the rule from the way he spoke. In the same way, if we archæologists want to understand primitive man from the odds and ends of things which he has left to us, we have got to approach them from the human side—and we may learn to do that from the men who work for and with us.

Chapter Three

CARCHEMISH ON THE EUPHRATES

IN 1911 the British Museum invited me to take charge of the excavations at Carchemish. Hogarth had done one season's work, to test the site, and now the Museum was prepared (thanks to a generous benefactor) to embark upon the biggest excavation it had yet attempted. Naturally I was delighted to agree to the offer. Hogarth had had T. E. Lawrence on his staff and suggested that I might like to continue the arrangement. I had known Lawrence since my time in the Ashmolean Museum when as a shy schoolboy, with a friend even more tongue-tied than himself, he used to bring me bits of medieval pottery found by workmen digging house foundations in Oxford, and I was very glad to have him now as my sole assistant. Of course the expedition was, by modern standards, most inadequately staffed. There were only the two of us, myself not nearly as experienced as I liked to think, Lawrence virtually new to the job. I had to be my own architect for the drawing out of plans, Lawrence took over the photography—I brought two trained Egyptian photographers with me but soon had to send them home as the exile in a strange land proved too much for them—and although Gregory of Cyprus was a tower of strength both for the technique of digging and for guiding the men yet, thrown as we were on our own resources, conditions were difficult enough.

From Aleppo to Jerablus, the modern village on the site of Carchemish, was a long two-days' journey (there was no railway then) done in *yailias*, light covered cars shaped like a drain-pipe in which one lay at full length on one's bedding, each drawn by three horses; there was a little platform at the back of the car on which the servant travelled, with a charcoal brazier on which he could keep coffee going and cook a meal of sorts when the time came. We passed through the village of Bab, being stoned *en route* by the villagers, and the country grew more desolate and more savage as we went; the only other village was Membidge, where we had some trouble with an officious policeman, and when we reached Carchemish, just in time to pitch our tents before night fell, it seemed like the ends of the earth. There however we got a welcome from the men Hogarth had employed. Jerablus could produce good-will, if little else; we had plenty of helpers, and when next morning I started to measure out the foundations of our expedition house to be, and enrolled a gang of men greeted by Lawrence as friends, I already felt at home. But it was far from easy going. In 1912 Syria was a province of Turkey, and Turkey was still governed, or misgoverned, by a Sultanate in the last stages of decay.

It is almost impossible for anyone who knows only modern Turkey to imagine what was the state of the country in those days. Semi-independent provinces were ruled by Valis whose term of office was uncertain (a hostile whisper in the ear of the Sultan and the Vali was dismissed) and their salaries *nil*; the Vali's object therefore was to collect as much money for himself as he could in a short time. His example was followed by all his subordinates, and the corruption was unspeakable—it was not an abuse, it was a system. For instance, the head of the Customs, so far from being paid an official salary, himself paid for his job; his duty was to send a certain amount of money annually to Stambul, and if he exceeded the minimum he acquired favour and a prolongation of office; but there was no limit to what he might impose as customs dues, and he was expected to live on bribery. My own difficulties with the government, and I had many, were due simply to the fact that I refused to give bribes. Then, too, there was complete anarchy in the country's finances.

I had travelled to Aleppo by land from Beyrouth, spending a certain amount of money on the way. When I came to draw up my accounts—which had to be audited by the Treasury—I found that it was impossible to say how much I had spent. I invoked the help of an Aleppine banker, and he drew up a formal statement for me. Every coin current in Turkey had five different values in the city of Aleppo alone—the *medjidiyeh* was worth so many piastres at the State bank, double as many at the railway station, half as much again in the bazaar and rather less at the post-office, etc., but even so it was more complicated than appeared, because your change would include various coins of smaller denomination—five-piastre pieces, for example—and each of these had its widely different values, so that merely counting the piastres did not help at all. Even in the tiny village of Jerablus the gold pound had a shifting value in piastres according as you paid it to one of the three little shops, to the tax-collector or at the station where the German engineers were building the Baghdad Railway. All I could do was to invent a fourth value and stick to it. But this financial problem was a sad headache for the director of an archæological expedition who, on the top of his other responsibilities, had to satisfy an incredulous auditor at home.

One is in duty bound to make the most economical use of one's archæological fund which is meant for digging and ought to be employed on digging, so far as possible directly; while there are all sorts of "overhead expenses" such as equipment and travelling, about two-thirds of the total spent ought to go in wages to the men. But the work of the staff is no less essential, and men cannot do their best work unless they are well fed and reasonably comfortable. Anything imported is certain to be expensive, but one can live well and cheaply if one makes proper use of local produce and sees to it that it is well cooked; and a house, adequate but not luxurious, should represent a real saving of money. Our Carchemish house (planned for a ten-years' dig) was of rough stone collected from the site, and mud-brick, one story high with a flat roof made native fashion of earth spread over poles and matting.[1] It was built round a courtyard and contained, apart from little bedrooms, a bathroom and the kitchen and servants' quarters, a museum storeroom (which could be expanded indefinitely), photographic darkroom, mapping office, and a large living-room where we could eat, read and entertain guests. The last was a

[1] This was the kind of roof which the people who brought to Christ a man sick of a palsy "dug through" in order to let down the bed before Him. (Mark 2 : 4.)

source of pride to us. There was a good open fireplace, a bookcase recess for our small library, we hung rugs (our personal property) on the walls, and when the railway employees digging the foundations of the station found a large and very fine Roman mosaic we lifted it, glueing canvass on to the *tesserae* and under-cutting and then rolling the whole thing up on a pole, like a sheet of linoleum, and relaid it in new cement in our sitting-room, and so could boast of a floor-covering which was a real museum exhibit. One piece of decoration however was less genuine. The lintel over the entrance door was made of a single big block of soft limestone, and Lawrence amused himself by carving on it the winged sun-disk which was the emblem of Hittite god-head. Only a month or so ago a distinguished archæologist sent me a photograph of the doorway anxiously inquiring what had happened to this fine and unpublished monument of Hittite sculpture! Lawrence would have enjoyed the joke immensely. Altogether ours was a very nice house, and since the total cost of it to the expedition was only £140 we could scarcely be accused of extravagance.

At Carchemish, as previously in Nubia, I was dealing with a civilization about which nothing was known, so that on the one hand my own ignorance was excusable and, on the other, every object that turned up was a novelty in itself and a new piece of evidence for the building up of history. About the later history of Carchemish a little was already known from Assyrian sources, but of the earlier periods nothing at all; it was tantalizing to find inscriptions which, one felt, must contain just the information that one wanted, but not be able to use them; they were written in the Hittite

(*top*) Sitting-room of the Carchemish expedition house, showing part of Roman mosaic floor

(*bottom*) Carchemish: the Temple of the Storm-god, looking towards the sanctuary from the Inner Court, with the great bull laver

hieroglyphic script, the translation of which still baffled all the efforts of scholars.

One of the greatest excitements and bitterest disappointments I have ever had was when we were digging at the Water Gate of the city and found fragments of a big basalt lion which had been the cornerstone flanking a gateway in the Hittite royal palace; on its flank had been carved a Hittite hieroglyphic inscription and above this was another inscription but this time in the familiar cuneiform of Mesopotamia and in the Assyrian language; here then was the bilingual, the key that we had hardly dared hope to find. But the lion was in fragments and of the Assyrian text only a few disconnected bits survived—groups of two or three signs that told nothing and could not by any ingenuity be associated with the Hittite version. The sad thing about it was that only sixty years before the sculpture had been intact; discovered in 1854, it had been dragged down to the riverside for transportation to the British Museum and then left there by the incompetent Aleppine in charge, and the village miller had smashed it up to make mill-stones. So the key was lost, and not until 1935 was another found, when a Turkish expedition unearthed at Karatepe in Cilicia a long inscription in parallel versions, Hittite and Phoenician; the many inscriptions which we brought to light—we more than doubled the number of Hittite texts previously known—did not at the time help us at all. Actually they gave us a lot of extra work. All the texts would have to be published and for that photographs alone were not sufficient, for many signs would be indistinct and the more so when, as often was the case, the inscriptions were on curved surfaces, while mere hand-copies could not be trusted.

For study the next best thing to the stone itself is a "squeeze", made by beating wet pulped paper with a brush on to the face of the stone, for this when the paper dries gives in reverse a faithful mould of the original; but for reproduction in a book the squeeze is useless. Since something had to be done I tried making the squeeze with a single thickness of paper (sticking on extra bits where the paper broke) and letting it dry on the stone, then sizing it with white of egg and painting in the background and the detail with Indian ink, so that the hieroglyphs stood out in white against a black ground. This of course could be photographed, and even when it was reduced to a tenth of its size the text was perfectly legible.

I was encouraged by the success of this experiment to try another. The British Museum wanted plaster casts of some of the sculptures found, and I had made a piece-mould of one monument carved in the round, a column-base supported by lions, but for somebody as inexperienced as myself the technical difficulties of making such a mould were very great and the time taken by it very long. Most of the things required were reliefs, about a yard square, which were standing upright, and plaster moulds of those would again be difficult to make and, if made, would almost certainly be broken before they reached England. So I made the moulds after the fashion of a squeeze but reinforcing them with constant additions of fresh sheets of paper, and then varnishing the inside; they were quite light and, provided they were kept flat, not liable to damage, and although the plaster-workers at home

A Hittite hieroglyphic inscription, the "blacked squeeze"

were very contemptuous and assured me that paper moulds were useless they none the less made from them an admirable series of casts which are shown in the British Museum to-day. It was fortunate, for since that time most of the reliefs have been terribly damaged and the casts are the more valuable as preserving the effect of the intact monuments.

The casts were wanted because by the Turkish law all the objects found in an excavation belonged to the Turkish Government, and the *firman* authorizing my work emphasized that condition, to which naturally I had subscribed. The Turkish authorities were surprised and almost shocked to find that I kept my word and Fuad Bey, the Commissaire, who had been instructed to act the part of a policeman and spy on everything I did, reported to Stambul that his job was a farce because there was not the least risk of theft. But I told him that the promise I had given referred only to the dig, and if I chose to buy antiquities anywhere else I considered myself free to do so, and as for smuggling them out of Turkey I had no objection to breaking the law and it was up to the authorities to catch me if they could. The challenge was accepted, and my smuggling became a recognized game. Since the British Museum bore the whole expense of the dig and got nothing out of it in the way of objects it seemed only fair that they should get things from elsewhere whatever the law might say—though of course the law-breaking was entirely my affair. Most of the things I bought were small and the smuggling of them was easy, but in the spring of 1914 I was faced with a real problem.

The natives of Amarna, a village ten miles away, had been plundering an ancient cemetery, and they brought everything they found to me and I bought the lot; then I divided it into two parts, presented one half to the Turkish Government and retained the other half for export. At the same time another cemetery was plundered by villagers at Deve Huyuk, about twenty-five miles away, and this stuff too came to me. After sunset there would arrive a little train of men with loaded donkeys; we would send Fuad Bey to bed and then in our sitting-room the antiquities would be unpacked and carefully arranged by the finders into the respective tomb-groups (they were very good about that) and then I would fix the price, which no one was allowed to dispute, and the objects would be stowed away out of sight. This went on for weeks, and at the end we had a large collection of great scientific value, a unique illustration of North Syrian culture in the sixth and fifth centuries B.C. For the sake of easy handling we packed the contents of both cemeteries in small cases measuring two feet by eighteen inches, and when all was done found that we had sixty-four boxes to smuggle out of the country!

I got them, without any trouble, as far as Aleppo and there handed them over to the British Consul and asked him to do the rest. He was about to move into summer quarters in the mountains above Alexandretta, so asked the Vali for an escort of Turkish soldiers as some of his baggage-carts would contain, among other things, consular archives; so a few account books, etc., were dumped into the carts containing my antiquities, and as the "archives" were to go to the British Vice-Consulate at Alexandretta the soldiers duly deposited the boxes in the Vice-Consul's shed on the beach. The Vice-Consul was a shipping agent and the shed normally contained goods for export, so it looked as if all would be plain sailing, but unluckily the truth leaked out, as truth will, and reached the ears of the Kaimakam or Governor of the province of Alexandretta. He could not remove the boxes because the shed, being Consular property, ranked as extra-territorial—was British, not Turkish ground—but he did the next best thing, he put an armed sentry at the door to see that no one else moved them and announced that once outside the shed they would be seized forthwith. This was check-mate.

I was at Beyrouth, knowing nothing of what had happened, when I went to the British Consulate and found the Consul-General deep in a discussion with the Commander of H.M.S. *Black Prince*, which was lying off Beyrouth, over instructions to be sent to our Vice-Consul at Alexandretta referring to a report just received from him. Now this was in 1914, when owing to the disasters she had suffered in the Balkan war Turkey was in a greater state of turmoil than usual; nobody was much surprised therefore when a telegram came from Alexandretta saying that there were rumours in the bazaar of a threat to massacre the Armenians. A second, more urgent telegram, arrived and H.M.S. *Black Prince* went at full steam up the Syrian coast; when she reached Alexandretta the situation seemed so serious that a force of marines was landed to safeguard the British Vice-Consulate, and immediately the storm clouds dispersed and there was no more risk of bloodshed; the marines returned on board ship, and with them they took sixty-four packing cases. The horrified Turkish sentry ran to report to the Kaimakam. The Kaimakam summoned the Chief of

Police and the Commander of the Forces and together they went to protest to the Vice-Consul. They did not have to go far. He was hurrying to meet them, and at the top of his voice he poured out his grievances: "Was he not the British Consul? Were not they the Kaimakam, the Chief of Police and the Army Commander? What were they doing? What were they going to do? Would they stand aside and let the representative of Great Britain be robbed in broad daylight by a lot of rascally sailors? Where were the police? Where was the army? Why did no one shoot the sailors? Why did they not open fire on the cruiser?" It took the agitated officials a long time to calm him down, and by that time they had forgotten all about the antiquities. When, later on, they remembered them they were content to regard the whole affair as an excellent joke.

That was the sort of thing that could happen in Turkey in the days of Sultan Abdul Hamid. It was a state of anarchy in which one had to fend for oneself. On my first arrival in Aleppo I took Lawrence with me to pay an official call on the Vali. Attended by two consular *kavasses* in their magnificent full dress of scarlet and gold we were shown in to the Vali's office and duly announced. Without a word the Vali got up from his chair and walked to the window and stood looking out with his back to us; it was a deliberate insult, for what reason offered I could not imagine, but something drastic had to be done. When at length he turned round it was to see me sitting in his place. "I think," I said gently, "that Your Excellency forgot to ask me to sit down." The Vali apologized for his "absent-mindedness" and sent for coffee.

At Jerablus the only writ that ran was my own, and

that made for simplicity in the work and things really went very easily after a few preliminary skirmishes at which one could afford to laugh. My Arab and Kurdish workmen were a fine lot, very high-spirited but easy to manage if you took trouble to understand their points of view and so could be regarded as a friend, and the work was fascinating. Carchemish had been a big town in the Roman period and the site was littered with column-shafts and fragments of architraves bearing imperial inscriptions, and only too often when one started to dig one came on enormous building foundations in solid concrete which had to be dynamited before one could get at the Hittite remains buried beneath them. After the work that I had done at Corbridge and at Teano it seemed rather queer to be blowing up Roman remains, even though they were all carefully planned before destruction, but it was quite obvious that provincial Roman buildings were of little importance compared with those of the capital city of the Hittites; so they had to go. And the Hittite buildings were splendid. Our work inside the old city was for the most part concerned with temples and palaces and such were generally adorned with sculptures; gateways were carved or inscribed with hieroglyphic texts, along the base of the walls ran a line of big stone slabs, three feet high, forming a sort of dado, and very often these were carved in relief with scenes of mythology or history.

The upper parts of the walls, built of mud-brick masked perhaps by coloured tiles or by a panelling of cedarwood, had fallen and perished, but the debris of them had preserved the lower stone courses. Where the deep-sunk Roman foundations had not made

Carchemish: (*top*) The "Royal Buttress" representing Araras,
King of Carchemish, with his family
(*bottom*) The long row of sculptured slabs in the King's Gate

havoc of the underlying Hittite work we might find a continuous row of twenty or thirty reliefs; often black basalt stones were used alternately with others of white limestone (the latter at least originally painted, but the paint had vanished) and the effect of those bizarre scenes in changing colours was most striking.

The finest series was a set of four slabs, all basalt, which we named "the Royal Buttress"; there was a long inscription and then figures of the king of Carchemish and the whole of the royal family, down to the baby in arms. It was found on a day on which there had turned up a party of American tourists, and I think it made the "high light" of their tour. When the top corner of the inscription appeared there was much excitement and the stone was duly honoured, according to the custom of the dig, with a fusillade from Hamoudi's revolver. Another stone was traced next to it, and Hamoudi, groping with his fingers through the loosened earth, pronounced it a relief with figures—he could feel a human head—and there were more shots. Almost immediately there came a third stone and a fourth. All the men were yelling at the tops of their voices, the earth was flying in every direction, American hats and Arab cloaks were flung into the air and American revolvers swelled the salute which Hamoudi was firing with every cartridge he possessed. It was a mad scene, most un-archæological, but very funny. One of our visitors was a newspaper correspondent, and I wish that I could give as picturesque an account of the day's doings as he printed in a San Francisco paper.

Beyond the Royal Buttress came a long series of slabs sculptured with figures of priestesses and temple servants carrying offerings, and as more and more reliefs appeared in what seemed an endless row the competition among the workmen to be put on to a site so rich in glory and *baksheesh* grew very keen. A pick-man working in another part of the dig came to me and reported that his job was finished; could his gang be moved to "the wall of pictures"? I had an idea that we were almost at the end of the reliefs and that there would be another buttress, this time ending in a door-jamb, and that the door to which this fine approach led might well be a double one with a decorated central jamb; so I put the gang not quite on the line of the reliefs but where I thought the door opening might be. Great was the pick-man's disappointment as he pointed out that the wall didn't run in that direction at all, so what chance had he of finding anything? Drawing a bow at a venture I said that I was getting tired of the reliefs and was now after something different. What was that? "Well," I said, "the reliefs are only reliefs; what about a statue of a lion carved in the round?" "A lion!" "Yes, but let's make it two lions," and the men started in joyfully. Another gang came with the same request and I put them just in front of the first lot. "Is there another lion here?" they asked anxiously and I told them, no; two lions were enough, and their job was to find a statue of a man, also in the round; and they were quite happy. A third gang was put ahead again, and I explained to them that the statue was of course broken and the middle gang would only get the body but the head would be in their patch of ground. Of course all this was pure guess-work, and although one may legitimately put forward theories to be tested one has no business to state them

Çarchemish; statue of the god Atarluhas on his lion throne

as facts, and even Lawrence was rather shocked at my presumption. Actually I was wrong. There *was* a doorway, with inscribed door-jambs, and it was where I had expected, but it was a single doorway with no decorated central jamb at all. But on the far side of the entrance (where I had thought the centre would be) there had been a great statue in basalt of the god Atarluhas carved in the round, a seated statue on a throne supported by two lions; and the first gang found the lions, the second the god's body and the third his head, just as if I had known all about it, which I hadn't.

The statue was broken and a few bits were missing, so we stuck it together, with cement to fill the gaps. In order that the cement might not crack by drying too quickly Lawrence draped the figure in a very splendid Arab cloak that he had, to keep off the sun; our men seemed curiously impressed. Naturally what we wanted was a good photograph of it, but as it faced south and the sun was always behind it this was difficult, and Lawrence, who was then acting as photographer, decided to try it by magnesium light, so that night after dark we went down and with a succession of magnesium flares took several photos. From the village the men could not see what we were doing, but they did see the flashes which like summer lightning illuminated the hollow in which the statue sat, and there was a real panic. The English had known, mysteriously, just where the thing lay, they had dressed it in a cloak of honour and now with their spells had brought the old god to life. He was Lord of the Storm, and what would he not do? We had a lot of trouble in allaying their fears, and they always looked upon Atarluhas with a certain suspicion. Now the statue has been broken up again and only a few fragments of it are preserved in the museum at Ankara, and I fancy that the destruction was deliberate.

Actually we did find the Temple of the Storm-god. There was an outer court with its range of service chambers and sculptured reliefs on its walls, and behind it an inner court at a slightly higher level in a corner of which was the altar of burnt offerings; in the middle, facing the door of the shrine, was a great basalt basin supported by two bulls carved in the round. The shrine was quite small, an exact square with inscriptions on the basalt door-jambs but the walls proper of polished limestone slabs, perfectly plain, above which had been mud-brick faced with glazed tiles with patterns of rosettes in white and yellow on a blue ground; in the wrecked interior a basalt column-base was found which implied one if not a pair of columns (the shafts would have been of wood) but gave no idea of where they would have stood; judging by such analogies as we possess they would have been outside the shrine, flanking its doorway. The interesting thing was the resemblance of this building to the temple of Solomon at Jerusalem; there too there was an outer and an inner court, the former decorated with reliefs; the Holy of Holies was a true square of almost identical size with that at Carchemish, absolutely plain but its façade adorned with hangings of coloured needlework; in front of the door was a bronze laver, or basin, supported by figures of oxen, and the altar of burnt offerings was in much the same position as in our temple; and if I am right in assuming two columns flanking the door they would correspond to the two columns, Jachin and Boaz, on either side of the door of the Holy of Holies. The Carchemish temple was an old one restored by King Katuwas in the ninth century B.C., very probably on the original lines; Solomon's temple was built only a little earlier and it was built not by the Hebrews, who had never learnt to build in stone, but by the Phoenician craftsmen of Hiram king of Tyre, and if, as is likely, his architects supplied the plan they may well have combined the ritual requirements of the Hebrew priests with the current fashions in temple construction. Solomon, having no local precedents to fall back on, would want a temple *à la mode*, and an adaptation of the Hittite model would suit his purpose admirably.

It is always a pleasure to dig up something new and then to realize that the novelty has yet familiar associations. When we were tracing the walls of the Outer Town we took the opportunity of clearing two or three private houses and one of them gave us ample reward. It was quite a large house, standing back a little from the town wall; it had been destroyed by fire, but it had also been the scene of a fierce battle; the floors were littered with weapons, and close to every door there were quantities of arrow-heads, many of them bent or broken, showing how the defenders had barricaded themselves inside the rooms and the attackers had carried one room after another by storm. Other objects gave us the date and the entire story. A clay tablet with a cuneiform text was an order from the Assyrian king for the collection of taxes, Carchemish being then subject to Assyria. But there were several Egyptian objects, among them a ring inscribed with the name of Psammetichus king of Egypt, from which

it was clear that the city had been intriguing with the
enemies of its overlord, and sealings from letters written
on papyrus bore the cartouche of Pharaoh Necho;
lastly, among the weapons, there was a broken bronze
shield decorated with rows of animals and a Gorgon's
head in the style of the Ionian Greeks. Our house
dated to the very last days of Carchemish, for the
battle had taken place in the year 604 B.C. when the
prophet Jeremiah thundered in triumph "against
Egypt, against the army of Pharaoh Necho king of
Egypt, which was by the river Euphrates in Carchemish, which Nebuchadnezzar king of Babylon smote";
and the bronze shield had belonged to one of the
Greek mercenaries who, as Herodotus tells us, served
in the Egyptian army and dedicated the spoils taken
from Gaza in the temple of Apollo at Branchidae in
Ionia. So, quite unexpectedly, something turns up in
the ground and there are the Hebrew Prophet and the
Greek "Father of History" brought together to bear
witness.

Unfortunately the excavations at Carchemish were
fated never to be finished. We had planned for a long
term and worked therefore systematically, clearing the
outsides of buildings so as to get the general plan before
starting to look inside them; we traced the Outer Wall
and cleared the defences of the Inner Town and we
excavated a number of early graves on the Acropolis,
leaving most of its buildings to be examined later, and
in 1914 the war interrupted everything. I returned to
the site at the end of 1919, this time with P. L. O. Guy
instead of Lawrence, and we worked through one ex-
traordinary season with war raging all around us,
French headquarters actually in our expedition house,

The author's goodbye to Carchemish

(*A caricature by a French archæologist*, M. L. Brossé)

and their enemies, Turks, Arabs and Kurds, just across the river. In self-defence I had to make a rule that there should be no fighting within four miles of Carchemish and was able to get that rule observed, but all the same it was archæology under difficulties. Some of my workmen lived outside the trucial limit so, when they came to work in the morning, left their rifles with the French outposts and recovered them again in the evening—occasionally, I'm afraid, turning round before they had gone very far to have a friendly pot-shot at the said outpost; but nothing serious happened. I had laid down my terms at a council of war which I summoned to meet me in the desert; most of the assembled chiefs were friends of mine and did not want to give trouble, but they protested that they were under orders to fight the French and did not see why they shouldn't. There was, of course, no valid reason other than my convenience, so at last I said, "Right, you have come to fight, but what are you fighting for?" To which they replied with the glib catchwords, "For the Turkish Government and for Liberty!" "Exactly," I answered, "and I have come here to dig for the British Museum and for Archæology. Tell me, which is greater, the British Museum or the Turkish Government?" and ordinary politeness obliged them to say "the British Museum". "And which is the greater thing," I continued, "Liberty or Archæology?". They had not the least idea of the meaning of either word, both strange to their vocabulary, but they did know their manners; "Archæology, by God!" they said in chorus, and so we were able to dig in comparative peace. When our season ended and we left Jerablus the truce ended also and the French were driven back and the ruins of Carchemish passed into Turkish hands. Since the mound, commanding as it does the great bridge over the Euphrates, was a valuable strategic point it became in fact, as it had always been in name, a military stronghold and forbidden ground for the archæological digger. This minor war left me thus at a loose end, and I returned to Egypt, putting in the season's work at Tell el Amarna of which I have told already; but just at this time the British Museum and the Museum of the University of Pennsylvania planned a joint expedition to Ur of the Chaldees, and a new chapter in my life began.

Chapter Four

UR OF THE CHALDEES

EVER since the middle of the last century it had been known that the mound of Tell al Muqayyar in southern Mesopotamia was the ruins of Ur, the city from which Abraham came. In 1854 the British Consul at Basra, working for the British Museum, had unearthed there inscribed clay cylinders, the text on which, when translated, proved the identity of the site. The object of the joint expedition therefore was not to discover Ur of the Chaldees but to learn as much about its character and history as excavation could teach. It was to be excavation on a large scale and spread over a number of years (actually I spent twelve years there), but from the outset I realized that it would be no use drawing up in advance a hard-and-fast programme of work. The site was so extensive that no expedition could ever clear the whole of it; one would have to select those parts which would give the best results from a historical point of view, and that meant that one must in some degree be guided by one's discoveries. One thing however was quite clear. The main mound, called by the Arabs "the Mound of Pitch" because the walls that showed in its sides were of burnt bricks laid in bitumen mortar, had been proved by the excavations of 1854 to be the Ziggurat or Staged

Tower which was the religious centre of the city; preliminary work carried out in 1919 by H. R. Hall of the British Museum had further proved that there was, connected with the Ziggurat, a large walled enclosure which one could safely take to be the Temenos or Sacred Area containing the principal temples. Obviously this area must take precedence over any other quarter of Ur.

Hall's experimental work had also brought to light a building whose sculptural remains marked it out as being of supreme importance, while the character of its architecture implied for it a date of very great antiquity; and as this little mound—Tell al 'Ubaid, it was called—lay some four miles away from the Mound of Pitch it was equally obvious that our efforts could not be confined to one spot. Tell al 'Ubaid had to be excavated, the Temenos of Ur had to be cleared; for the rest, we must wait upon events.

Before the expedition started, the outlines at least of the history of Ur were known as far back as 2150 B.C. At that time there began an epoch named after the Third Dynasty of kings who with Ur as their capital reigned over the whole Mesopotamian river-valley; the line had been founded by King Ur-Nammu and had been maintained through five generations, and those kings had left written memorials from which a fairly detailed account of their times could be made out. After the fall of the dynasty Ur ceased to be the chief city of an empire and its history had to be gathered from the more or less chance mentions of it made by the rulers to whom it was in turn subject, so that the record possessed little interest; of the time before Ur-Nammu nothing really was known and though the

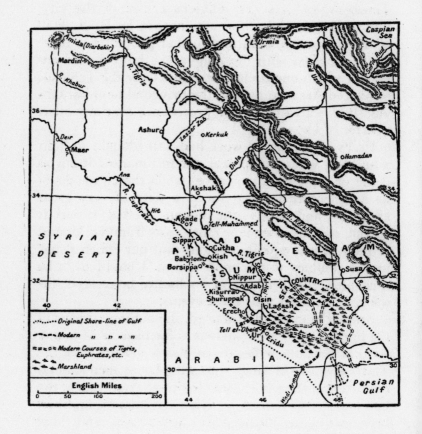

Map of Mesopotamia

names of earlier kings had been listed by the ancient compilers of the Babylonian "Outlines of History" they were not supposed to have had any historical existence but were regarded by modern scholars as mythological inventions. I was assured that I should undoubtedly find monuments of the Third Dynasty and possibly something a little earlier, of the time of Sargon of Akkad, a great ruler of the north country who reigned about 2385 B.C. and conquered the whole of Mesopotamia, but that would be my limit; most of the discoveries would relate to the later history going down to the days of Nebuchadnezzar and his successor Nabonidus, the last king of Babylon, in the sixth century B.C.

In the first season we dug only at Ur. We had to train our men, and for that it was necessary to concentrate; we ourselves had to learn something of the topography of the site; we had to learn something about the character of the antiquities of the historic periods, about which nobody knew a great deal and about which I was completely ignorant; incidentally we had also to build an expedition house. In the second season we finished the work Hall had begun at Tell al 'Ubaid and, at the same time, started to clear the Ziggurat. The last was a colossal piece of work, for the tower, still standing to a height of fifty-five feet, was so buried in fallen rubbish and drifted sand that one could ride up its sides without difficulty, and many thousands of tons of sand and rubbish had to be carried off in little baskets and then moved to a distance by our Décauville railway; fortunately much of this navvy work could be done with a minimum of supervision on our part and we were therefore free for the very intri-

cate work at Tell al 'Ubaid. Before the dig was ended
we had cleared the whole of the Temenos area suffi-
ciently to get its history from Ur-Nammu to Nabonidus, and in the neighbourhood of the Ziggurat we had
gone down to earlier levels; we had traced the defences
of the Inner City belonging to the early days when Ur
was a walled town; we had dug a considerable area in
that city, in, that is, the residential quarter, illustrating
the private life of the citizens during all the periods
from the Third Dynasty to the final desertion of Ur;
and we had excavated a vast number of graves of the
"historic" periods and two great cemeteries of what
had hitherto been reckoned as "pre-historic" date, and
below those had dug down to the levels that gave us the
foundation of Ur some time in the fifth millennium
before Christ.

I took with me to Ur, Hamoudi, my Carchemish
foreman, and a second sub-foreman from Jerablus to
help in the training of the men. We were warned that
the Muntafik Arabs from whom the gang would be
enlisted were the wildest and most unruly of the Mesopotamian tribes, and there was a good deal of truth in
the warning, but none the less they proved a likeable
and a trustworthy crowd. A day or so after reaching
Ur Junction we pitched our camps out in the desert,
enrolled our men and started work. I had arranged
terms with Munshid, the chief of the tribe, and among
other things he was to provide a guard for our safety;
the guard of five men duly appeared, but unarmed and
demanding rifles—which was a most transparent trick,
for they all had rifles of their own but wanted to increase the tribal armoury with a few British army
weapons; so I refused, saying that they would have to

bring their own the next day. But that night, or rather in the early hours of the next morning, I was awakened by shots and found that bullets were coming through the canvas of the tent. I went out and saw half a dozen men shooting at us from a slope thirty yards away; after emptying their magazines they rushed into the camp shouting "Rob, Rob!" and disappeared into the tents, from which everybody had now emerged. We had only two revolvers in the camp and my main concern was to prevent anyone shooting, since we were no match for six men with rifles. I was standing beside the (unarmed) head of the new guard when one of the robbers coming from my own tent passed close to us, carrying my suitcase; the guard rashly called out "I have seen you, I know you!", upon which the other turned and shot him through the stomach, killing him almost immediately. Then they all vanished with their loot.

The sequel was interesting. The thieves belonged to a sub-tribe of Munshid's Muntafiks and the dead man was his cousin; the murder meant a blood-feud, and in this the entire tribe was involved; the murderers therefore had no chance, and after three days they surrendered and threw themselves on Munshid's mercy. Tribal law was still allowed by the Government in cases between tribesmen, so the sheikh held his court and assessed the blood-money, which was promptly paid by the relatives of the guilty men, and, having thus secured his own interests, he handed the prisoners over to the State police, explaining in answer to their indignant protests that while the murder charge had been properly disposed of they had, unfortunately, also been guilty of armed robbery of Englishmen, and

87

for that must be tried by the Government courts; so tried they were and sentenced to two year's imprisonment. Two years later four men turned up at my house and demanded to be enrolled on the dig, claiming that they were old hands. They were; they had worked for me for one day and then shot me up! Sheikh Munshid's brother was at that time the head of my guard so I asked him whether he had any objection to my enrolling the men who had shot his cousin; he said, of course not; they had paid blood-money and he had nothing against them; crime was absolved by punishment. I agreed with his virtuous sentiments and the four men were at work the next morning.

That was the only serious trouble we ever had. I have already told how we overcame the initial propensity to steal; in a very short time there was no more danger of theft because the men had come to regard us as friends. When, years later, we dug the Royal Cemetery and the expedition house was full of gold objects worth some thousands of pounds even as bullion and an incredible amount as antiquities, none of it was even locked up; we kept it in cardboard boxes in the "antika-room" which had an outside door that wouldn't shut. I did however send for Sheikh Munshid and asked him whether, since the responsibility was his, he was quite satisfied with having only five guards on the site. As he seemed surprised at the question I produced several gold vases, remarking that they were a sample of the kind of thing that had to be looked after. The sheikh smiled and getting up from his chair walked to the window and pointed to the Ziggurat. "You see that brick tower?" he said; "if every brick in it were of solid gold and all the bricks were loose, I should still be

The Ziggurat of Ur

content with a guard of five men." The guard was, of course, a symbol; our real protectors were Munshid himself and the whole of his tribe.

It was not until the winter of 1926-7 that we dug the Royal Cemetery, but the existence in that area, not indeed of royal tombs but of graves richly furnished with gold objects, had been known since the first week of our first season when we had the minor trouble of thefts which I have already described. The real reason for postponing the excavation of the site was that we had to train the men, for the delicate work of tomb-digging cannot be done with raw labour, and we had to train ourselves also. So little was then known about Mesopotamian antiquities that it was impossible to date the things we found; thus, jewellery that turned up in that first season was taken to be late Babylonian, i.e. of the sixth century B.C., whereas some of it was in fact of the Sargonid period, seventeen hundred years earlier; and when we found the gold dagger, one of the finest objects from the Royal Cemetery, a very well-known authority pronounced it to be Arab work of the thirteenth century A.D., a judgment more than 3,000 years wide of the mark. If our discoveries were to have their proper historical value we had to work out some kind of archæological framework into which those discoveries could be fitted; it was therefore best to dig not graves but buildings, for buildings could, more often than not, be dated by inscriptions, and so any objects found in them could be put in their true horizon. So we left the Royal Cemetery alone for four years and dug elsewhere.

Even so we were not immune from mistakes. The clearing of the Ziggurat was, as I have said, a colossal

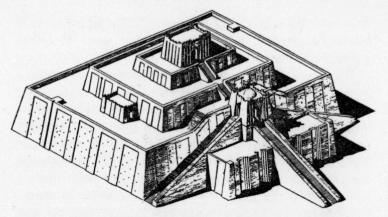

Reconstruction of the Ziggurat at Ur as built by King Ur Nammu, *Circ.* 2100 B.C.

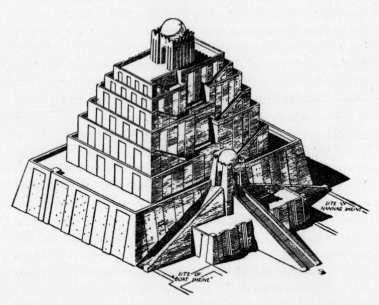

The Ziggurat as remodelled by King Nabonidus in the sixth century B.C.

task and work was done on it intermittently for many
years, but by the close of our second season so much
progress had been made that, since I had the invaluable help of Newton, perhaps the most experienced of
archæological architects, I was encouraged to put out
a conjectural restoration of the building as it was
originally. There had been Ziggurats in all the great
cities of ancient Mesopotamia but, of them all, that of
Ur was the best preserved, and so the Government
had very rightly insisted that our excavations should
not do any damage to its structure; none of the existing brickwork was to be removed. Now the existing
Ziggurat was built by King Ur-Nammu in about 2100
B.C. and many later rulers had repaired or altered it,
and traces of their work survived; not only were we
forbidden to move any of it so as to see what might
be below, but very often we could not recognize that
it was not original. Everything was of burnt brick, and
to us, in those early days, one brick, unless it was con-
veniently stamped with a king's name, was just like
another; apart from inscriptions, we had no means of
fixing dates. Consequently my "restoration" was far
from correct. Only when the experience of years had
taught us to distinguish the unstamped bricks of different periods was I able to unravel the difficulties of the
Ziggurat patchwork and to publish a restoration of it
that was reasonably close to the truth.

What really gave us a firm basis for archæological
dating was the excavation of Tell al Ubaid. There we
were continuing the work which Dr. Hall had begun,
and to his remarkable discoveries we added a great
deal more—copper statues and reliefs, mosaics in limestone and in shell, all of a kind new to Mesopotamian

archæology—and then had the crowning luck of finding an inscription which dated the building and all the
objects connected with it. I can remember few occa-
sions more exciting than that on which the workman
handed to me the little foundation-tablet of grey soap-
stone covered with what even I could see was very
archaic writing; I passed it on to C. J. Gadd, who was
standing beside me, for his verdict, and that usually
staid epigraphist executed a *pas seul* of triumph before
he could so much as tell me what he was triumphing
about. The text might not seem to have warranted
such enthusiasm—"A-anni-padda, King of Ur, son of
Mes-anni-padda King of Ur, has built this for Nin-
khursag his Lady"; that was all. But Mes-anni-padda
was recorded as the first king of that First Dynasty of
Ur which scholars had rejected as a mythological invention, and here was his name and that of his son on
a contemporary document to prove that the supposed
myth was sober history; we had rescued a whole
period from oblivion and carried back the history of
Ur by many hundreds of years. Our inscription would
have done that much if it had been an isolated discovery, but as the foundation-tablet of a building so
rich in objects of art it did much more; it enabled us
to put those objects in their right place in the historical
sequence and make the First Dynasty of Ur the
starting point for the systematic archæology of the
Euphrates valley.

What the field worker wants to establish is a sequence
so that he may arrange all his material in correct order
to illustrate the progress of culture, and with that done
his immediate task is finished. But if the cultures of
different countries have to be compared, a mere se-

quence is not enough; for such comparison the time
relation is all-important, and therefore you want not
only to define your periods but also to date them in
terms of years. You cannot do that on the basis of
pottery types or what-not; exact dates must depend on
literary evidence, and therefore the establishment of a
fixed chronology is the task not of the field worker as
such but of the historian. The task is not an easy one,
nor is the first solution necessarily correct. In 1924 it
was thought that the First Dynasty of Ur must have
started about 3100 B.C. and my publication both of
Tell al 'Ubaid and of the *Royal Cemetery at Ur* proceeded on that assumption. Now it is agreed that the
date 3100 B.C. was too early by two centuries at least
and my chronology—for which I was not responsible—
must be revised accordingly; that is a common experience, but the change of date ought not to affect at all
the truth of the sequence which the archæologist has
evolved from the material which is properly his own.

Although the discovery of the First Dynasty of Ur
was literally "epoch-making", yet Tell al 'Ubaid is
best known for something of a completely different sort
and of much greater antiquity. Little more than fifty
yards from the ruins of the temple which A-anni-padda
built we found the remains of a village which must at
one time have been pretty deeply buried but now, owing to the denudation of the mound by wind action,
lay almost at ground surface. The village houses had
for the most part been built of reeds or matting plas-
tered with mud—mud bricks were known but used,
apparently, only for such details as fireplaces—but
were none the less permanent structures having wooden
doors that turned on stone hinges. We found no trace

of metal, but quantities of stone implements, most of them chipped from the chert and flint that is common in the higher desert plateau, some of imported obsidian or volcanic glass; there were numerous flaked knives and scrapers, awls, etc., used for all sorts of purposes; arrow-heads for war or for hunting; large spoon-shaped hoe-blades for tilling the soil and small flakes with serrated edges that may have been let into wooden sleighs for threshing the grain; there were net-sinkers for the fisherman, loom-weights for the weaver and ear- or nose-studs of polished obsidian for personal adornment; the commonest instruments of all were sickles for cutting corn which were made of clay very hard-fired—they were sharp enough to be practical, but very brittle, and the fact that they would so easily snap in use would account for the number that we found, invariably broken. And everywhere there was pottery, fragments of hand-made vessels of a pale coloured clay, off-white or pinkish or greenish, decorated with simple designs in black or brown paint.

It was quite clear that the village belonged to the Chalcolithic Age, to the time, that is, when the Stone Age proper was past and metal was just coming into use but was still so rare and so costly that for all ordinary purposes men continued to employ the stone implements which had served their forebears. Consequently it was older, by an incalculable amount, than the First Dynasty of Ur which had produced the copper statues and reliefs of the Nin-khursag temple; those bore witness to a highly developed civilization far removed in character and in time from our primitive village, and the latter gave us a new and much earlier chapter in the history of the Euphrates valley. Thus it came about that in the technical jargon of the modern archæologist the term "al 'Ubaid" is used to denote not the treasures of A-anni-padda's building, which is properly described as of the First Dynasty of Ur, but the period and the culture of the early village with its distinctive painted pottery. Since 1923 similar pottery has been found throughout the Mesopotamian valley, from Eridu in the extreme south to Nineveh in the north, and westwards as far as the Amq plain near Antioch; but wherever it occurs it is called "al 'Ubaid ware".

Our work at the outlying site of al 'Ubaid had given us extremely important results concerning two disconnected periods; it had therefore set us a fresh problem which was bound to influence profoundly all our future work at Ur. Our original purpose had been to throw light upon the city's history back to the rise of the Third Dynasty in the twenty-second century B.C.; now we saw that we must also try to find material which would link up the Third Dynasty with the First and, again, the First Dynasty (of about 3000 B.C., as we then thought) with al 'Ubaid.

During the next ten years we went a fair way towards fulfilling that ambitious project, but if it is to-day possible to give a detailed account of the stages of man's cultural progress throughout that long period of time, that is not due simply to the excavation of Ur; the picture is a composite one, pieced together from the results obtained by many excavators excavating on different Mesopotamian sites. For it is a fact (which we archæologists are only too prone to forget) that no one excavation is going to yield all the truth. Supposing that we have a very well stratified site, rich in objects

95

of a historical character, and by digging carefully from top to bottom satisfy ourselves that we have an ordered and continuous record which can be put in historical form; then we may reckon ourselves fortunate indeed. But—and this is the important point—we shall be courting trouble if we assume that our record is either complete or universally true. If we do assume that, it is certain that sooner or later someone else working on another site will discover facts just as well established as ours which simply cannot be reconciled with our historical scheme. An excavation deals with a single town (if it be a town site) and in most cases with a relatively small part of the town's area; it is very likely that certain phases of the town's history happen not to be represented in the part excavated, sometimes because in a time of adversity whole quarters may have been uninhabited, sometimes because an important building within the excavated area survived through several historical phases without showing any traces of their passage, sometimes because the builders, preparing to erect a new building, have dug deeply for their foundations or artificially levelled the site and in the process have obliterated all evidence of former constructions. Our record therefore is liable to be incomplete. But however continuous it may seem to be, it is the record of one town only, and that town may have had a history very different from that of its neighbour. The facts that we have noted must stand, but the final interpretation of them must take into account all the known facts from other sites. Let me give an example of what I mean. Had I been asked to estimate the length of the al 'Ubaid period on the evidence afforded by the Ur excavations I should have said that it ap-

Hamoudi, foreman of excavations (from a bronze bust by Lady Woolley)

chana: the stone por-
it of a king, probably
rim-Lim, eighteenth
century B.C.

peared to have been relatively short; at al 'Ubaid itself there was no stratification and therefore no means of judging time, while at Ur the whole period was represented by not more than four occupation-levels, and for those a century and a half would be ample allowance. But at Eridu, close by, the Iraqi excavators found fourteen superimposed temples of which the uppermost was still of al 'Ubaid type, and at Warka (the Biblical Erech) the Germans found forty feet of al 'Ubaid deposit. Similarly at Warka there are at least twelve occupation-levels belonging to the Uruk period which succeeded the al 'Ubaid, and its buildings are the finest on the site, whereas at Ur that period was represented by a stratum of broken pottery and, as it happened, not by any buildings at all. If we had been digging in a different part of Ur we might very probably have obtained evidence of a different sort, conforming to that of Eridu and Warka, but we did not. It is possible that the Uruk period really was much shorter at Ur than at Erech, i.e. that the distinctive culture of Erech developed locally and took a long time to penetrate into the south country; but that is only a surmise, and for the working out of general history the testimony of Ur must be corrected by the witness of others.

The time-gap between the First and the Third Dynasties of Ur is a long one, and it would not be true to say that we filled it, but we did a good deal in that direction. Thus, at the back of the Ziggurat we discovered a headless statue on the shoulder of which was an inscription stating that it was a portrait of Entemena, who was king of the city of Lagash—not very far from Ur—about 2500 B.C., and ruler also of Ur, which his grandfather had conquered. Possibly he set up in the subject city his statue, which had certainly been made for use at home, or, possibly, after the people of Ur had won back their freedom they brought the figure home as a trophy to be set up in token of victory. But however the sculpture came to be at Ur there it was, in a public place, actually in a gateway of the Ziggurat enclosure, and to celebrate their triumph the townsmen knocked off its head. Not only was the break an ancient one, but the broken surface of the hard diorite was worn smooth and polished; I imagine that everybody who came through the gate contemptuously patted the top of the headless image of the former enemy of Ur.

The temple of the goddess Nin-gal, an ancient building many times restored by successive rulers, was a very precious source of historical information because in its treasury there had been preserved objects of all sorts dedicated to the goddess by great men of the past. The treasury of a Sumerian temple, just like that of a modern cathedral, was a regular museum of antiquities and in the present case accident had resulted in the survival of many of them. One of the most important was a terribly damaged disk of alabaster having an inscription on one side and a carving in relief on the other; the carving showed a priestess taking part in a libation ceremony before the statue of the goddess, and the inscription told us that it was dedicated by the daughter of Sargon the Great, King of Akkad. Not so very many years ago scholars were inclined to think that Sargon was a legendary character who had never actually lived; later his reality had been rather doubtfully conceded; but when the Princess Enheduanna is thus brought to life he becomes a very real person indeed. We can safely assume that the relief represents the princess, for she calls herself "priestess and wife of Nannar". Right down to the last days of the city's existence it was a common thing for the daughter of the reigning king (whether he were king of Ur, of Larsa or of Babylon) to be High Priestess of the Moon-god at Ur; it was so important a position—and the revenues attached to the Moon-god's temple were so great—that it was just as well to keep the job in the royal family, and this was already the custom in Sargon's time, in the twenty-fourth century B.C. If anyone were to doubt that this is what our alabaster disk implies we have virtual proof of it from another quarter. In the Sargonid graves which lay above the Royal Cemetery we recovered two seals and a seal-impression giving the names of three members of the Princess's household, her major-domo, her scribe and her officer of the harem; it is obvious therefore that Enheduanna lived at Ur, and the only reason for her doing so would be that she held some post which required her presence in the Moon-god's city.

There were many other inscriptions, not of great interest in themselves but important in that they helped to fill the gap in our record. One stone bowl bore the name of Naram-Sin, King of Akkad, the great-grandson of Sargon, and a second inscription, added later, by the daughter of Shulgi, one of the kings of the Third Dynasty of Ur; the bowl seems to have been kept as an heirloom in the royal house for a hundred and fifty years and then to have been dedicated in the temple by a princess who was perhaps in her turn the High Priestess of the Moon-god.

Isolated objects such as these are, of course, the "high lights" which memory retains; most of one's results are built up painstakingly from the routine work of every day. But when we came to deal with the periods before the First Dynasty of Ur, hoping to discover how there had developed the civilization which could produce A-anni-padda's gay temple at al 'Ubaid, then the routine work itself was memorable indeed. The clearing of the vast cemetery kept us busy for many months and from beginning to end there was not a day which would not have been a red-letter day in an ordinary excavation; if one remembers specially the royal tombs it was not so much because others were unexciting as because of the extra labour these involved. The normal graves, individual burials in coffins of wood or reeds, were often richly furnished, and as everything that they contained was new to archæology a very complete record had to be made; and they lay so thick in the ground (we excavated about 1,800) that it was difficult to keep pace with them; each had to be plotted in on the map, each had to be drawn and perhaps photographed, every object noted and numbered and—what was not always easy —removed safely from the ground, and it was generally when we were feeling most hard-pressed that the men would report a royal tomb. The character of any one of those was immediately obvious, for a royal tomb consisted of two parts, in the first place a tomb-chamber built of brick or stone, in which the king or queen was buried, and in the second place, connected with the chamber, a great shaft or pit in which would be found the bodies of those members of the court who were privileged to accompany their master to the other world. In one "death-pit" there were laid out in rows the bodies of sixty-four court ladies all wearing head-dresses of gold or silver and elaborate necklaces of gold, lapis lazuli and carnelian beads; they were undisturbed, and although everything was crushed flat by the weight of the soil it was yet possible—and therefore necessary—to recover everything in its proper order and so to have not merely a collection of beads, gold ribbon and what-not, but the complete head-dress as it was originally worn. We did not know how many of them there were, but the sides of the pit had been traced and then, at the bottom, strands of gold ribbon showed, first in one spot and then in another.

Most of the workmen were sent away and the few picked men who were left were told to clear away the earth down to the gold, but no farther, and then they too were sent off so that the final work with knives and brushes could be done by my wife and myself in comparative peace. For ten days the two of us spent most of the time from sunrise to sunset lying on our tummies brushing and blowing and threading beads in their order as they lay. Sometimes an exceptionally good head had to be cleaned for photographing and then "waxed", the whole thing—fragments of bone, gold ribbon, gold ear-rings, beads and all—fixed together with hot paraffin wax and muslin so that it could be lifted intact for exhibition in a museum case; there were lyres of silver or of mosaic work and gold which were in sorry condition and called for elaborate methods of salvage: it was an engrossing task, complicated by the fact that at any moment one was summoned away to look after something in another part of the dig, and it seemed unending. You might suppose that to find three-score women all richly bedecked with jewellery would be a very thrilling experience, and so it is, in retrospect, but I'm afraid that at the moment one is much more conscious of the toil than of the thrill. An incident not at all to my credit will show this. However careful we might be in rethreading the beads of the necklaces in their original order there were bound to be some that had slipped out of position; we contented ourselves with threading those of which we were sure and simply collecting the displaced ones in boxes, but as some of these might escape our notice altogether it was our rule that as soon as a head was finished the soil from that patch of ground was swept into a basket and taken off to be sifted by a workman appointed to the task. Passing him as I came back from a visit to another part of the field I asked him whether he had found anything, and he proudly showed me quite a number of gold and other beads, remarking that his was a fine job, just to sit still and earn *baksheesh*. I answered, as I thought, in like vein, "More of those cursed beads? I think that instead of a *baksheesh* you'll get a fine for every one you produce!" and went back to my threading.

Half an hour later there was a sudden uproar and I saw a number of men, shouting and waving picks, rush out from the work and lay violent hands on the earth-sifter; as they looked like murder I ran too, to stop them, but they had only laid him out and were searching his clothes. In great excitement they told me that they had been watching him and had seen him putting things into his pockets, he was a thief, a disgrace to the tribe and deserved death; he *was* a thief, for see what they had found; and they showed me beads, twelve of lapis lazuli, twelve of carnelian and twenty-four of gold. Of course I taxed the man with his guilt, but he seemed merely puzzled. "Yes, I took them," he said, "but you didn't seem to want them. You said you'd fine me for them, and I didn't want to be fined; but they were there, so I took them as a present for my wife, who would like them very much. I am fond of my wife." There was nothing for it but to assure my self-righteous pickmen that there had been a misunderstanding for which I was solely to blame and to tell the "thief" privately that he was a fool for not seeing a joke and would of course get his *baksheesh*; but I felt that the real fool was myself. In any case it is not fair to the workmen to underrate their finds, and it does not encourage them to be careful in their work; the opposite policy pays much better. When, for example, we were digging the "Flood Pit" and there was little to be found other than broken pottery—but the pottery was invaluable, for it gave us precisely the historical sequence of which we were in search—I paid out quite a lot in *baksheesh*, often making a parade of enthusiasm over what was really of no interest at all, simply in order that the men might not, through boredom, grow careless and fail to put aside *all* the fragments. They had of course no idea as to what was important, and we could not be sure of our results unless we passed in review everything, common and rare alike, so we played our comedy and the men neglected nothing, hoping always that the most ordinary-looking potsherd might for some incomprehensible reason prove a gold-mine.

That was the most "exciting" work that we did at Ur, more so than the Royal Cemetery with all its

wealth of treasure. We knew what we were after, for
a little shaft which we had sunk below the Royal
Cemetery had already given us the bed of silt which I
had recognized as evidence for the Flood, but now we
were to test it on a larger scale and put it in its correct
historical setting. Our pit measured at the top about

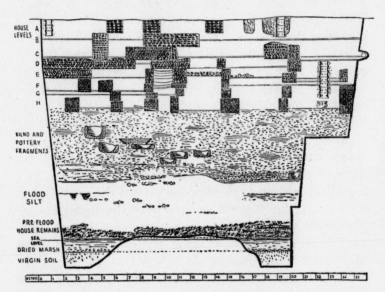

Section of the flood pit

twenty-seven yards by seventeen, and we dug down to
a depth of over sixty feet. At the top we had houses
roughly contemporary with the First Dynasty of Ur.
Below them came more house ruins, and below those
again six other building levels; and as we went down,
the character of the pottery found in the successive
houses changed and the early Dynastic wares were replaced by types which at Ur we had found in graves

lying below the Royal Cemetery, the Jamdet Nasr types (so called after the Mesopotamian site where they were first found) which are the hall-mark of a historic period very much older than the First Dynasty. But below the eighth range of buildings everything changed suddenly. Here there were no walls at all, but we were not digging into barren soil; in fact, there was very little soil, but a stratum seventeen feet thick made up almost entirely of broken pottery. As one examined the sherds one could see that a great many of them came from pots which had been overbaked or distorted by the heat of the kiln; they were in fact "wasters", vessels which had gone wrong in the firing and had no commercial value, so the potter had smashed them and thrown them away; we were digging through the rubbish-heaps of a factory which had been in business for a very long time. And as we dug we found, at different levels, the brick-built kilns in which the pots had been fired; each had in turn been buried beneath the accumulating sherds, and the potter had built a new one higher up. In the upper levels the pottery was of the Jamdet Nasr type; gradually this gave place to a plain ware, red or dark grey, which is equally distinctive, the "Erech" pottery first found by the German excavators on that site, which fills the gap between Jamdet Nasr and al 'Ubaid. It was in the Erech level that we found a potter's wheel, a thick disk of baked clay, made to turn on a pivot and heavy enough to keep on spinning of its own weight while the pot was being turned; it was the oldest potter's wheel known.

In the lowest levels of potsherds the Erech ware was first mixed with and finally replaced altogether by al 'Ubaid pottery, hand-made without the wheel, the product of the early and still barbarous villagers who first settled at Ur. Then we came to the flood deposit, eleven feet of clean silt, disturbed only by a few graves dug into it by the late al 'Ubaid people whose pottery we had just found; silt left piled up against the mound whereon the primitive town had stood by an inundation that must have overwhelmed all the low-lying villages of the river valley and destroyed what for those people was the world. Under the eleven-foot stratum lay the ruins of the houses in which had lived the antediluvian inhabitants of the Lower Town; they had, we may suppose, taken refuge on the mound, the Inner City, and from its walls watched their homes disappear beneath the muddy waters of the flood. This was the flood, coming in the latter part of the al 'Ubaid period, which the ancient Sumerians regarded as the outstanding disaster in their country's history, and out of the historic fact grew the legend which in the course of time the Hebrew people incorporated in their own sacred writings and handed on to us to-day, the story of Noah's Flood.

During the twelve years in which we worked at Ur we had not a few dramatic surprises and brought to light a vast amount of material of absorbing interest; but the most satisfying if not the most thrilling episode was the digging of the great pit which gave us in ordered sequence the whole record of history from the time when the first immigrants set up their huts of mud-daubed reeds on the drying marshland to that when, to the music of lyres, the men and women of the royal court went down into the death-pit that they might minister in another life to the dead King of Ur.

Chapter Five

TELL ATCHANA IN THE HATAY

WHEN, after the Ur expedition was over, I set about finding another site for excavation, my wife laughingly said, "First and foremost, of course, it must be a good site archæologically. But it *must* be in a green country, in sight of mountains, and not too far from the sea." Until then I had scarcely recognized what a strain Ur had been; twelve years in an absolutely barren desert, with its flat expanse of yellowish grey extending virtually unbroken to the horizon; but I did most heartily agree. And the spot I chose fully met our requirements.

The archæological problem on which I hoped to throw light was the connection between the Asiatic mainland and early Greece, particularly Crete. I could not believe that the wonderful civilization to which Arthur Evans's excavation of the Palace of Minos at Knossos bore witness was due entirely to the genius of the people of a small and isolated island; they must, I felt, have had something to go upon which derived from the older civilizations of the great countries of Asia. There was no literary evidence or early tradition to guide me, but a variety of arguments, largely geographical, led me to the Amq plain. This lies in the extreme north-west of Syria, in what is now the Hatay,

Early painted pottery showing the influence of al 'Ubaid

a province of Turkey; it is a hollow land between Aleppo and the sea, a fertile land watered by the river Orontes, closed in on the west and north by mountains, the Amanus and the Anti-Taurus ranges, and by rough hill country on the east and south. Here the Orontes turns west to break through the Amanus chain, past the site of that famous city Antioch, where the Christians were first so called, and a road, following the river, leads by one of the very few practicable passes, to the sea, and the river mouth makes one of the very few safe harbours on the inhospitable Syrian coast. Among the hundred and eighty ancient mounds that litter the Amq plain and testify to a past when it was rich and densely inhabited (in 1935 there were perhaps a score of squalid hamlets dotted over the fever-stricken marsh) I chose one, Tell Atchana, which from its shape and position was likely to have been the chief city and, since according to my theory it was to have Aegean connections and therefore needed an outlet to the Mediterranean, I took in addition a little mound, al Mina, at the mouth of the Orontes river. We had therefore all that we could ask in the way of amenities—a green and fertile plain, river, mountains and sea—but these made precisely the conditions required by our archæological problem; what appealed to us would have appealed equally to, and served the purpose of, ancient man.

Seven seasons of work, starting in 1936 and continued after the interruption of the war, more than fulfilled our hopes. We unearthed the royal city of Alalakh, whose ruins form the Atchana mound, and we were able to trace its history, and that of its port at al Mina, sometimes in great detail, over a vast expanse of time. The kingdom of which Alalakh was the capital was not a very large one, but it was a buffer state and the meeting-place of the great powers of the old world. At the very start, just after the close of the Stone Age, we find the people here making painted pottery which is in part at least derived from the painted al 'Ubaid ware that we found in Ur below the level of the flood. Because Alalakh commanded the route of the important hard-wood trade it was always in touch with Mesopotamia, and in very early days we find the local king building his palace after the fashion of the great Mesopotamian overlords.

About 2000 B.C., the city becomes for a time either the subject or the ally of Pharaoh, and its rulers put themselves under the protection of Egyptian gods, only to switch over in the eighteenth century and become the friends of Babylon, so that a royal portrait is now carved in the style of Mesopotamian art. As early as this we find just those connections with Crete which we had hoped to discover, connections which help to explain the growth of Cretan civilization, for the methods of building and the art of fresco decoration on the walls of the royal palace at Alalakh are exactly those which were to be employed in the palace of Knossos at a later date. In the fifteenth century B.C., in particular, the picture of the place given to us by the private houses and the graves of the citizens, by the city temple and the well-preserved palace of the king is made even more detailed and complete by written tablets and, above all, by the autobiography of one of the kings, Idri-mi by name, inscribed on the front of a statue which is a most unflattering portrait of a none-too-successful ruler. Right up to the end Alalakh

Local painted pottery of the fourteenth century B.C.

maintained its connections with the Greek islands of the Aegean Sea; Mycenæan vases were freely imported, and, about 1300 B.C., whereas the bulk of the painted clay vessels made at Alalakh itself were decorated with designs in the local Asiatic tradition we find side by side with these an elaborate pattern of papyrus flowers and double axes which is unquestionably borrowed from Crete.

Alalakh was destroyed about 1200 B.C. and after that the story is carried on by the harbour town, al Mina, where we have a wholly unexpected record of Greek trade down to the time of Alexander the Great. The most surprising thing is that Athens was busily exporting her manufactures to Persia throughout all those desperate years when she was fighting for her life against the Persians, and the most intriguing thing was to find quantities of duplicates of the familiar red-and-black painted Greek vases, proving that the Athenian factories went in for mass production and export on wholesale lines. Our record did not stop even there, and the last phase came when the Christian crusaders built their Port of St. Symeon over the ruins of the Greek harbour. Right up to the end this was the open gateway between East and West, and always the intercourse was fruitful, from the time when king Minos learnt from Asia how to decorate the walls of his palace with frescoes, to the time when crusaders sent home examples of the locally made glazed earthenware and by so doing started the manufacture of Italian majolica.

Once again we had to begin our work with inexperienced workmen who had to be properly trained. It was a strangely mixed gang that we enrolled—Moslem

Atchana: statue of King Idri-mi inscribed with his autobiography

Arabs, Turks and Kurds, pagan Alaouites, Greek
Orthodox Syrians and a few Armenians—but far more
intelligent than the Muntafik of southern Iraq, and
luckily I still had as foreman Hamoudi, the veteran
of Carchemish and of Ur, assisted now by two sons
trained to follow in his steps. Foremen make or mar
a dig, and it is not only technical skill that one requires
from them but also, or even more, character and ability
to deal with men. In 1936 politics intruded unpleas-
antly on our work. Syria, newly independent, claimed
the Hatay for its own, and Turkey claimed it too; in
the country, and on our work, everyone took sides and
passions ran high, and one Sunday propagandist
agents from Syria distributed pamphlets urging the
Arabs to rise in arms—"the land was Arab; the Turks
were the enemy; every Arab must now fight and, if
need be, die gloriously for his country"—half our men
had the illicit broadsides hidden in their breasts and
eyed the Turks askance, gripping their picks or fumb-
ling at their long knives, and things looked dangerous.
Hamoudi gathered the Arabs round him and producing one of the pamphlets proceeded to read it aloud;
he read with dramatic eloquence and with obvious
approval, and excitement rose high. "Splendid," cried
Hamoudi as the reading closed on the note of battle.
"Splendid! Who wrote this, and where is he?" There
was a puzzled silence and then one said, "He is a
leader of the Nationalist Party in Aleppo". "But where
is he now? I want to follow him. Surely he is about to
march and to die gloriously for the country; where is
he?" Someone volunteered, "In Aleppo". "And what
is he doing there? He tells us to die, isn't he going to
set the example?" There was an awkward pause and

then somebody laughed. Hamoudi changed his note:
"When the man who writes so beautifully about dying
comes here and dies himself, perhaps I shall do the
same," he said caustically, "but until he does I shall
just get on with my work. And you, what are you
idling for? Grrr, on to the job, all of you!" and shouting with laughter the men went off and fraternized
with "the enemy".

Hamoudi could even turn the situation to our advantage. At the end of the season we had the dull
task of filling in the trenches and levelling the ground
for agriculture, which I reckoned at five days' work.
Hamoudi formed the pro-Arabs and the pro-Truks
into two parties, one for filling the wagons from
the spoil-heaps, the other for running the cars,
and explained that there was to be a competition
as to whether the filling would go too fast for the cars
or the cars run too fast for the fillers. "This", he said,
"is war between the two nations, and the prize is the
Hatay; on you it depends whether the Hatay is to be
Turk or Arab," and he solemnly produced Turkish
and Arab flags. He gave the Turkish flag to the Arab
party: "You", said he, "are Turks," and the Turks
received an Arab flag and were told that they were
fighting for the Arab Government; "I myself am a
Turk," he added. The men entered into the jest with
enthusiasm. The dirt flew, the wagons ran as they had
never run before and if they ran off the rails were
lifted back by sweating and screaming wagoners; the
Arabs were shouting "Down with the Arabs, the Hatay
for Turkey!" while the Turks yelled "Death to the Turks,
long live Damascus!" and men worked till they dropped,
and the ground was smooth and level in two days and

Atchana: clay goblet painted
with a design derived from
Cretan art

An Athenian vase
from al Mina

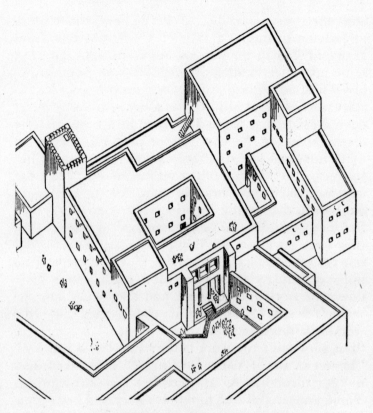

Reconstructed view of the fifteenth century palace of
King Niqmepa

Hamoudi proclaimed a dead heat which, he explained,
meant peace for the Hatay. The Turkish Vali afterwards told me that it was an incredible performance
and the most effective piece of diplomacy that he had
come across.

After the war Yahia, the eldest son, took Hamoudi's
place because his father was really too old for the work

and also was a member of Parliament and had to attend the sittings. Yahia is of a different type from Hamoudi but in his way no less competent. In 1948 some misunderstanding about his Syrian passport delayed him at the beginning of our season and I had to start work without him. It was a heavy programme of deep digging that we had in hand and I was bitterly disappointed at the slow rate of progress. I enrolled more men and still it looked as if the work could not be finished by the end of the season, in which case the expense would have been in vain. All the men were old hands, thoroughly experienced and good workers, but they had fallen far below standard; it was not that they were obviously slacking but simply that they did not get on. At last I told them that if there was no improvement by the end of the week I should close down the work and go home, and they would lose the season's wages. "You are quite right," they said, "the work is a disgrace." "It *is* a disgrace," I answered, "but why don't you work better? You can if you try." "How can we, if Yahia isn't here?" they asked, and to that there was no answer. But the next morning Yahia appeared. I told him that things had been going badly but that he must let the men down gently at first, not drive them too hard; he agreed and going on the work just greeted the men cheerily as they flocked to kiss his hand and then stood about making an occasional jest. Half an hour later one of the Turks on my staff came to me to ask what had happened, for the men were working as he had never seen them work, and I told him it was because Yahia was back. "Yes," he said, "he's back, but he isn't doing anything, and he hasn't said a word about working." "No," I

(*top*) Athenian oil flasks illustrating methods of mass production
(*bottom*) Painted and glazed bowl made at al Mina in the crusading period

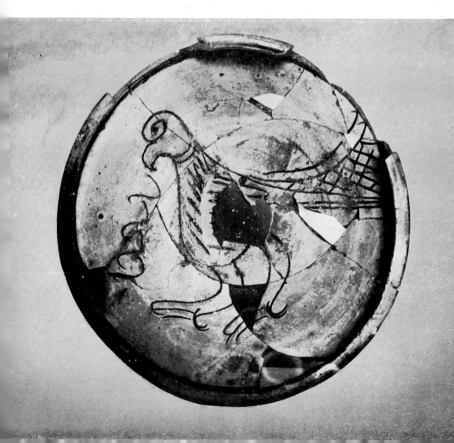

answered, "but he's back," and for the men that was everything. Actually I sacked nearly half the men and we finished the work with the remainder well before the end of the season.

In most cases an archæologist is using public money, and he is in honour bound to make the best use of it. He cannot in advance guarantee scientific results to the value of his expenditure, but he must see that there is no waste. If his men do not work well then the wages represent a sheer loss, and it is there that a good foreman can assure economy both by getting a proper return for wages and by enabling the director to give more time to the scientific side. In any case the unfortunate man has his hands more than full with jobs of every kind, and I know very well that I could never have coped with the digs at Ur and at Atchana if I had not been blessed with admirable assistants and with foremen on whom I could rely absolutely. The digging season in the Middle East is short—largely because of the weather, but there are other good reasons—and the overhead expenses are heavy; therefore the work must be done at high pressure. In my own experience this means for the director a working day of fifteen hours, seven days in the week; he has to be on the dig all day long, from six o'clock or earlier till about four-thirty, and after tea there is the indoor work which will keep him busy till midnight; and even at meals the talk will generally be of a business nature. At home, naturally, he will keep shorter hours, but working over his material and writing up his reports is an unending job, and he will look forward to his retirement from digging as an opportunity to catch up with arrears. It really is a strenuous life, and looking back on it I feel immense gratitude to the various members of my staff who have relieved me of so much that I could ill have done myself, and have made possible such success as I have enjoyed.

APPENDIX

Since this book deals in a rather haphazard way with many different historical periods in different countries, it may help the reader if these are arranged in a more or less chronological scheme.

MESOPOTAMIA	SYRIA AND AEGEAN	EGYPT	B.C.
The al 'Ubaid Period			(?) 3500
The First Dynasty of Ur			c. 2800
Sargon of Akkad			c. 2385
The Third Dynasty of Ur			c. 2150
		The Twelfth Dynasty	c. 2000
Hammurabi of Babylon			c. 1780
	King Yarim-Lim of Alalakh		c. 1780
		The Eighteenth Dynasty	from 1580
	The Great Palace of Knossos		from 1500
	King Niqmepa of Alalakh		c. 1450
	King Idri-mi		c. 1400
		Tell el Amarna	1370
	The Hittite Empire		c. 1400-1200
	The End of Alalakh		1194
	The Kings of Carchemish		from c. 1000
Nebuchadnezzar destroys Carchemish			604
Nabonidus			555
	Athens secures the port of al Mina		525
			A.D.
		The Meroitic Period	from c. 300
	Crusaders at al Mina		from 1097

INDEX

ON YOUR MARKS

Ready, set – learn how to get a good education

DETROIT FREE PRESS

DEDICATION

To the hands that rock the cradle

FOREWORD

When Free Press staff members decided in 1992 to produce a special section on elementary education, little did we realize we were setting in motion a three-year effort that would culminate in this book.

The 1992 special section — "It's Elementary" — was wildly successful. Parents loved it, teachers loved it. Through the education pipeline, it made its way around the country. It won awards. It sold out.

The next year, it seemed only logical to tackle the next segment — middle school. "The Kids in the Middle" appeared in October 1993. Parents loved it, teachers loved it — you get the idea. The die was cast. The 1994 special section would be about high school. And to satisfy the continuing interest in the previous sections, all three would be compiled into a book.

"On Your Marks" is designed to help parents better understand what their children need to learn in school and how they should be learning it.

Articles from the 1992 and 1993 sections are reprinted here with only minor changes. Some of those quoted may have changed jobs or schools; students have advanced. Those changes are not reflected.

What is reflected are the ideals of educators today — the changes they advocate in hopes of stimulating kids to think more creatively. Educators are trying to adjust to a dramatically changing world — one where rote learning and hidebound teaching no longer are prized. They believe today's students should be challenged to explore, to think critically, to be active learners.

As you read about what is happening in schools all over Michigan, make comparisons to your own schools. How do they stack up? Are they where you want them to be — or where they should be? What can you do about it?

Knowledge, after all, is power. With this book, we hope to place a little more of both in *your* hands. Then it's up to you. ○

Kathleen O'Gorman
October 1994

THE STAFF

EDITOR: Kathleen O'Gorman

DESIGNER: Tim Oliver

COPY EDITOR: June Day

REPORTERS: Debra Adams, Amber Arellano, Emilia Askari, Cami Castellano, Marian Dozier, David Everett, Robin Fornoff, Dan Gillmor, Marty Hair, Stephen Jones, Wendy Warren Keebler, Bill Laitner, Robert Musial, Craig Porter, Joan Richardson, Cassandra Spratling, Linda Stewart, Margaret Trimer-Hartley, Mike Williams

PHOTOGRAPHERS: William Archie, Patricia Beck, Duane Burleson, John Collier, William DeKay, Timothy D. Easley, Hugh Grannum, George Gryzenia, Daymon J. Hartley, Alan Kamuda, Richard Lee, Daniel Lippitt, Pauline Lubens, John Luke, Steven R. Nickerson, Craig Porter, Mary Schroeder, John A. Stano, Cathy VanSchwartz

PHOTO EDITORS: Marcia Prouse, Robert St. John

PRODUCTION ASSISTANCE: Diane Bond, Mike Floyd, Andrew J. Hartley, Jessica J. Trevino

ACKNOWLEDGMENTS: The Free Press is grateful to the many parents, teachers, educators and others who assisted our staff. This effort would not have been possible without their support. In addition to those named elsewhere in the book, the Free Press would like to acknowledge these sources:

American Association for the Advancement of Science
American Association of University Women
"Creating a Classroom Climate of Equity: A Look at Teacher Behaviors," by Alberta Dory
Creative Classroom magazine
"The First Grade Readiness Checklist," by John J. Austin
Gesell Institute of Human Development
"Growing Up Confident: How to Make Your Child's Early Years Learning Years," by Melitta Cutright
Michigan Department of Labor
North Central Regional Educational Laboratory
"Ready for School? What Every Preschooler Should Know," by Marge Eberts and Peggy Gisler
U.S. Bureau of Labor Statistics
U.S. Commerce Department
Universities of Michigan and Houston

ON THE FRONT COVER: On their marks and ready to learn are (l-r) Khary Hobbs, 11, from Malcolm X Academy in Detroit; Megan Opie, 6, from Springfield Plains Elementary School in Springfield Township; and Maysan Haydar, 17, from Carman-Ainsworth High School in Flint Township. (Maysan, who is Muslim, wears a traditional hair covering.) Photo by Steven R. Nickerson

CONTENTS

IT'S ELEMENTARY   1-65

CHAPTER 1

CONTENTS

CHAPTER 2

CONTENTS

HIGH SCHOOL, HIGH STAKES 129-207

CHAPTER 3

IT'S ELEMENTARY

Megan Opie
with one of her
favorite possessions.

Your child's future is at stake

Nuthin'.

Chances are you've heard that response or some version of it when asking a child, "What did you learn in school today?"

Yet you know they should be learning *something*.

What they should be learning, or how they should be learning it, may not be so clear.

Take reading, for example. Dick and Jane are long gone.

Many educators, in fact, are moving away from teaching children to read with text-books. Instead they're using good literature — storybooks, fables, fairy tales and other material.

This section on elementary education is intended to help guide parents through the confusion. It leads off with lists of elementary-level skills and behavior traits. The experts who provided the information would agree, however, that it doesn't matter so much when children acquire skills — just that they do.

Children are individuals. Some learn faster or slower than others. Some excel early in one area while picking up another much later. That's OK.

More important than learning particular skills is learning how to learn — how to get and use information, think critically, question, solve problems and work and play cooperatively with others.

Not every school teaches the skills at the same grade level. Ask for your school's curriculum to find out when skills will be taught. If the curriculum is hard to understand, ask the principal or teacher to clarify it.

And, of course, ask the teacher what skills he or she expects children to master by year's end. Find out what activities you can plan at home to assist. Don't be shy. Remember, your tax or tuition dollars pay the bills and your child's future is at stake.

Look for articles in this section on the academic reforms that are changing elementary schools. The articles are designed to help your child meet the educational challenges that will be expected of him or her.

Despite changes in what children are learning and the way they are learning it, one fact remains: The surest way to develop a love of learning in young children is to be active, enthusiastic learners yourselves.

Read regularly to your children. Let them see you reading and learning — and enjoying it. And show them how what they're learning applies to their lives — something the very best classroom teachers are doing. O

BUILDING CONFIDENCE

A foundation for success

Like "The Little Engine That Could," children aren't going to do well in school unless they think they can.

To get them on the right track, moms and dads can create a supportive environment at home, one where their children learn to have faith in themselves and their abilities.

They can help them develop a positive self-concept or a feeling of self-worth and self-competence. It's called self-esteem.

And it's elementary. People who feel good about themselves — who have high self-esteem — are more likely to do well in school and life, studies show.

Their counterparts, those on the low end of the self-esteem scale, are usually the ones who become teenage drug abusers and dropouts. They're more likely to get pregnant or father a child before they get their driver's license, or to join gangs or kill themselves.

"The self-image influences who you are and what you do," says Garry Walz, an education professor at the University of Michigan and coauthor of a book, "Students' Self-Esteem: A Vital Element of School Success," published by the Educational Resources Information Center, a nonprofit government agency housed at U-M.

"We've got to help people look at that self-image and polish it," Walz

Kary Hatcher, 5, skips as Eben Levy, 8, turns the rope at Cathedral School.

says. "The time to intervene is at an early age. At that age, parents and teachers are particularly important. But as they grow older, particularly among males, peers assume greater importance."

So, while they've still got their attention, parents should let their children know they're loved — not for what they can do but for who they are.

They also can encourage children to set goals and work hard to achieve them, take appropriate risks so they can learn their potential, handle failure so the next time they can profit from what they've been through and dream about success — not just in material terms but in

HOW TO BUILD IT

Psst! Want to know one of the most important things you can do for your children? Help them develop good self-esteem.

That's a person's feeling of self-worth. People with high self-esteem make good decisions. They're proud of their accomplishments, willing to take responsibility and able to cope with frustration. They also are likely to be creative because they'll meet challenges and take risks in new situations.

Good feelings about oneself begin at home. When children feel they are listened to, taken seriously and genuinely cared for, their self-esteem is high.

Here are some ways parents can help children to like themselves:

☆ Self-esteem is a byproduct of accomplishment. Involve young children in simple projects such as making cookies, letting them do more of the steps each time. For older kids, skiing, hiking or acting accomplish the same thing. Don't overlook the deep satisfaction that

continued ▶

HOW TO
BUILD IT

continued ▼

skill development, such as mastering a musical instrument. To find your child's talents, provide as many different kinds of experiences as possible.

☆ Reward children. Give praise, recognition, a special privilege or increased responsibility for a job well done. But don't go overboard because it can backfire; some children might think they are worthwhile only when praised.

☆ Focus on the positive. Say, "You're good at picking up" or "You're terrific at sharing." When a report card has five A's and a C, say, "Five A's! This is wonderful!" Later say, "Let's see how we can turn the C into an A."

☆ If your child has behaved badly, criticize the behavior, not the child. When a parent says, "You are a bad boy" rather than "What you did was bad," it can be devastating. Discuss problems without placing blame or commenting on a child's character. If chil-

continued ▶

4

BUILDING CONFIDENCE

terms of how they can help others.

"Ultimately, the responsibility for self-esteem rests with the person himself," Walz says. But "one needs to look at the environment and culture in which a person functions to understand both their level and source of self-esteem."

Children who come from families or communities where education isn't valued, or who have peers who think it's nerdy to do well in school, might have a difficult time academically. It isn't that they're intellectually inferior, but they've tied their self-worth to other areas, such as acceptance by friends or playing roles they think society expects.

Such is the case with black students who may have high self-esteem but who buy into negative stereotypes of black people, says Chicago educator Jawanza Kunjufu, author of "To Be Popular or Smart: The Black Peer Group."

Because some of these children fear that being smart is "acting white," they choose not to try to excel in class. Others are afraid to try because they fear failure.

The consequences are frightening; much potential is lost.

To counter the negative forces, Kunjufu and other counselors say students must be taught their history so they can take pride in their cultural identity. They need to know the advantages of doing well in school — that their odds of success are better with a good education and hard work than with drugs or crime — and they need to see and meet positive black role models.

In short, they need to know that being smart and being black complement, rather than contradict, each other.

Role modeling is important for girls, too. A 1991 report from the American Association of University Women found that girls, especially after they reach high school, are most afflicted by low self-esteem.

As a result, they are less likely to tackle more challenging or male-dominated courses such as math or science. They're afraid to take the risk or be seen as different.

"If they feel good about themselves, they're not going to care that much if it's nontraditional to take advanced math," says Jeanne Bleuer, associate director of the Educational Resources Information Center, a nonprofit government agency housed at U-M.

A person with high self-esteem also is less likely to give into peer pressure to please others.

"A person with high self-esteem will say, 'I am a person who is worthy of being loved by myself and by others?'" Walz says. "'I am competent to deal with challenges and problems which I experience on a daily basis?'"

Researchers emphasize that building self-esteem is a great deal more than giving pats on the head. Bleuer, who wrote the self-esteem book with Walz, says high self-esteem comes from true achievement, from

BUILDING CONFIDENCE

hard work.

"It's so important in the early years to build in experiences for kids in which they can succeed so that they can feel good about themselves," she says.

But experts discourage teachers from lowering their expectations to give students a false sense of accomplishment. That can do more damage in the long run when children are unable to compete, or devastated because they never learned to deal with and overcome failure.

In addition, schools must place more emphasis on encouraging all students to study hard, rather than focusing on those for whom learning comes easy.

"We have to create rewards and respond in ways that say we appreciate the effort you put into that," Walz says. "We value your persistence and ability to keep working until you get it right."

Bianca Pritchett, 3, left, and Dorothy Thompson, 5, have a snack break at the Cathedral School in Detroit's Cultural Center.

HOW TO BUILD IT

continued ▼

dren know of a problem but don't feel attacked, they are more likely to help look for a solution.

☆ Define limits and rules clearly, and enforce them. But allow leeway within the limits.

☆ Be a good role model. Let your children know that you feel good about yourself. Also let them see that you too can make mistakes and learn from them.

☆ Be available. Give support when children need it. Spend time together and share favorite activities.

☆ Use phrases that build self-esteem. "Thank you for helping" or "That was an excellent idea!" Avoid negatives: "Why are you so stupid?" ○

WHAT KIDS ARE LIKE

Most children start preschool at age 4. These characteristics describe a typical 4-year-old:

☆ Egocentric, but usually involves others in play and talk.

☆ Boastful: "I'm bigger than you are." "I can jump higher than you."

☆ Loves words, word play and silly language.

☆ Asks questions. Endless "whys" and "hows."

☆ Highly confident. Loves adventure, excursions, anything new: games, people, places.

☆ Loves humor.

☆ Speedy — not interested in perfection, but keeps moving to the next activity.

☆ Loves to run, jump, climb and gallop.

☆ Prone to hitting, kicking and spitting.

☆ Loves to talk about and make big or

continued ▶

Little ones play, share, solve problems

Pupils in prekindergarten programs should:

■ Be curious: Ask many questions and express interest in how things work.

■ Be able to choose between at least two outfits, two meals, two activities.

■ Solve problems: Know what to do if something is out of reach; know what to do if lost or if something spills — for example, to ask for help.

■ Begin to engage in complex play, as in playing with puppets or creating skits or building a city with blocks.

■ Participate in routines: Songs before story time, show and tell, cleanup.

■ Develop a positive relationship with adults: Accept input, directions and questions.

■ Begin relating to other children by listening, respecting and asking questions.

■ Develop friendships with other children.

■ Begin to solve minor social problems and skirmishes.

■ Begin to share things with other children, take turns.

■ Begin to understand and express feelings.

■ Seek assistance when necessary.

■ Imitate adult behaviors, play make-believe games.

■ Speak and listen for variety of purposes.

■ Contribute relevant information to conversation.

■ Understand the meanings of "big" and "small," "up" and "down," "top" and "bottom."

■ Understand spatial relations, such as above, below, beside, inside, under, close, far away.

■ Begin classifying things such as farm or zoo animals or big and little things.

■ Relate personal experiences in simple drawings, speech or other ways.

■ Identify major body parts.

■ Know age.

■ Be comfortable with numbers.

■ Begin to understand one-to-one correspondence, such as setting the table for four people with four plates.

■ Develop more complex sentences, with some descriptive words and details.

■ Show interest in reading activities, such as story time, looking at illustrations and telling stories.

MASTERING SKILLS

- Demonstrate knowledge about books, such as how to hold them.
- Know names of basic colors.
- Build with blocks, boxes and other materials.
- Draw and paint. Enjoy working with a variety of media, such as crayons, clay, finger paint and construction paper.
- Begin using writing tools.
- Sort objects by color, shape, category or size.
- Begin to recognize likenesses and differences in pictures and designs, recognize patterns.
- Begin to take pride in work.
- Begin to understand rhythm.
- Begin to follow music and movement directions.
- Enjoy listening to and making music.
- Take care of toilet needs.
- Dress themselves (except for tying shoes and zipping).
- Know parents' names.
- Run, jump, hop, walk down stairs.
- Throw a ball underhand.
- Know how to use a tissue.
- Separate from parents with ease.
- Clean up toys, tidy messes.
- Understand basic safety rules: no biting, no jumping, no running in class.
- Know simple ways to help others.
- Enjoy school.

WHAT KIDS ARE LIKE

continued ▼
ENORMOUS things.

☆ Also loves detail and prefers books with highly detailed illustrations.

☆ Shows little self-restraint and appreciates when boundaries are set: "You may go as far as the tree."

☆ Exaggerates and even lies: "High as the sky," "10 million bugs."

☆ Can be persistent to the point of being obnoxious.

☆ Has a wild imagination and concocts elaborate play scenarios.

☆ Becomes more aware of good and bad in the world.

☆ Loves stories about how good or how bad parents were when they were young.

☆ Fascinated by bowel movements and bathrooms.

☆ Loves other children, especially 4-year-olds. ○

Busy, busy, busy learning the basics

What can kindergartners learn? The following skills have been compiled from various educational sources in Michigan and are intended as a broad picture. In kindergarten, children are learning to:

MATH

- Write numbers 0 through 9.
- Count spontaneously 0 through 20 and backward, 10 to 0.
- Count objects, up to about 15 or 20.
- Recognize and say numbers 0 through 20.
- Match a specific number of objects with a numeral. For example, place 10 beans on 10 dots drawn on a piece of paper. Or demonstrate the number 10 by creating a pile of 10 beans.
- Add whole numbers, up to 10, using objects. Example: Add a pile of three beans to a pile of four beans and count the total number of beans.
- Estimate which set has more or less. Example: Which pile has more beans? Which line is longer? Which rod is smallest? Which object is heaviest?
- Compare objects by size.
- Place objects in sequential order by size.
- Identify ordinal numbers — first, second, third, etc. — by using objects.
- Measure lengths using nonstandard units (toothpicks, string, interlocking cubes, craft sticks, etc.).
- Identify basic shapes. Example: circle, square, triangle, rectangle.
- Classify and sort objects. Example: Separate orange and blue buttons.
- Sort the same collection in more than one way. Example: Separate the buttons by size or shape.
- Recognize simple patterns, continue them and make up new ones.

LANGUAGE ARTS

- Follow simple two- and three-step directions.
- Learn songs, poems and rhymes.
- Speak in complete sentences and so others can hear.
- Listen when somebody is talking.
- Begin to speak with ease before peers and adults.
- Listen for a variety of purposes, such as for facts, for directions.
- Understand and use some nonverbal communication: hand signals, facial expressions.
- Begin to describe events in correct sequence.

WHAT KIDS ARE LIKE

These characteristics describe the typical 5-year-old kindergartner.

☆ Wants to be and usually is very good. It's called the "golden age."

☆ Usually is very positive. Frequently uses words such as "sure," "wonderful" and "lovely," and phrases such as, "I love you."

☆ Is very close to mom. Many prefer following their mothers around to playing with friends.

☆ Lives in the here and now.

☆ Knows limits and usually lives within them.

☆ Loves to be read to.

☆ Loves to tell stories.

☆ Is developing restraint and an ability to sit still for longer periods.

☆ Loves to talk.

☆ Still has trouble distinguishing between fact and fantasy.

continued ▶

MASTERING SKILLS

- Begin to describe events in correct sequence.
- Participate in mini-plays, puppetry and dramatizations.
- Be familiar with the library.
- Identify parts of a book, title, author, illustration.
- Name some authors and illustrators.
- Understand concepts of print: front and back of book, left to right progression of text, return sweep, word-space relationships.
- Understand that print is speech written down.
- Know that people read for different reasons.
- Know that there is a variety of types of literature and be familiar with poetry, fairy and folk tales, informational text and biography.
- Show interest in a variety of literature.
- Retell a story chronologically, orally and through drawings.
- Begin to describe the main idea or problem of a story.
- Make simple predictions about stories.
- Begin to name characters in a story.
- Identify mood of a story.
- Begin to understand setting of a story.
- Distinguish who, what, where and when in a story.
- Recognize many letters and numbers.
- Know many letter sounds when experienced in familiar contexts, such as favorite stories, billboards, etc.
- Recognize words in the environment.
- Distinguish rhyming words and be able to name some.
- Be able to classify words, letters, pictures, objects in a variety of ways, such as putting things that begin with "B" in one group and those that begin with "M" in another; list all words that relate to a farm.
- Use letter recognition, context, topic knowledge, illustrations and other clues to decode new words.
- Print name.

S O C I A L S T U D I E S

- Begin to consider other viewpoints relating to gender, race, religion or disability.
- Show respect for differences among people.
- Begin to accept responsibility for behavior.
- Begin to develop a sense of past.
- Begin appreciating the environment and develop awareness of responsibility for the future.
- Begin to understand that everybody must follow rules for safety and order.
- Begin to learn how to gather information from a variety of sources.
- Begin to understand the difference between wants and needs.

WHAT KIDS ARE LIKE

continued ▼

☆ Often makes generalizations based on inadequate evidence: all brown dogs are female; fathers die before mothers.

☆ Is modest about body and bathroom functions.

☆ Loves television; prone to ask for every toy and item seen in advertisements.

☆ Gets choosy about friends.

☆ Is sensitive and protective of younger children and pets.

☆ Begins to accept that mistakes are part of learning.

☆ Concentrates on tasks for 10 to 15 minutes. ○

Julia Kelly, *5, of Harper Woods, drew this self-portrait.*

IS YOUR CHILD READY?

☆ Has the child passed a thorough physical exam? Does the child have all immunizations required by school?

☆ Does the child uses rest room without assistance?

☆ Does the child ask for help when necessary?

☆ Can the child use a tissue or handkerchief when needed?

☆ Does the child play well with other children, share toys, handle conflict?

☆ Is the child content in group activities?

☆ Can the child make simple decisions about such things as what to play or how to organize time? Can the child make simple choices?

☆ Does the child speak clearly and without using baby talk?

☆ Can the child repeat a sentence with five to eight words?

continued ▶

MASTERING SKILLS

- Begin to understand the difference between wants and needs.
- Begin to understand what people need to survive.
- Begin to be able to resolve minor conflicts.

V I S U A L   A R T S

- Distinguish between bright and dull colors.
- Be able to name and identify colors (red, yellow and blue, orange, green and violet).
- Work with paint, clay, chalk and many other media.

M U S I C

- Enjoy listening to and making music.
- Become aware of expression, melody and rhythm in music.
- Recognize the difference between high and low tones, loud and soft.
- Recognize fast and slow tempos.
- Understand that melody is the arrangement of pleasing sounds.
- Explore sound using a variety of sources other than voice.

F I T N E S S   *(Kindergarten and first grade)*

- Walk, run, hop, jump in place, leap horizontally.
- Twist, bend, stretch, push, pull, kick.
- Throw underhand.
- Kick a stationary ball.
- Participate in daily vigorous physical activity.
- Identify body parts, skills and movement concepts.
- Understand safe use of play equipment.
- Enjoy participating in physical activities alone and with others.

☆ Does the child speak in complete sentences?

☆ Does the child understand and follow rules?

☆ Can the child complete a series of three directions?

☆ Has the child been taught basic safety rules: Look both ways before crossing street, understand some traffic signs and signals?

☆ Does the child adapt well to being away from home? Tantrums and tears should not occur when separated from mom and dad.

☆ Does the child know right hand from left?

☆ Is the child able to use crayons, paste, clay and such items comfortably?

☆ Can the child tell and retell stories?

☆ Does the child sit still and listen to a story for five to 10 minutes?

☆ Can the child work independently for at least five minutes?

☆ Can the child copy simple shapes: square, triangle, circle?

☆ Can the child bounce and catch a large ball? Can the child throw it overhand?

☆ Does the child recognize similarities and differences in sizes, shapes and colors of objects? ○

10

First grade goes beyond ABC, 1, 2, 3

What can first-graders learn? The following skills have been compiled from various educational sources in Michigan and are intended as a broad picture. In first grade, children are learning to:

R E A D I N G

- Follow multistep directions.
- Give simple oral presentation to a group of people.
- Begin to read orally with expression.
- Begin to understand library rules, care of books.
- Begin to find their own books in the library.
- Use title page and table of contents.
- Read frequently and more independently.
- Begin to distinguish between a story and a factual book about a subject, for example a story about rabbits versus an encyclopedia account.
- Recognize moral of a story.
- Understand cause and effect, even if they can't name it.
- Identify and describe basic story structure such as characters, setting and plot.
- Begin to identify poetry, fiction, mysteries and nonfiction.
- Make predictions about stories.
- Discuss similarities and differences in characters, settings and problems/resolutions.
- Begin to use a variety of sources — such as books, magazines, Weekly Reader — to deepen knowledge of topics.
- Know that many words have more than one meaning.
- Begin alphabetizing.
- Form upper and lower case letters.
- Use simple nouns in written sentences.
- Prewrite by collecting ideas orally or on paper through drawings, words or diagrams.
- Write simple sentences expressing complete thoughts using phonetic spelling.
- Begin to punctuate the ends of sentences.
- Begin to write short, simple stories.

M A T H

- Use problem-solving strategies: logical reasoning, acting out or using objects, using or drawing a picture, finding a pattern or guessing-and-checking.

WHAT KIDS ARE LIKE

These are characteristics displayed by typical 6-year-olds. As first-graders go through the year, they may developmentally turn 7 before their actual birthday. Six-year-olds are likely to be:

☆ The center of their own universe. They want to be first, be the best, always win and have the most of everything.

☆ Stubborn, bratty and arrogant.

☆ Ambivalent: want both of two opposites.

☆ Prone to reverse letters and numbers.

☆ Anxious, in need of constant reassurance that they're loved.

☆ Trying to be independent.

☆ Smart-alecks: "Why should I?" "Why do you want to know?"

☆ Demanding and difficult because they're so insecure and have great emotional needs.

continued ▶

WHAT KIDS ARE LIKE

continued ▼

☆ Very vulnerable. They can be warm, and extremely enthusiastic for new games and new ideas. They love to practice and show off academic abilities.

☆ Full of questions.

☆ Eager to read or learn about things.

☆ Smiling, laughing, giggling or dancing with joy when happy.

☆ In need of praise and compliments.

☆ Wonderful companions, but parents must have tremendous patience.

☆ Adoring of their mothers, but will blame them for anything that goes wrong. "Mommy, I love you!" can change in a flash to "I hate you!"○

IS YOUR CHILD READY?

☆ Does your child's kindergarten teacher recommend the child go on to first grade?

continued ▶

MASTERING SKILLS

■ Count spontaneously from zero through 100 and backwards from 15 to zero.
■ Read, write, compare and order numbers zero through about 100.
■ Count by ones, twos, fives and 10s to 100.
■ Use ordinal numbers — first, second, third.
■ Recognize and use +, - and = symbols.
■ Demonstrate basic addition and subtraction facts up to 9 + 9 = 18 and 18 - 9 = 9.
■ Demonstrate that whole things can be divided into two, three or four equal parts.
■ Practice estimation skills.
■ Tell time to the hour or half-hour.
■ Recognize, name and describe the value of pennies, nickels, dimes and quarters.
■ Recognize and use calendars, days of the week and months.
■ Estimate lengths and measure items with nonstandard units. Example: Use a paper clip or coin to measure linear objects.
■ Recognize, repeat and make up geometric and numeric patterns.
■ Make and interpret simple graphs, using blocks or people or everyday things. Example: Collect and graph information about birthdays or pets. Interpret the results of the graph.
■ Identify numbers on a calculator. Locate and use the on, off, plus, minus, equal and clear keys.

G E O G R A P H Y

■ Know geographic location of home in relation to school and neighborhood.
■ Know the layout of the school campus.
■ Use simple classroom maps to locate objects.
■ Identify state and nation by name.
■ Identify seasons of the year.
■ Describe characteristics of seasons.
■ Follow and give verbal directions such as here/there, left/right.
■ Distinguish between land and water symbols on maps and globes.
■ Construct and interpret single concept maps and other simple data.

S O C I A L   S T U D I E S

■ Identify family structures and discuss how families are alike and different.
■ Explain why rules are often necessary within families and at school.
■ Discuss ways that people resolve conflict and interact.
■ Appreciate cultural, ethnic, racial and religious similarities and differences in the family and school environment.
■ Express their ideas about society, both orally and in writing.

MASTERING SKILLS

■ Demonstrate the ability to participate cooperatively in large and small groups in the classroom.

■ Demonstrate knowledge of current events from watching television.

■ Use clock and calendar time in daily activities.

■ Compare family life today to families in other times and places through group performances and discussions.

■ Express opinions on issues involving honesty, fairness and the rights of others.

■ Match visuals of baby animals with those of parent animals.

V I S U A L   A R T S

■ Identify basic shapes (circle, triangle, square or rectangle) as they

appear in two- and three-dimensional forms.

■ Recognize differences in texture by sight and touch.

■ Identify these textures: hard, soft, smooth, rough, coarse and fine.

■ Describe qualities of lines: curved, straight, wavy, zigzag.

■ Continue to develop fine muscle coordination by using scissors, brushes, crayons, markers and wire to make art and crafts.

■ Continue to cut, fold, weave, paste and shape art materials.

■ Paint and sculpt art objects that reflect themes from nature and literature.

Michael *Williams, 6, of Detroit drew this self-portrait.*

■ Develop and apply a visual-arts vocabulary on which to build.

■ Use imagination to create art.

M U S I C

■ Distinguish between loud and soft tones and fast and slow tempos.

■ Expand music vocabulary.

■ Discern sounds made by different instruments, such as a piano, drum or bells.

■ Create sound patterns by playing simple classroom instruments.

■ Read some music symbols and identify classroom instruments.

■ Know that a note represents sound and a rest represents silence.

■ Respond to music through physical movement.

■ Enjoy listening to and making music.

IS YOUR CHILD READY?

continued ▼

☆ Will the child be 6 or older before school begins?

☆ Does the child seem as mature as other children that age?

☆ Does your child show some signs of becoming a rebellious, argumentative 6?

☆ Can your child copy a circle counterclockwise, starting at the top? A triangle? A divided rectangle?

☆ Does your child hold a pencil in a good two- or three-finger grasp?

☆ Can your child print his or her first name?

☆ Does your child know upper and lower case letters out of context?

☆ Can your child count to 30?

☆ Can your child write numbers up to 20?

☆ Does your child know right from left? ○

Second-graders grow in reading

What can second-graders learn? The following skills have been compiled from various educational sources in Michigan and are intended as a broad picture. In second grade, children are learning to:

R E A D I N G

■ Work cooperatively in groups, listen to others, ask questions when things are unclear.

■ Assess more aspects of own work.

■ Start reading in different ways, such as skimming, to get different information.

■ Give simple directions.

■ Distinguish different types of writing.

■ Become familiar with genres, such as mysteries, fables.

■ Use many strategies, including context and phonics, to figure out new words.

■ Begin to recognize an author's writing style and purpose, such as humor or mystery.

■ Discuss story structure and details with others.

■ Summarize a story orally.

■ Understand and describe stories with multiple or complex problems.

■ Increase their understanding of cause-and-effect relationships.

■ Discuss feelings about literature; make connections with own life experiences.

■ Find plots, settings and styles of stories; compare and contrast stories; find descriptive passages and rhyming verses.

■ See that the setting of a story is related to the theme.

■ Recognize character traits and values in stories.

■ Begin to imitate various writing styles in their own writing.

■ Begin using commas and apostrophes.

■ Listen and take simple notes.

■ Begin cursive writing.

■ Use many pronouns in writing.

■ Use adjectives in writing.

■ Revise and proofread writing.

G E O G R A P H Y

■ Make and use simple maps of school and home neighborhoods.

■ Use compass directions — north, south, east, west.

WHAT KIDS ARE LIKE

The typical second-grader is 7 years old. In general, this is the age of withdrawal and calming down. If you're dealing with 7-year-olds, you'll find they are likely to:

☆ Be silent and often moody, morose and melancholy.

☆ Worry about everything. They worry that the family doesn't have enough money or that school might be too hard. They worry that they'll be late for school or that the teacher won't like them.

☆ Think that people are mean, hateful, unfriendly and always picking on them.

☆ Think that people don't like them, or fear that people may not like them.

☆ Be afraid of many things, including the dark. Might mistake clothes hanging over a chair for a burglar, ghost or spy. But at the same time have conquered

continued ▶

14

MASTERING SKILLS

■ Locate one's community, state and nation on maps and globes.
■ Identify a variety of types of transportation and communication within the community.
■ Differentiate between maps and globes.
■ Locate other neighborhoods studied on maps.
■ Compare pictures and maps of same area.

M A T H

■ Read, write, compare and order numbers up to four digits, or about 1,000.
■ Count by twos, fives and 10s.
■ Identify a number as odd or even.
■ Use ordinal numbers, such as first, second, third.
■ Use symbols for greater than and less than.
■ Know addition and subtraction facts through $9 + 9 = 18$ and $18 - 9 = 9$.
■ Use seven problem-solving strategies: make a table, make a list, act out or use objects, use logical reasoning, find a pattern, guess-and-check, use or draw a picture.
■ Estimate answers to addition and subtraction problems.
■ Use a calculator for simple addition and subtraction problems.
■ Begin multiplying and dividing.
■ Identify fractions, such as halves, thirds, quarters.
■ Estimate the number of objects in a given setting. Example: How many beans are on the plate?
■ Compare the length, area, weights of different objects.
■ Measure objects using standards units, such as inches or centimeters.
■ Identify congruent shapes — geometric figures that are the same size and shape.
■ Recognize and name squares, rectangles and circles.
■ Recognize that an object is divided into equal parts (line of symmetry).
■ Read temperature on a thermometer.
■ Tell time to the nearest quarter hour.
■ Make change with coins and bills.
■ Identify coins by heads and tails.
■ Identify days of the week and months.
■ Find a specific date on a calendar.
■ Use tally marks to keep track of information being collected for graphing.
■ Make and interpret simple graphs.
■ Do simple probability activities.
■ Work with patterns of numbers, shapes, colors, sounds, etc. Add to existing patterns, complete missing sections, make up new patterns.

WHAT KIDS ARE LIKE

continued ▼

earlier fears, such as fear of the dentist or swimming. And they are now more willing to tackle other scary situations, such as using a flashlight to face frightening shadows in the closet.

☆ Feel that he or she has "all the bad luck." Actually it may be little more than having to go to bed.

continued ▶

Neice *Wilson, 6, of Detroit, drew this self-portrait.*

WHAT KIDS
ARE LIKE

continued ▼

☆ Feel strongly that parents like the child's brothers or sisters better and that they do more for others in the family.

☆ Frown or cry easily.

☆ Withdraw or just quit when things don't go their way.

☆ Be able tell time by the clock. Many are eager to have their own wristwatches.

☆ Keep working at a task until it's finished.

☆ Be very serious, have high standards and ideals and be ashamed of mistakes. This might be the reason why, when doing desk work, the child erases so much. They are eager to do things right. ○

MASTERING SKILLS

SOCIAL STUDIES

■ Arrange and interpret social studies information in various forms, including prose, maps, graphs, tables, charts and globes.
■ Recognize that holidays are celebrated to honor certain people or events.
■ Discuss certain current events.
■ Cooperatively plan and implement a project that contributes to the well-being of a group of people.
■ Identify, chart and compare differences between colonial times and the present.

VISUAL ARTS

■ Use drawing and painting techniques to depict ideas, feelings and moods.
■ Describe differences between two- and three-dimensional objects.
■ Create two- and three-dimensional art that relates to familiar places, activities and events.
■ Describe expressive characteristics of lines: smooth, jagged, thick, thin, dark, light.
■ Experiment with dark and light values.
■ Become acquainted with works by artists.
■ Become familiar with art forms from a variety of world cultures.
■ Recognize that artists make art for different purposes.

MUSIC

■ Recognize the volume, pace and range of music.
■ Identify the sound of various instruments.
■ Create sound patterns using a variety of sources.
■ Enhance a song by using an instrument.
■ Sing melodic patterns.
■ Understand the quarter note, quarter rest and eighth note.
■ Recognize fast, moderate and slow tempos.

HEALTH AND PHYSICAL EDUCATION

■ Change direction and speed of travel quickly and safely.
■ Forward roll.
■ Throw overhand.
■ Dribble a ball.
■ Jump a self-turned rope.
■ Cooperate, take turns, share and demonstrate safety when participating in physical activities with others.
■ Name major body parts and their functions.
■ Understand the benefits of a balanced diet.

Rhyme and reason are on the horizon

What can third-graders learn? The following skills have been compiled from various educational sources in Michigan and are intended as a broad picture. In third grade, children are learning to:

L A N G U A G E   A R T S

- Manage time, make reasonable guesses and follow written directions.
- Understand the purpose of a reading, writing or listening exercise and set their own purposes for reading for pleasure.
- Use various methods for reading and writing.
- Begin to understand and use prefixes and suffixes to determine meaning of words.
- Read several books by the same author.
- Read for pleasure.
- Pose questions about literature and read to answer them.
- Be familiar with historical fiction.
- Begin to identify rhyme, punctuation and capitalization patterns in various kinds of poetry: limerick, haiku, couplet and riddle.
- Analyze characters, their actions, motivations.
- Begin to understand figurative language: simile, metaphor, personification.
- Identify topic sentence and supporting details in text.
- Read a newspaper article and name the five W's: who, what, where, when and why.
- Use dictionary, glossary, encyclopedia and other reference books.
- Use library for simple research projects.
- Write simple informational pieces.
- Use card catalog.
- Paraphrase an author's ideas.
- Spell conventionally on final drafts of work and spelling tests. Invented spelling is still OK on first drafts, journals, etc.
- Begin to use quotations.
- Use common, proper, singular and plural nouns and verbs and their regular past, present and future tenses. Children don't need to be able to name them.
- Use proper verb agreement, but not necessarily be able to name it.
- Use subjects and predicates, but not necessarily be able to name them.
- Capitalize geographical names, languages and titles of people.
- Use descriptive language in writing.
- Develop questions to guide simple research, such as "Why do bears

WHAT KIDS ARE LIKE

These characteristics apply to the average 8-year-old. As the school year goes along, they may developmentally be turning 9 before their actual birthdays. The typical third grader is:

☆ Enthusiastic about school.

☆ Fond of bringing things home from school.

continued ▶

Lalee *Xiong, 8, drew this self-portrait.*

WHAT KIDS ARE LIKE

continued ▼

☆ More likely to be interested in reporting about what happened at school than second-graders are.

☆ Beginning to compare abilities to other children's.

☆ Still fond of and admires the teacher, but loves to catch the teacher in a mistake.

☆ Less reliant on the teacher than in earlier grades.

☆ Interested in geography. Grasps a sense of the whole country, the whole world.

☆ Aware of the opposing forces of good and bad; wants to be good. Beginning to think in terms of right and wrong.

☆ Easily able to copy material from the board — shifting eyes from board to paper and back again.

continued ▶

MASTERING SKILLS

hibernate?"

■ Begin writing simple paragraphs that include topic sentences and supporting details.

■ Distinguish between fact and opinion.

■ Compile and use information from more than one source.

■ Give and receive help revising and editing writing.

■ Respect comments and opinions of others.

MATH AND SCIENCE

■ Use estimation with all problems.

■ Use problem-solving strategies: choose the method, solve a simpler problem, use logical reasoning, use or draw a picture, brainstorm, work backward, act out or use objects, guess-and-check, find a pattern, make a list and make a table.

■ Read, write, order and compare numbers through 10,000.

■ Count by twos, fives and tens.

■ Round two-place numbers to the nearest 10 and three-place numbers to the nearest 100.

■ Construct and compare fractions in physical form, such as half is greater than a quarter in a pizza pie.

■ Identify fractions of a whole number. Example: Half of 8 is 4.

■ Explore concepts of decimal numbers, using money to represent values. Example: .25 is more than .05, a quarter is greater than a nickel.

■ Use symbols for greater than and less than.

■ Solve simple addition and subtraction problems mentally.

■ Demonstrate the concept of division through repeated subtraction and pictorial expression.

■ Recognize and name shapes, such as triangles, squares, rectangles, circles.

■ Identify three-dimensional shapes: cubes, cylinders, spheres, cones, cylinders.

■ Demonstrate the concept of figures that are the same shape, same size.

■ Estimate before measuring.

■ Identify metric or standard unit of measure to be used for determining length, weight, volume or capacity. Example: A glass of milk would be measured in milliliters, the student's desktop in centimeters.

■ Use concrete models to compute perimeter and areas of a square and rectangle.

■ Interpret temperature from everyday situations. Example: What is a comfortable room temperature? 50 degrees C, 70 degrees C or 20 degrees C. (Answer: 20 degrees C).

■ Tell time to the nearest minute.

■ Use calendars for problem solving. Example: Jane is born in March. Her friend Nyasha was born 15 months later. In what month was Nyasha

MASTERING SKILLS

born?
- Express value of money in decimal form. Example: Two dollars and 35 cents = $2.35.
- Explore concepts of probability, such as the chance of something happening. Example: If you toss a penny 10 times, how often will it land heads? Tails?
- Interpret the results when given tally marks.
- Make, read and interpret simple bar graphs, picture graphs and tables.
- Use calculator in problem solving involving one or two operations. Example: 4 x 5 + 3 = ??? (Answer: 23).

SOCIAL STUDIES

- Describe problems in various communities and suggest solutions.
- Describe similarities and differences between communities in terms of age, size, location and culture.
- Explain the importance of urban, suburban and rural areas both past and present.
- Develop a sense of pride in their local community and an appreciation for communities unlike their own.
- Define and contrast the terms: goods and services, public and private services, consumer, producer, taxes, sales, property and income.
- Name and describe some services provided with tax money.
- Identify at least three ways in which technology has resulted in community changes.

FINE ARTS

- Identify and describe themes in specific works of art.
- Use more complex color systems.
- Appreciate and differentiate textures in art.
- Understand and use principles of composition.
- Begin to develop a visual arts vocabulary; know the proper names of basic tools, such as a paintbrush, and use words that relate to or describe a process, characteristic or trait of works of art, such as painting or watercolor.
- Create two- and three-dimensional works of art.
- Use imagination, sensory awareness and personal experience in creating art.
- Recognize the functions, cultural origins and relative age of artworks.
- Appreciate different artistic expressions in society.
- Demonstrate an appreciation of design and craftsmanship in man-made objects.
- Recognize, count and apply some rhythmic notation (such as whole, quarter, half and eighth notes).
- Begin to control vocal expression and sing using accurate pitch.

WHAT KIDS ARE LIKE

continued ▼

☆ Able to understand money has meaning and will buy things.

☆ Far more outgoing than 7-year-olds.

☆ Emotionally impatient and demanding.

☆ Strongly interested in adults. Relationship with adults is close but complex.

☆ Secretive and self-critical. Feelings are easily hurt.

☆ Less self-centered than earlier. Recognizes the views of others.

☆ A talker. Seems just to like to hear his or her own voice.

☆ Able to see ways in which objects are alike and different.

☆ Able to apply simple logic to reach a conclusion. Can reason deductively. Can classify.

☆ Able to picture a series

continued ▶

WHAT KIDS ARE LIKE

continued ▼

of actions, such as going on an errand and returning.

☆ Becoming aware of impersonal forces of nature. Example: Understands that wind, which is invisible, makes a sailboat go.

☆ Often able and willing to work out problems alone, needing only a hint from an adult.

☆ Interested in code language, like pig Latin or double Dutch. Enjoys using secret passwords.

☆ Likely to use considerable slang and profanity, although family and school influences can limit this.

☆ Generally truthful, but prone to exaggeration, boasting, telling tall tales. Most can differentiate fact from fantasy. ○

MASTERING SKILLS

■ Describe music in terms of expression, rhythms, instruments and form.
■ Recognize a change of dynamics and of tempo within a piece.
■ Understand that music may have different purposes.
■ Read some music symbols and identify many instruments.
■ Respond to music through physical movement in terms of expression, melody and rhythm.
■ Enjoy listening to and making music.

HEALTH AND PHYSICAL FITNESS

■ Climb rope.
■ Dodge a ball.
■ Jump down from a height.
■ Understand how the body is organized into cells, tissues, organs and systems.
■ Recognize the major parts of the skeletal and muscular systems.
■ Review the use of the four food groups.

Adverbs, story problems add to challenges

What can fourth-graders learn? The following skills have been compiled from various educational sources in Michigan and are intended as a broad picture. In fourth grade, children are learning to:

L A N G U A G E   A R T S

■ Put in sequence and summarize information that is presented orally and in writing.
■ Be familiar with tall tales, adventures and other genres.
■ Refine reading strategies: Read for details, skim, identify main ideas, make connections among the characterization, setting and plot.
■ Recognize implied meaning of words.
■ Draw conclusions from information.
■ Use and understand graphics in informational writing.
■ Do many kinds of book reports.
■ Use biographical information and nonprint resources such as videos and computer programs.
■ Use irregular present, past and future verb tenses, but not necessarily be able to name them.
■ Define and identify comparative forms of adjectives.
■ Use "a" and "an" correctly with nouns.
■ Use adverbs.
■ Understand compound subjects and predicates.
■ Understand idioms.
■ Recognize and begin using similes and metaphors.
■ Develop research skills: note-taking, evaluating information, summarizing, using many forms of information.

M A T H   A N D   S C I E N C E

■ Identify and use 11 problem-solving strategies: choose the method, solve a simpler problem, logical reasoning, use or draw a picture, brainstorm, work backward, act out or use objects, guess and check, find a pattern, make a list and make a table.
■ Analyze story problems to find information, question and process.
■ Solve problems using estimation and mental arithmetic in addition, subtraction, multiplication and division.
■ Read, write, order and compare numbers up to one million. Demonstrate where commas should be placed in those numbers.
■ Round off numbers to facilitate estimation.
■ Recognize equivalent fractions. Example: 1/2 = 2/4

WHAT KIDS ARE LIKE

The typical fourth-grader is:

☆ Reading to learn instead of learning to read.

☆ Soaking up information and memorizing facts.

☆ Ready to tackle anything and persistent in practicing skills.

☆ Able to focus on and stick with a task, not needing as much variety as previously.

☆ Writing rather than printing.

continued ▶

Matthew *Heredia drew this self-portrait.*

WHAT KIDS ARE LIKE

continued ▼

☆ More partial to written rather than oral arithmetic.

☆ Becoming less self-centered.

☆ Very interested in history and in ancient times. Biographies are popular with this age group. Likes to study cultures other than own.

☆ Interested in community problems: health, business, seasonal activities, transportation.

☆ Applying simple logic to reach a conclusion, reasoning deductively and classifying information.

☆ Improving ability to think abstractly.

☆ Talking less just for the sake of talking. Seeing language as a tool.

☆ Less prone to wild exaggeration, fantasizing and tall tales.

continued ▶

MASTERING SKILLS

■ Find fractions of whole numbers. Example: 1/5 of 100 = 20.
■ Add and subtract decimal numbers.
■ Identify simple percentages — such as 10 percent, 50 percent and 100 percent — using pictures and relate them to decimals.
■ Use geometric shapes to find patterns of corners, diagonals, edges, etc.
■ Identify right angles.
■ Locate more than one line of symmetry in a given figure.
■ Identify coordinates in a simple map or graph.
■ Explore how different shapes cover a flat surface.
■ Construct and identify parallel, perpendicular and intersecting lines.
■ Read and draw simple maps using coordinates.
■ Make simple scale drawing, like a drawing of a bedroom.
■ Use sampling techniques to collect information or conduct a survey.
■ Make, read and interpret bar, line, tally and pie graphs.
■ Use a calculator to correctly solve one- and two-step problems and to check mental calculations.
■ Demonstrate an understanding of a calculator's function keys.

VISUAL ARTS

■ Use vocabulary to identify or describe artwork.
■ Use the principles and elements of art (line, shape, color, pattern and texture) in creating art.
■ Recognize that each culture has its own aesthetic values.
■ Make an informed response to works of art by using objective criteria for analysis, interpretation and judgment.
■ Understand the techniques and methods of various art forms.
■ Use art supplies in an efficient and inventive manner to create art.
■ Explore techniques for producing the illusion of space in two- and three-dimensional modeling.
■ Recognize works of individual artists.
■ Know that learning about art is important.

MUSIC

■ Understand vocal techniques and control dynamics and tempo.
■ Sing in a two-part round.
■ Identify basic symphonic instruments by family.
■ Recognize basic symphonic instruments by sight and sound.
■ Distinguish types of music, i.e., march, lullaby.
■ Identify the verse and refrain of a song.
■ Read and write some musical symbols and interpret basic notational symbols.
■ Sing in tune.
■ Recognize the basic features of an unfamiliar song.

MASTERING SKILLS

G E O G R A P H Y

- Interpret pictures, charts, graphs and tables.
- Work with distance, direction, scale and map symbols.
- Relate similarities and differences between maps and globes.
- Use maps of different scales and themes.
- Demonstrate how people interact within and between state, nation and world.
- Compare countries with different people, cultures and environments.
- Discuss how personal behavior could be changed to solve an environmental problem.
- Discuss how people of the world are linked by transportation and communication.

S O C I A L   S T U D I E S

- Describe the basic functions of local and state government.
- Describe the relationship among federal, state, county and local governments.
- Identify contributions of significant men, women and cultural groups, to the development of Michigan, the United States and the world.
- Express an informed and reasoned position on a state and local issue.
- List the rights that are guaranteed in the Michigan Constitution and identify responsibilities that go with them.
- List the three branches of government and their roles.
- List ways citizens can participate in the legislative process.
- List factors influencing voter behavior in elections.
- Create a chart that shows the types, terms and qualifications of specific political offices.
- Describe nonviolent, legal actions one can take to protest an issue.

H E A L T H   A N D   P H Y S I C A L   E D U C A T I O N

- Catch overhand.
- Do a backward roll.
- Hit a softly thrown ball with a bat or paddle.
- Develop patterns and combinations of movements into repeatable sequences, as in simple dancing or aerobics routines.
- Jump a rope turned by others, entering and exiting.
- Balance on moving objects, such as skates, scooters, balance boards.
- Do basic swimming stroke and survival skills, such as treading water and floating.
- Understand game rules and principles of fair play.
- Understand the structure of the heart, circulatory and respiratory systems and how they work.
- Understand the effects of smoking and drugs, including alcohol, on the body.

WHAT KIDS ARE LIKE

continued ▼

☆ More grounded in reality; has less interest in fairy tales, less belief in magic.

☆ Competitive. Likes to be graded and compare himself or herself with other students.

☆ Trying to be independent. Less reliant on the teacher. Relationships with teachers are much less personal than in earlier grades.

☆ Seeing school as a matter of business. ○

5TH GRADE!

WHAT KIDS ARE LIKE

These characteristics describe the typical 10-year-old. As they go through the school year, 10-year-olds may turn 11 developmentally before their actual birthday. Most fifth-graders:

☆ Love their life — their family members, their teachers, their friends.

☆ Respect the teacher's word as law.

☆ Like school and their teacher and are easy to teach.

☆ Like to talk and listen more than they like to work.

☆ Show good, intellectual enthusiasm for their favorite subjects.

☆ Enjoy the social aspect of school as much as the academics.

☆ Are interested in learning specifics.

☆ Enjoy geography, especially the names of states and capitals; love to place states, cities,

continued ▶

24

Similes, metaphors, puns — what fun!

What can fifth-graders learn? The following skills have been compiled from various educational sources in Michigan and are intended as a broad picture. In fifth grade, children are learning to:

LANGUAGE ARTS

- Give oral presentations.
- Identify techniques that make a speaker effective.
- Participate in group discussions: summarize discussion, reinforce comments from others, involve others in discussion, limit remarks to purpose of discussion, use names of group members in discussion.
- Read variety of books including historical fiction, legends and myths.
- Use maps, appendixes, prefaces, introductions and tables in reference material.
- Draw conclusions and form opinions based on reading.
- Recognize turning points in stories.
- Compare and contrast characters from different stories.
- Identify and understand themes in literature and expand on such themes in written work.
- Begin to write descriptive paragraphs, reports, essays, business letters, reference pieces, poetry, etc.
- Use dialogue properly in writing.
- Use helping and main verbs in writing.
- Use simple note-taking techniques.
- Cite resources for reports.
- Use similes, metaphors and puns.

MATH AND SCIENCE

- Read, write, order and compare two numbers of up to six digits.
- Solve problems using estimation and mental arithmetic in addition, subtraction, multiplication and division.
- Recall multiplication and division facts through 12.
- Multiply two digits by three digits.
- Divide using a two-digit divisor.
- Use models and pictures to explain problems using a two-digit divisor.
- Identify and use problem-solving strategies, including solving a simpler problem, logical reasoning, using or drawing a picture, brainstorming and working backward.
- Recognize the use of letters as variables in simple equations and solve them.

MASTERING SKILLS

- Round and estimate an answer to an assigned problem.
- Know and use the correct order of operations in an equation.
- Recognize and use the terms: mean, median and frequency.
- Recognize and name two- and three-dimensional shapes.
- Identify and use points; circles, radii and diameters; line segments; parallel, intersecting and perpendicular lines; rays; planes; and angles.
- Accurately use a calculator to solve computation problems.
- Expand understanding of prime numbers, composite numbers, squares, common divisors, common multiples.
- Compare and order fractions and mixed numbers.
- Master addition and subtraction of fractions with common denominators.
- Multiply and divide fractions.
- Add, subtract, multiply and divide decimal numbers.
- Compute percentages. Relate percentages to fractions and decimals.
- Calculate averages.
- Develop an understanding of ratio and proportion.
- Identify and use metric measurement in millimeters, centimeters, decimeters, meters and kilometers.
- Measure, draw and identify various angles.
- Identify shapes that are congruent (same shape, same size).
- Identify shapes that are similar (same shape, different size).
- Demonstrate coordinate graphing.
- Draw and read maps.
- Use hands-on tools to measure, always estimating first, for length, area, volume, mass or weight, temperature.
- Tell time accurately.
- Collect and organize data. Display data in graphic form: picture, bar, circle, line charts and graphs.

S O C I A L   S T U D I E S

- Understand the rights and responsibilities of citizens in a democracy.
- Create a chart that indicates the types, terms, and qualifications of specific offices.
- Acquire a knowledge of the structure and function of federal, state and local governments.
- Interpret social studies data from charts, graphs, maps, tables, and various articles.
- Present the contributions of significant men, women and cultural groups to the development of the United States and Canada.
- Differentiate between goods and services, import and export, public and private services.
- List the liberties that are guaranteed in the U.S. Constitution and Michigan Constitution.

WHAT KIDS ARE LIKE

continued ▼

mountains and rivers on maps.

☆ Are often better with oral and pictorial presentations than with the written word.

☆ Write book reports in short, choppy sentences but with enough punch to interest the reader.

☆ Like school but hate some subjects.

☆ Love to memorize and recite with good expression.

☆ Have difficulty connecting two facts and prefer to take things as they are.

☆ Like oral arithmetic and long strung-out arithmetic problems.

☆ Develop self-consciousness about reciting and singing.

☆ Like to take dictation, though handwriting is often sloppy.

continued ▶

WHAT KIDS ARE LIKE

continued ▼

☆ Like to read to younger brothers and sisters.

☆ Read as much as they watch television.

☆ Say they plan to go to college.

☆ Are unable to plan their own work; need structured schedules.

☆ Can manage homework with little help and without much complaint.

☆ Want to be kept interested and motivated.

☆ Hate to miss school for fear that they won't be able to catch up.

☆ Like to listen to stories; like to tell stories about things they've seen, heard or read about; they see and listen well and want to discuss.

☆ Focus little on spelling.

☆ Are comfortable with themselves.

continued ▶

MASTERING SKILLS

- Recognize and appreciate the diversity of American society.
- Explain the voting process.
- Show legal ways to protest a national issue.
- Respect the right of all to present different points of view in the classroom and community.
- Recognize examples of equity and justice.

GEOGRAPHY

- Recognize distance, direction, scale, map symbols and the relationship of maps and globes.
- Work with latitude and longitude.
- Use maps, charts, graphs and tables to display data.
- Map the link between resources and industry.
- Compare physical and cultural areas and regions within the United States.
- Outline regions within the United States and Canada based on movement and concentrations of different cultural groups.
- Discern ways that personal choices and public decisions influence environmental quality.
- Explain how Michigan's Native Americans, explorers, immigrants and community builders influenced the development of the state.
- Demonstrate knowledge of the products, natural resources and industries of Michigan.

Dominic *Magni drew this self-portrait.*

VISUAL ARTS

- Make and justify aesthetic judgments about one's own work, the artwork of peers, visual forms in daily life and works of art.
- Demonstrate an open-mindedness toward visual art.
- Use the following art concepts to produce images: rhythm-movement, balance, contrast, emphasis, proportion, unity, pattern-variation, repetition, harmony.
- Apply these art elements to make images: line, shape, color, texture, value, space and form.
- Demonstrate versatile use of colors.

MUSIC

- Recognize parts of a song: refrain, verse, solo, chorus.
- Recognize terms and musical forms for concerto, theme and variation.
- Change tempo within a song and exhibit good posture and breathing while singing.

MASTERING SKILLS

- Distinguish between soprano and bass voices.
- Recognize various instruments such as the harp, organ and snare drums.
- Read and write music symbols.
- Distinguish a beat from the melodic rhythm of a musical selection.
- Recognize melodic changes within a piece of music.
- Develop musical knowledge about one's own and other cultures.
- Discuss some major compositions, composers, performers and styles of music.

HEALTH AND PHYSICAL EDUCATION

- Demonstrate tumbling and balancing skills with and without apparatus.
- Develop understanding of team sports.
- Design own games and gymnastic or dance sequences.
- Throw a variety of objects (football, Frisbee, etc.) for accuracy and distance.
- Hand dribble and foot dribble a ball.
- Understand principles of training and conditioning, including warming up and cooling down.
- Distinguish body changes as adolescence approaches.
- Understand the use and abuse of drugs, including alcohol.

WHAT KIDS ARE LIKE

continued ▼

☆ Are enthusiastic about sharing things.

☆ Don't usually resist parental directives.

☆ Tend to be restless and have short attention spans.

☆ Shrug off responsibility.

☆ Don't take kindly to jokes.

☆ Value fairness and demand fair treatment from teachers.

☆ Are easily hurt and upset by criticism.

☆ Are poised, friendly, secure, outgoing, trusting of others.

☆ Take a turn for the worse as the year moves on, becoming casual, restless, careless, forgetful and rude. ○

GOOD STUFF TO READ

Former U.S. Education Secretary William Bennett offered these lists as a guide to choosing reading for elementary school children.

Kindergarten to Grade 3

☆"Behind the Back of the Mountain: Black Folktales from Southern Africa,"
Verna Aardema

☆ "Aesop for Children,"
Aesop

☆ "Hans Christian Andersen's Fairy Tales,"
Hans Christian Andersen

☆ "Anno's Alphabet and Anno's Counting House,"
Mitsumasa Anno

☆ "Wiley and the Hairy Man,"
Molly Bang

☆ "Once in Puerto Rico,"
Pura Belpre

☆ Madeline books,
Ludwig Bemelmans

continued ▶

Powerful tools for the information age

Your second-grader disagrees with her teacher about a story's meaning. She has more questions than answers. She misspells many words and even turns to her classmates when looking for solutions.

What should you do?

Applaud her. She is probably on track.

Reading and writing aren't a tidy collection of letter sounds, spelling lists, sentence diagrams and right answers.

And they definitely don't involve the follies of Dick and Jane, as they did when many of today's parents were in school.

Now, those first two R's are a complex process of digesting, dissecting and delivering ideas.

"Reading and writing are not passive. We're not just pouring information into children like they were empty vessels anymore," says Elaine Weber, reading consultant for the Michigan Department of Education. "Now, the learner is a real participant."

That might not sound like a startling idea. But it wasn't until about 1980 that educators embraced research that shows children don't come to school as blank slates.

They come loaded with diverse ideas and experiences that influence everything they do in school.

"Now, we see children as rich pots with lots of substance," Weber says. "That has changed everything."

But why throw out our old friends Dick and Jane? And why lighten up on those tried-and-true grammar exercises?

Because those things don't help children express themselves or understand what they read or, more importantly, what to do with it.

Proof the old-fashioned methods are failing comes year after year in dismal test scores that show too many children do not comprehend what they read.

The 1985 report from the national Commission on Reading, "Becoming a Nation of Readers," says nearly 40 percent of 13-year-olds who took a national test could not locate information within a paragraph or make simple generalizations based on what they read.

They do pretty well at naming and defining nouns, verbs, subjects and predicates. "They just can't use language," Weber says.

Children wouldn't memorize the parts of a bicycle before learning to ride it, Weber says. So why should they spend so much time memoriz-

READING AND WRITING

ing the parts of speech before learning to interpret and analyze stories?

In the Information Age, language is a powerful tool for workers who can think deeply, solve problems and work together.

It has become a necessary tool for anyone who must interpret complicated food and drug labels, bus or airline schedules or VCR instructions. And, one hopes, for anyone who writes them.

Children need to learn strategies to help them get the most out of what they read.

They should learn to ask questions about subjects before they begin to read about them: "What do I know about wolves?" "Have I ever seen a wolf?" "Wolves look like dogs. Are they related?"

They should discover how to read for different purposes: to get facts, to sequence events, to compare characters, to write a report, to enjoy.

Reading lessons shouldn't happen just once a day anymore; they should be happening across all lessons.

Perhaps most shocking and foreign to parents is the theory that children should be allowed to spell words the way they sound — with only consonants at first — until about third grade.

Then they should spell them correctly most of the time.

Pupils shouldn't agonize over spelling at the expense of conveying and analyzing ideas, educators say. Spelling the way words sound is also natural and similar to the way children learn to speak.

In the age of computers that can check spelling, what's more impor-

Katie *Afendoulis gives her students a language lesson at Collins Elementary School in Grand Rapids.*

☆ "The Three Billy Goats' Gruff,"
Susan Blair

☆ "Freddy the Detective,"
Walter R. Brooks

☆ "The Pied Piper of Hamelin,"
Robert Browning

☆ "The Story of Babar, the Little Elephant,"
Jean de Brunhoff

☆ "Mike Mulligan and His Steam Shovel" and "The Little House,"
Virginia Lee Burton

☆ "The Very Hungry Caterpillar,"
Eric Carle

☆ "Jack and the Three Sillies,"
Richard Chase

☆ The Ramona and Henry Huggins books,
Beverly Cleary

☆ "Adventures of Pinocchio,"
Carlo Collodi

continued ▶

GOOD STUFF TO READ

continued ▼

☆ "Chanticleer and the Fox,"
Barbara Cooney

☆ "The Courage of Sarah Noble,"
Alice Dagliesh

☆ "Book of Nursery and Mother Goose Rhymes,"
Marguerite DeAngeli

☆ "Drummer Hoff,"
Barbara Emberley

☆ "Ask Mister Bear,"
Marjorie Flack

☆ "The Whipping Boy,"
Sid Fleischman

☆ "Millions of Cats,"
Wanda Gag

☆ "The Three Bears,"
retold by Paul Galdone

☆ "Stone Fox,"
John Reynolds Gardiner

☆ "Grimm's Fairy Tales,"
Jacob and Wilhelm Grimm

☆ "The Wonder Book,"
Nathaniel Hawthorne

continued ▶

30

READING AND WRITING

tant for children to learn, how to spell or how to think?

A thinking child, educators say, will be able to analyze and articulate complex ideas — and look up words he or she can't spell.

Children who are bombarded with lots of fun and interesting literature and guided through meaningful reading and writing activities early will learn to spell correctly and use proper grammar smoothly.

Trust them, educators are saying.

That may be the most difficult part of the new approach to reading and writing. It's not as measurable as mastering rules and sounding out words was. In fact, literacy today is downright messy.

But it's a lot more meaningful, educators say.

Michigan's statewide reading test changed in 1989 to reflect the new thinking. Scores on the new test generally have showed steady improvement.

But there is still a long way to go before all children are taught that it's OK to have opinions about what they read. It's OK to misspell words at first. It's OK to discuss stories with peers.

And, most importantly, it's OK to not know who the best and worst readers are. "Parents are our biggest inhibitor," Weber says. "They want their kids to be in the top reading group, almost like a caste system."

The new tack removes some of those comparisons that many educators believe are harmful to self-esteem and progress. It measures children in terms of individual growth, like a parent may measure a child's height against a mark on a wall, Weber says.

Ways to help a child become a good reader

☆ Diversify the reading material, including a variety of nonfiction and fiction.

☆ Ask questions about books and encourage children to relate what they've read to real-life situations.

☆ Read aloud to children.

☆ Make children reason through and solve everyday problems, such as what to do if locked out of the house. ○

The equation now includes thinking first

P at Huellmantel flips through several versions of "The Three Little Bears."

"Have them read and compare them. Have them find similarities and differences. Don't let them just whip through a book. Get them really examining the book, the paper, the printing, how the characters are drawn.

"Is the sequencing the same? Is the story the same? Do you know who belongs to whom? Can you predict what's going to happen?"

Reading lesson? Wrong. That's a math lesson.

"We're trying to get away from teaching math in isolation," says Huellmantell, a math consultant for Flint Public Schools who trains other teachers for the revolution in the way math is taught in U.S. schools.

"By integrating into content areas, we begin to show kids that these things work in connection with each other, not in isolation."

The math revolution began in the 1980s. Jolted by comparisons of young Americans to their counterparts in other countries, educators began to re-examine the American way of doing math. They learned that American kids excelled at solving equations but weren't so good at thinking.

Consider this problem from a national assessment of math skills:

An Army bus holds 36 soldiers. If 1,128 soldiers are being bused to their training site, how many buses are needed?

Most of the students did the division correctly, dividing 1,128 by 36 to arrive at 31 with a remainder of 12.

But two of every three students then went on to answer that the Army needed 31 1/3 buses to move those soldiers.

A third of a bus?

Ouch.

Given answers like that, U.S. educators began to wonder: What do we want children to learn? Do we want them to learn to solve equations that can be solved more accurately and faster by a calculator? Or do we want them to learn how to think creatively, to see their way through a problem?

The answer was that we want students who can think and solve problems, who feel so comfortable with math that they can use their skills quickly and creatively. We want students who have the consumer skills needed for a world that includes retail sales, confusing economic news, federal deficits and newspapers that routinely present information in graphs and charts.

GOOD STUFF TO READ

continued ▼

☆ "One Fine Day," *Nonny Hogrogian*

☆ "Little Red Riding Hood," *retold by Trina Schart Hyman*

☆ "John Henry: An American Legend" and "The Snowy Day," *Ezra Jack Keats*

☆ "Pecos Bill," *Steven Kellogg*

☆ "Just So Stories," *Rudyard Kipling*

☆ "The Arabian Nights" and "Aladdin and the Wonderful Lamp," *Andrew Lang*

☆ "Piping Down the Valley Wild," *Nancy Larrick*

☆ "The Story of Ferdinand," *Munro Leaf*

☆ Pippi Longstocking books, *Astrid Lindgren*

☆ "Swimmy," *Leo Lionni*

continued ▶

GOOD STUFF TO READ

continued ▼

☆ "Frog and Toad Together,"
Arnold Lobel

☆ "Mrs. Piggie-Wiggie,"
Betty MacDonald

☆ "Make Way for Ducklings" and "Blueberries for Sal,"
Robert McCloskey

☆ "Every Time I Climb a Tree,"
poems by David McCord

☆ "Anansi the Spider: A Tale from the Ashanti,"
retold by Gerald McDermott

☆ "When We Were Very Young" and "Winnie-the-Pooh,"
A.A. Milne

☆ "Amelia Bedelia,"
Peggy Parish

☆ "Cinderella,"
Charles Perrault

☆ "The Tale of Peter Rabbit,"
Beatrix Potter

continued ▶

ABOUT MATH

Michigan's statewide math exam was changed in 1991 to reflect the changed emphasis. It was a way to send the message to the state's 2,040 elementary schools that they need to change their instruction.

In today's grade schools, math should be a lot more than addition, subtraction and multiplication. Children should be taught to look for patterns, to compare, predict, estimate, solve problems and, above all, ask questions.

When today's parents were in grade school, teachers believed they were preparing the next generation of mathematicians and scientists for the Cold War. Students learned math by flash cards and classroom drills. Teachers believed they were teaching math so students could study more math, with little regard for the way it would be used in everyday life.

"It was computation driven, recipe-oriented," says Bob Peterson, math consultant for the Macomb Intermediate School District. He was honored in 1985 with the highly prized Presidential Award for Excellence in Mathematics.

Under the old version of math education, there were exact answers and exact ways to solve problems.

No more.

In cutting-edge classrooms today, math is a science. That means it is exploration and discovery. It is learning what questions to ask and which

What to look for during your child's math instruction

☆ Most math work should be done in the classroom. So, don't expect a lot of math homework, especially dittos. Some teachers even say that if you see too many of those, start asking questions about what's going on in the classroom.

☆ Students should sit in groups during most math exercises. They should be encouraged to work together to solve problems. Research indicates children learn math best when they work with other children.

☆ Children should use good math vocabulary to describe what they're doing.

☆ Problems and examples should be drawn from everyday life rather than using contrived problems from textbooks or worksheets. Problems should be personalized. For example: Students can measure themselves and each other and learn to chart that. They can collect information about the daily temperature and chart that.

☆ Problems should have a practical significance and should be written in natural language and reflect a student's culture.

☆ Class projects should connect math to the real world, such as running a class store, a school bank or bookstore. ○

tools to use to find the answer. Often, asking the right question counts for as much as finding the right answer.

Does that mean kids don't learn addition facts anymore? No, but it does mean they may learn them in a different way. Instead of being expected to learn those facts in their heads alone, children are given objects, known as manipulatives, to handle to help them out. Children learn to count by counting out buttons or keys. They learn to add, subtract, multiply and divide in the same way.

"Math should not be just a paper and pencil subject. Children need to experience math," says Patricia Jones, a math specialist at Wilkins Elementary School in Detroit. Jones was a 1991 presidential award winner.

Does it mean they'll be using calculators more often? Yes. But it means they'll also be learning to make decisions about when using a calculator

GOOD STUFF TO READ

continued ▼

☆ "Ride a Purple Pelican" and "Read Aloud Rhymes for the Very Young," *Jack Prelutsky*

☆ "Clementine" *and other books by Robert Quackenbush*

☆ Curious George books, *H.A. Rey*

☆ "The Dancing Stars: An Iroquois Legend," *Anne Rockwell*

☆ "Where the Wild Things Are" and "Chicken Soup with Rice," *Maurice Sendak*

☆ "The Cat in the Hat," "Green Eggs and Ham," "Horton Hatches the Egg" *and others by Dr. Seuss*

☆ "Caps for Sale," *Esphyr Slobodkina*

☆ "Noah's Ark," *Peter Spier*

continued ▶

Books to help children see patterns in math

For kindergarten-grade 3

☆ "Chickens Aren't the Only Ones," *by Ruth Heller (Grosset & Dunlop, 1981).*

☆ "Corduroy," *by Don Freeman (Puffin Books, 1968).*

☆ "Freight Train," *by Donald Crews (Puffin Books, 1987).*

☆ "Hailstones and Halibut Bones," *by Mary O'Neill (Doubleday, 1961).*

☆ "I Can't Get My Turtle to Move," *by Elizabeth Lee O'Donnell (Morrow Junior Books, 1989.)*

☆ "Over in the Meadow," *by Ezra Jack Keats (Scholastic, 1971).*

☆ "The Day Jimmy's Boa Ate the Wash," *by Trinka Hakes Noble (Dial Books, 1984).*

☆ "The Grouchy Ladybug," *by Eric Carle (Scott, Foresman, 1971).*

☆ "The Important Book," *by Margaret Wise Brown (Harper & Row, 1949).*

☆ "The Mixed-Up Chameleon," *by Eric Carle (Crowell, 1975).*

☆ "The Very Busy Spider," *by Eric Carle (Philomel Books, 1984).*

☆ "The Very Hungry Caterpillar," *by Eric Carle (Putnam, 1987).*

☆ "Who's in the Box, Bobby?," *by Pat Paris*

For number development

☆ "How Many Bugs in a Box," *by David Carter (Intervisual Communications, 1988).*

☆ "Moja Means One," *a Swahili counting book by Muriel Feelings (Pied Piper Books, 1976).*

☆ "One Crow: A Counting Rhyme," *by Jim Aylesworth (Harper & Row, 1988).*

☆ "One Watermelon Seed," *by Celia Barker Lottridge (Oxford University Press, 1986).*

☆ "Ten in the Bed," *by Penny Dale (Discovery Toys, 1988).*

☆ "Ten, Nine, Eight," *by Molly Bang (Puffin Books, 1983).* ○

GOOD STUFF TO READ

continued ▼

continued ▶

ABOUT MATH

makes more sense than doing the problem in their heads or on paper.

"We used to suffer at the computational gate. Now, we can be error-free" by using a calculator for the most complicated equations, Peterson says.

That means today's teachers often stop where teachers of yesteryear might have forged ahead.

Instead of giving fourth-graders an equation for figuring out the area of a square, today's teacher might simply provide the tools and encourage children to figure it out for themselves.

Lynn Royer, a math consultant and teacher in the Waverly schools west of Lansing, compares it to being a passenger or a driver in a car: "If I drove you somewhere, you wouldn't remember the route nearly as well as if you were in the driver's seat and did it yourself.

"We fill a child's math basket with the appropriate tools," says Royer, a presidential award winner in 1990. "We give them a scientific method. We give them strategies they can use. That allows them to approach math problems with power, with reasoning."

Improving American math education means overcoming a significant obstacle: elementary school teachers who generally have strong backgrounds in language arts but lack confidence in math and science.

Most grade school teachers lack confidence because they didn't feel comfortable with the way they learned math. Peterson says they warm to the new methods quickly.

Using literature breaks down a lot of the barriers for teachers. "The teachers already know these books. They can do this without being threatened," Huellmantel says.

In her training sessions, Huellmantel says she is ever conscious that teachers need to ensure that children understand the math they're learning as well as perform it well.

Her goal is to make sure no American leaves those poor Army soldiers stranded with only a third of a bus.

Hands-on activities lead to learning

Hands on her hips, Shelly Potter bites her lip while her fourth-grade students try to figure out what went wrong.

Her class at Midvale Elementary School in Birmingham has designed cars using milk cartons for the body, round plastic pieces from an ice cream treat for wheels and straws for axles. They roll their cars down an incline and measure how far they traveled. They could choose any power source.

One group of students used two foot-long solar panels. Each time their car starts off, it sags to a quick halt.

The dilemma is clear to Potter: The solar panels are too heavy for the tiny car.

But she doesn't tell them how to solve their problem. She asks questions.

"They have to find the answers for themselves," she says.

Lessons like Potter's reflect science education today.

In excellent science classrooms, children are encouraged to put their hands on science. As the saying goes, if their hands are on science, their minds will be, too.

"Kids have to have stuff. They have to have things to put their hands on. They have to have materials to work with, things to look at and touch and manipulate. They need time to fuss with stuff, too," says Joseph Riley, science coordinator for the Ann Arbor Public Schools.

It's impossible to teach anyone all there is to know about science. But it is possible to train children to think like scientists, to give them ways to

Fourth-graders at Midvale Elementary prepare a self-propelled car of their own design for an auto derby.

GOOD STUFF TO READ

continued ▼

☆ "Owl Moon" and "The Seeing Stick," *Jane Yolen*

☆ "Rumpelstiltskin," *retold by Paul O. Zelinsky*

Grades 4 through 6

☆ "Born Free," *Joy Adamson*

☆ "Little Women," *Louisa May Alcott*

☆ "Sounder," *William H. Armstong*

☆ "Tuck Everlasting," *Natalie Babbitt*

☆ "Peter Pan," *J.M. Barrie*

☆ "Crickets and Bullfrogs and Whispers of Thunder: Poems and Pictures," *Harry Behn*

☆ "Stories of the Gods and Heroes," *Sally Benson*

☆ "Sundiata: The Epic of the Lion King," *Roland Bertol*

continued ▶

GOOD STUFF TO READ

continued ▼

☆ "The Dog Days of Arthur Cane,"
T. Ernesto Bethancourt

☆ "Doctor Coyote: A Native American Aesop's Fables,"
retold by John Bierhorst

☆ "The Secret Garden,"
Frances Hodgson Burnett

☆ "The Summer of the Swans,"
Betsy Byars

☆ "A New Treasury of Children's Poetry: Old Favorites and New Discoveries,"
edited by Joanna Cole

☆ "Prairie Songs,"
Pamela Conrad

☆ "James and the Giant Peach" and "Charlie and the Chocolate Factory,"
Roald Dahl

☆ "The Black Stallion,"
Walter Farley

☆ "Thor and the Giants,"
Anita Feagles

continued ▶

ABOUT SCIENCE

see things that will last a lifetime.

That means children should be taught how to collect information and interpret it to solve problems. They should be encouraged to explore, to ask questions.

Perhaps most important, it is possible to nurture in them a love and respect for science. And elementary school is the best time to begin doing that.

"What I try to do is sharpen their senses. They see, they hear, they taste, they touch, they feel. We should fine-tune all of those senses," says Liz Barnett, a teacher at Haviland Elementary School in Waterford Township.

Elementary school science programs should not emphasize reading about science.

Ann Arbor's Joe Riley goes a step further: "They should emphasize not reading about science."

"Most elementary teachers are much more comfortable with paper. Most of the science that kids get is what they read about it. … That's not science," Riley says.

So far, the state's science Michigan Educational Assessment Program test has largely tested a student's knowledge of facts. But a new, improved science test will be introduced in fall 1995.

Students will do hands-on activities and experiments as part of the exam and will write essay-type answers to questions, says Diane Smolen, supervisor of the state's MEAP office.

Rather than asking students many questions that reflect a shallow level of science knowledge, the state wants to identify scientific concepts that

Home studies

Science invites parent participation. You don't have to be a forensic pathologist to have something interesting to share with your child's classroom. (Some teachers say the professionals are actually the least helpful because they talk way over the kids' heads.)

Maybe you're a gardener who understands how plants grow.

Maybe you're a cook who understands what happens when you put baking soda and vinegar together.

Maybe you're a scuba diver who has taken underwater photographs.

Maybe you collect butterflies or rocks.

Think about what you know and what you could share in your child's classroom.

Another tip: If you don't already have an area of expertise, find out what science units your child will be studying, find out where the teacher would like help, then pick one of those areas and become a mini-expert by reading and experimenting.

A free book published by the U.S. government will get you started: "Helping Your Child Learn Science." Ask for Document No. 611X. Send your request to Consumer Information Center, Pueblo, CO 81009. ○

all children need to know, Smolen says. The new test will zero in on those concepts.

What does your child

Michigan's science curriculum does not fit neatly into grade-by-grade packages.

Unlike other subjects, there is no agreement on what science a child should study in a given grade.

In mathematics, for example, educators agree children need to learn to add before they can multiply. Science isn't so simple. Educators say children don't need to learn how plants grow before studying rocks or about planets before studying weather.

The state makes no recommendations on what children should study in each grade. The only signal is that children need certain knowledge to be successful on the statewide science test at the beginning of fifth grade.

Using the statewide test as a guideline, children finishing fourth grade should be able to

demonstrate their knowledge in these areas in the following ways:

LIFE SCIENCE

☆ Describe cells as living systems.
☆ Compare and classify familiar organisms by observable physical characteristics.
☆ Describe vertebrates by observable body parts and physical characteristics.
☆ Describe life cycles of familiar organisms.
☆ Compare and contrast food, energy and environmental needs of selected organisms.
☆ Describe functions of seed plant parts.

Evolution

☆ Explain how fossils provide evidence about ancient life.
☆ Explain how living things adapt to their environments.

Ecosystems

☆ Identify familiar organisms as part of a food chain or food web; describe feeding relationships within the web.
☆ Explain common patterns of interdependence and interrelationships of living things.
☆ Describe basic needs of living things.

☆ Describe systems that encourage growth of particular plants or animals.
☆ Describe effects of humans on the environment.

PHYSICAL SCIENCE

Matter and Energy

☆ Classify common objects and substances by observable characteristics: color, size, shape, smell, hardness, texture, flexibility, length, weight, buoyancy, states of matter, magnetic properties.
☆ Measure weights, dimensions and temperatures.
☆ Identify properties of materials that make them useful.
☆ Identify forms of energy associated with common phenomena.
☆ Describe interaction of magnetic materials with other magnetic and nonmagnetic materials.
☆ Describe interaction of charged materials with other charged or uncharged materials.

Changes in Matter

☆ Describe common physical changes in matter (size, shape, melting, freezing, dissolving) and the heat energy that accompanies some changes.
☆ Prepare mixtures and separate them into their

GOOD STUFF TO READ

continued ▼

☆ Great Brain books, *John D. Fitzgerald*

☆ "Harriet the Spy," *Louise Fitzhugh*

☆ "Johnny Tremain," *Esther Forbes*

☆ Selections from "Poor Richard's Almanack," *Benjamin Franklin*

☆ "Lincoln: A Photobiography," *Russell Freedman*

☆"And Then What Happened, Paul Revere?" *Jean Fritz*

☆ "A Swinger of Birches: Poems of Robert Frost for Young People," *Robert Frost*

☆ "Julie of the Wolves," *Jean Craighead George*

☆ "The Wind in the Willows," *Kenneth Grahame*

☆ "Mythology," *Edith Hamilton*

continued ▶

ABOUT SCIENCE

What does your child

component parts.
☆ Construct simple objects that fulfill a technological purpose.

Motions of Objects

☆ Describe or compare motions of common objects in terms of speed and direction.
☆ Describe how forces (pushes or pulls) speed up, slow down, stop or change the direction of a moving object.
☆ Use simple machines to make work easier.

Waves and Vibrations

☆ Describe sounds in terms of their properties (pitch, loudness).
☆ Explain how sounds are made.
☆ Describe light from a light source in terms of its properties.
☆ Explain how light illuminates objects.
☆ Explain how shadows are made.

USING SCIENTIFIC KNOWLEDGE

Geosphere

☆ Describe major features of the Earth's surface.
☆ Recognize and describe different types of earth materials.
☆ Explain how rocks and fossils are used to understand the history of the Earth.
☆ Describe natural changes in the Earth's surface.
☆ Describe uses of materials taken from the earth.
☆ Demonstrate means to recycle manufactured materials.
☆ Describe how waters exist on Earth in three states.
☆ Trace the path that rainwater follows after it falls.

☆ Identify sources of drinking water.
☆ Describe the uses of water.

Atmosphere and weather

☆ Describe the atmosphere.
☆ Describe weather conditions and climates.
☆ Describe seasonal changes in weather.
☆ Explain appropriate safety precautions during severe weather.

Solar System, Galaxy and Universe

☆ Describe the sun, moon and Earth.
☆ Describe the motions of the Earth and moon around the sun. ○

What to ask about your school's science program

☆ Does your school or your district have a science specialist? If not, who oversees the science program in your school? Does that person have a science background? Only a relative handful of Michigan school districts have full-time science consultants.
☆ How much time do students spend on science each week? In kindergarten through third grade, children should spend 2½ hours a week on science; in fourth and fifth grade, at least 3½ hours a week.
☆ Does your child's teacher have a positive attitude about science? Do the children appear to like science?
☆ Do the children participate in science activities or experiments?
☆ Do the children explore science materials before they invent concepts to explain them?
☆ Does the teacher ask open-ended questions and give children time to respond?
☆ Does the teacher regularly combine science with other content areas — reading, mathematics, social studies, music, art? ○

Students need to know more about others

Social studies lessons that begin in kindergarten ought to prepare Michigan children "to be better citizens, know history, geography, and economics," says John Chapman, social studies expert for the Michigan Department of Education.

Such knowledge is critical in an increasingly diverse global community. But experts say the subjects that make up social studies are a low priority in too many Michigan elementary schools. That's because teachers generally stress what's on state exams. In elementary schools, that means math, reading and science.

There has been talk of developing a statewide social studies exam, but most experts say such a test is far in the future.

With so many demands on elementary school teachers' time, social studies "tends to be one of the subjects that gets pushed by the wayside," says Mel Miller, social studies consultant for the Macomb Intermediate School District.

Still the situation is improving, largely due to a growing, yet controversial, recognition that as the world gets smaller and becomes more diverse, students need to know more about themselves and other people.

Social studies themes for Michigan elementary school students center on four areas: knowledge, democratic values, skills and civic participation.

State guidelines recommend that in kindergarten, children focus on themselves and others. In first grade, the focus is school and family. In second grade, neighborhoods are stressed. In third grade, differences and similarities between school and community are the emphasis. Michigan history is studied in the fourth grade and U.S. history in the fifth grade.

Most Michigan students don't get significant doses of world history until middle school.

"There has been a deficiency in the way world history has been taught," Chapman says.

Besides the fact that there are no state exams in social studies to guide teachers, the subjects can be difficult to teach because controversy often tags along. Some teachers, for example, believe values should be a part of the social studies curriculum. But whose values?

There's also a national debate about multicultural education, which recognizes the history and culture of the various people that make up the United States.

"You take into account people who have come to the United States

GOOD STUFF TO READ

continued ▼

☆ The Rainbow Fairy books,
Andrew Lang

☆ "A Wrinkle in Time,"
Madeleine L'Engle

☆ "The Lion, the Witch, and the Wardrobe,"
C.S. Lewis

☆ "The Call of the Wild,"
Jack London

☆ "Castle" and "Cathedral,"
David Macaulay

☆ "Sarah, Plain and Tall,"
Patricia MacLachlan

☆ "Paul Bunyan Swings His Axe,"
Dell J. McCormick

☆ "Snow Treasure,"
Marie McSwigan

☆ "The Borrowers,"
Mary Norton

☆ "Hailstones and Halibut Bones," *poems by Mary O'Neill*

☆ "Bridge to Terabithia" and "The Great Gilly Hopkins,"
Katherine Paterson

continued ▶

GOOD STUFF TO READ

continued ▼

☆ "Tales of Mystery and Imagination,"
Edgar Allen Poe

☆ "The Merry Adventures of Robin Hood,"
Howard Pyle

☆ "The Westing Game,"
Ellen Raskin

☆ "Where the Red Fern Grows,"
Wilson Rawls

☆ "Bambi,"
Felix Salten

☆ "Abe Lincoln Grows Up" and "Rootabaga Stories,"
Carl Sandburg

☆ "Cricket in Times Square,"
George Selden

☆ "Black Beauty,"
Anna Sewell

☆ "A Day of Pleasure: Stories of a Boy Growing up in Warsaw,"
Isaac Bashevis Singer

continued ▶

40

ABOUT SOCIAL STUDIES

from different parts of the world other than Europe," including Africans, Asians, Middle Easterners, Native Americans and Hispanics, Chapman says.

Though a multicultural approach to social studies is supported by the state, it's far from being implemented statewide.

"Some districts have not done much," Chapman says. "We have not succeeded in multicultural education to the degree that we ought to."

The lack of appropriate textbooks is part of the problem.

That's why more schools and teachers are pulling away from textbooks and turning to supplemental literature, including newspapers and maga-

> ### *Parents can bring the world home*
>
> *Parents can help their children develop respect for:*
>
> ☆ Themselves as well as the rights and responsibilities of others.
> ☆ Cultural similarities and differences among people.
> ☆ Fair school and community rules.
>
> *Things parents can do:*
>
> ☆ Read the newspaper with your child. Choose a person of the week. Cut out a photo of the newsmaker and put it in a prominent place. Encourage the child to read as much as he or she can about the famous person. Try to include a range of male and female celebrities and world leaders of all nationalities and races.
> ☆ Use the newspaper to make charts and graphs. A sports fan can track batting averages. Someone interested in money can chart fluctuations in the stock market.
> ☆ Set rules at home and stress the importance of them.
> ☆ Hold family meetings. Discuss family problems and involve children in problem solving.
> ☆ Discuss an editorial on a controversial issue with your child. Discuss whether you agree or disagree with the viewpoint expressed. Then listen to your child's point of view. Encourage your child to write a letter to the editor.
> ☆ Teach your child to celebrate diversity. Learn more about other cultures. Watch television programs or read books about other countries. Try ethnic foods.
> ☆ Watch the evening news together. Talk about current events at the dinner table. Choose one or two issues to follow closely. Read more about them.
> ☆ Talk about your values and encourage your child to do so.
> ☆ Promote recycling or participate in other activities that protect the environment.
> ☆ Teach your child how to make decisions.
> ☆ Ask your child to think about the consequences of choosing one course of action over another. ○
>
>

zines, storytelling and artifacts from other countries. Some districts, including Detroit, are prodding textbook publishers to improve by withholding purchases until they do.

"Purists think we should center on our country and Americanize everything. The multiculturalists think we're a salad bowl-type country;

we should recognize the diversity," Miller says.

Charting a new course

☆ "Charting a Course: Social Studies for the 21st Century," by the National Commission on Social Studies in the Schools, a joint project of the American Historical Association, Carnegie Foundation for Advancement of Teaching, National Council of Social Studies and the Organization of American Historians, 1989. To order a copy, contact the National Council for the Social Studies, 3501 Newark St. NW, Washington, D.C. 20016; 1-202-966-7840.

☆ "Essential Goals and Objectives for Social Studies Education in Michigan K-12" and "Core Curriculum Outcomes for Social Studies." Contact the Michigan Department of Education, 608 W. Allegan, Lansing 48909;

Allegan, Lansing 48909; 1-517-373-3324.

☆ "Renewing the Social Studies Curriculum," Walter Parker, Association for Supervision and Curriculum Development, 1991. Contact the association at 1250 North Pitt St., Alexandria, Va. 22314; 1-703-549-9110.

☆ "Cultural Literacy: What Every American Needs to Know," E.D. Hirsch Jr., Houghton-Mifflin, 1987.

☆ "Dictionary of Cultural Literacy," Second edition, E.D. Hirsch Jr., Joseph Kett and James Trefil, Houghton-Mifflin, 1993. ○

GOOD STUFF TO READ

continued ▼

☆ "Call It Courage," *Armstrong Sperry*

☆ "Heidi," *Johanna Spyrl.*

☆ "Treasure Island," *Robert Louis Stevenson*

☆ "American Tall-Tale Animals," *Adrien Stoutenburg*

☆ "The Nutcracker: A Story and a Ballet," *Ellen Switzer*

☆ "What's the Big Idea, Ben Franklin?" and "Where Was Patrick Henry on the 29th of May?" *Margot Tomes*

☆ "Swiss Family Robinson," *Johann Wyss* ○

Hey PARENTS!

GOOD STUFF TO READ

These books come highly recommended as sources for parents seeking ways to help their children succeed in school:

☆ "The National PTA Talks to Parents: How to Get the Best Education for Your Child," *by Melitta Cutright (Doubleday for the PTA, $8.95).*

☆ "Growing Up Confident: How to Make Your Child's Early Years Learning Years," *by Melitta Cutright (Doubleday for the PTA, $12).*

☆ The National Committee for Citizens in Education Information for Parents series: 12 pamphlets on ways to help your children in school, available in English and Spanish, $4.95 for the series, plus $2.50 for shipping and handling. Make checks payable to: Center for Law and Education, and send to the center at: 1875 Connecticut Ave N.W., Suite 510, Washington, D.C.

continued ▶

ABOUT GEOGRAPHY

Small world gets closer

More than 23 million Americans couldn't find the United States on a map, according to the National Geographic Society. More than 44 million Americans couldn't find the former Soviet Union.

Despite the dismal findings from the society's 1990 poll, geography – what some call the "hidden child" of social studies – is gaining a new momentum in U.S. schools.

People are finding it's a small world after all – thanks to television that brings new events from around the globe into living rooms, computer technology that allows students in Michigan to chat with students in the remotest corners of the world and transportation that takes people from the United States to almost anywhere else in a matter of hours.

Geography educators are stepping up to the challenge by learning more about the world, pushing for more and better lessons in schools and striving to show how geography connects to other subjects, including current events and technology.

"You don't prepare students anymore to go to their little town and get a job in their isolated community," says Terry Kuseske, a teacher at Hamilton Middle School in Dowagiac and former president of the Michigan Council of Social Studies. "We're all interconnected."

The National Council for Geography Education, which includes educators from across the country and abroad, has been developing "world-

---

A global outlook right at home

☆ As a family, watch and discuss educational geography programs on television.

☆ Read geography books; have children point things out on maps.

☆ Put up a map in the TV room and point locations out as places are discussed.

☆ Read the newspaper; locate on maps places that make news.

☆ Make a map of the school and neighborhood, then take a walk through the school or neighborhood using the map.

☆ Use family trips as ways of exploring the environment. Use a map to show children where you're going and talk about what you see as you go there.

☆ Get a copy of "Helping Your Child Learn Geography," a 25-page booklet from the U.S. Department of Education. The cost is 50 cents. Write: Geography Consumer Information Center, Pueblo, Colo. 81009. ○

ON YOUR MARKS ○ IT'S ELEMENTARY

ABOUT GEOGRAPHY

class standards" that will give teachers more direction.

The standards would provide guidelines for the knowledge students should master in the fourth, eighth and 12th grades. The group hopes the standards will be used by districts nationwide.

Geography is an elective in Michigan high schools, though it often appears in world studies classes, says Joseph Stoltman of Western Michigan University, co-coordinator of the Michigan Geography Alliance.

"The strongest place for geography in the Michigan curriculum is grades six and seven," says Stoltman. "In many places in Michigan, the sixth-seventh-grade sequence is the last time they study geography."

Despite a renewed recent interest in geography, no standardized state tests exist. And some educators worry that many teachers don't know enough to provide intensive instruction, though state and national training programs have attracted many Michigan teachers.

"Most elementary teachers have backgrounds in the language arts; they really don't know a lot about world history," says Don Griffin of the Wayne County Regional Educational Service Agency, which assists local school districts.

Kuseske, a National Geographic teacher consultant who is among about 100 teachers in Michigan providing peer training, says the key is educating teachers on how to teach geography.

"As an elementary teacher, incorporating information is a big concern," Kuseske says. "Every time we turn around, there's a new subject that needs to have more attention. ... The bottom line is, you have to learn how to teach more than one subject at one time."

GOOD STUFF TO READ

continued ▼

Also available: "The Middle School Years: A Parents' Handbook," $9.95; the $2.50 shipping charge applies to orders under $25.

☆ "The Michigan PTA Parents' Answer Book" *by the advisory board of the Detroit Free Press Parent Talk Page, Alice McCarthy, executive editor (Bridge Communications, $5.95).* This 222-page, easy-to-read book is crammed full of information, references and support services that make being a parent easier. To order, call the Michigan PTA at 1-517-485-4345, weekdays 8-5, or write to the Michigan PTA, 1011 N. Washington Ave., Lansing 48906.

☆ "Empowering Your Child: How to Help Your Child Succeed in School and Life," *by C. Fred Bateman (Hampton Road Publishing, $7.95).*

☆ "MegaSkills," *by Dorothy Rich (Houghton-*

continued ▶

GOOD STUFF TO READ

continued ▼

-Mifflin for the Home and School Institute, $8.95).

☆ "Read to Me: Raising Kids Who Love to Read," *by Bernice Cullinan (Scholastic, $3.95).*

☆ "The School-Smart Parent," *by Gene Maeroff (Holt, $12.95).*

☆ "How to Get Your Child a Private School Education in a Public School," *by Marty and Barbara Nemko (Acropolis Books, $12.95).*

☆ "Your Child's Self-Esteem," *by Dorothy Briggs (Doubleday, $10.95).*

☆ "Teaching Children to Love Themselves," *by Michael Knight, (Simon and Schuster, $5.95).*

☆ "Taming the Homework Monster, How to Make Homework A Positive Learning Experience for Your Child," *by Ellen Klavan, (Poseidon Press, $10).*

continued ▶

Far from a frill, fine arts build minds

Deborah Katz opened her tiny mouth and sang "We are marching to Pretoria" ever so sweetly in a grade school music class 30 years ago.

Of course, back then the little girl from West Bloomfield Township didn't know where or what Pretoria was, much less why anyone was marching there. No need to let history or geography complicate a good song, her teacher probably thought.

Nonsense, says Katz, a music education coordinator for the Ann Arbor School District. What better way to expand students' knowledge of the world, other people and themselves than through the fine arts — music, art, drama and dance.

The fine arts are more than drawing cute ducks, making holiday trinkets or singing folk songs — at least, quality arts education should be more than that.

If Katz were to teach "Marching to Pretoria" now — and she says she would not because many consider it racist — students probably would discuss the war between the Dutch and British over control of South Africa in the late 1800s and the war's impact on people today. At the very least, students would learn Pretoria was a city in South Africa and that soldiers sometimes sang to lift their spirits or keep in step when marching.

The fine arts, progressive educators say, build the very skills that will be needed in the 21st Century: critical thinking, creativity, judgment and teamwork. They're as basic as reading, writing and arithmetic. Yet, across the state, the arts get short shrift and are swiftly slashed when school budgets tighten.

"Although there are wonderful ways to infuse the arts into other subjects, the thing you don't want is for the arts to become the handmaiden of other areas," says Carol Alexander of the Detroit Public Schools. "For obvious reasons, they should be allowed to stand alone."

Fine arts educators are not trying to train young people to become professional painters, singers, dancers or actors. But they do want to help all children have a better understanding and appreciation of the fine arts.

"But many arts programs have been superficial and fluff, spare time activities and those kinds of things," concedes Frank Philip, fine arts specialist for the Michigan Department of Education. "The new thinking about arts education has to do with helping children to be innovative, to use higher thinking skills."

Don't fret. Schoolchildren are still learning how to sing in tune and make works of art destined for refrigerator doors. But they're also listening to the music of diverse cultures, talking about mood as well as form and structure. Ideally, they're seeing more artworks — original and reproductions — and learning to say more than whether they like them.

In short, they're learning why the arts are important and have been valued through the ages.

And, if a school is following the state's guidelines, its students also are getting a taste of the philosophy of art or aesthetics. Students might grapple with questions such as "What is beauty?" and "Does art have to be beautiful?"

Parents viewing a student art show in an Ann Arbor elementary school, for instance, probably would be treated to something called an "informance," where information about the art or artist is posted next to the student's masterpiece, making it more understandable.

In a musical informance, parents who come to hear their little ones sing or play an instrument also might learn about the composer and type of song, or see the children doing vocal warm-up and breathing exercises on stage. As a result, the audience gains a little knowledge while enjoying the concert, play or show.

"In the new definition of arts education, the arts are every child's birthright," says Susan Wood, fine arts coordinator for Flint Community Schools.

And, to make sure that everybody understands the arts, the state's comprehensive curriculum plan encourages schools to cover four areas:

- Historical, cultural and social;
- Creating, producing and performing;
- Analyzing and critically examining,
- Aesthetics, the meaning, value and nature of the arts.

"We have many ways of knowing things," Philip says. "The arts are another way of knowing things."

Nonetheless, the arts don't get much respect in many school districts, especially in the lower grades. Dance and drama are rarely taught, and if an elementary school is lucky enough to have a music or arts specialist, the time they spend with an individual class might range from 25 to 50 minutes each week or every other week.

Some school systems don't even bother to teach the arts and some assume that a classroom teacher without any special training can handle the task.

Educators say the tenuous standing of the fine arts has frightening implications. People are just coming to realize that employers need workers who can do more than spew facts, push buttons or flip switches.

"We want creative and innovative thinkers," says Joann Ricci, executive director of the Michigan Alliance for Arts Education. "The arts are one of the few disciplines that allow that."

GOOD STUFF TO READ

continued ▼

☆ "Different and Wonderful," *by Derek and Darlene Hobson (Prentice Hall Press, $19.95).*

☆ "Developing Positive Self-Images & Discipline in Black Children," *by Jawanza Kunjufu (African American Images, $7.95).*

☆ "A Parent's Guide to Early Childhood Education," *by Diane Trester Dodge and Joanna Phinney (Teaching Strategies, $1.75).* To order, call Gryphon House at 1-800-638-0928, weekdays 8:30-5. Or send $3.25 (includes shipping) to Gryphon House, Box 207, Beltsville, Md. 20704. ○

☆ "101 Ways Parents Can Help Students Achieve," a pamphlet published in English and Spanish and edited by the American Assocciation of School Administrators. Costs $6, prepaid. To order, call 1-703-875-0748 or write AASA, 1801 N. Moore St., Arlington, Va. 22209. ○

ANSWERS YOU NEED

Q: *I've heard about Public Act 25 reports. What are they?*

A: The Public Act 25 reports are essentially annual reports for your local school and school district. Every Michigan school must prepare these reports for parents and present them at public meetings. In addition, they must be filed with the state Department of Education. Each report must include:

☆ Details on the school's three- to five-year improvement plan.

☆ What students are expected to learn in the core curriculum.

☆ Accreditation status.

☆ Dropout and graduation rates.

☆ Results of standardized tests, such as the Michigan Educational Assessment Program and various college entrance exams.

☆ The number of parents who participated in parent-teacher conferences.

To get the report, request a copy at your school.

continued ▶

ABOUT ART

There are other benefits, too. Performing arts, for example, can give a child a positive awareness of body, soul and intellect.

"It's interactive and expressive," says Julie Borik of the Center for Creative Studies Institute of Music and Dance in Detroit. "It develops your self-esteem and confidence as you practice and perform for others."

The ability to work well in groups is enhanced as children rehearse together. The skills learned in string orchestra class could come in handy in the corporate boardroom, Borik says.

Look around you for art

Here are a few ideas for artistic enrichment:

☆ Take a walking tour to identify and discuss the public sculpture in your community.

☆ Ask your children to plan entertainment for a family picnic. Everyone could get involved with creating a story or song, writing a poem about mom's potato salad or performing an acrobatic feat. If you don't think these activities are silly, the children won't, either.

☆ Bring a musical instrument into your home — perhaps a guitar, wooden flute, recorder, drums or even a piano. Have a family jam session.

☆ Listen to different kinds of music in your home. Tune the radio to the classical station or try some jazz, blues, country, folk, rock, gospel, etc. Expand your family's musical horizons.

☆ When looking at a child's art, don't put her or him on the defensive by asking "What is it?" Get the child to talk by saying something such as, "Tell me about your picture."

☆ Watch TV programs in which the arts and artists are introduced and explained. Such programs often air on public television.

☆ Take your child to art museums, concerts, dance recitals and plays. Those designed specifically for kids are the best. Encourage them to talk about the trip.

☆ Remember that even 5-year-olds can appreciate a walk through the museum, but because their attention span is short, don't force them to stay long. Allow them to direct the pace and what to look at. If there is something you don't understand, ask a docent.

☆ Check the arts and entertainment section of newspapers and other publications for reviews and suggestions on where to find events from gallery openings and ballets to bluegrass festivals and children's theater.

☆ Orchestras, theater groups and museums (including the Detroit Institute of Arts, Detroit Symphony Orchestra and Michigan Opera Theatre) have outreach programs. Some events are free.

☆ Fine arts classes for children are available through local art associations, museums, community cultural centers and city recreation departments. Many colleges offer programs for children. The Center for Creative Studies in Detroit offers arts programs for children, as well as private and group lessons. Scholarships may be available. ○

Kids find new uses for high technology

wenty-six fifth-graders bolt toward the computer terminals, flip a switch and bring the blank video screens to a brilliant blue life.

It's their first day back in the high-tech classroom at Farmington's Highmeadow Elementary School after summer vacation, but these students act as if they've been using computers for years.

Most of them have.

"They're the Nintendo generation," says Highmeadow's media specialist, Peggy McKinley. "They're used to it. They assume the technology is going to be there for them."

And, in a growing number of classrooms, it is.

Media-savvy grade schoolers are using computers and an array of sophisticated audio-visual equipment to perform science experiments, solve math problems and as an outlet for creative and artistic talents.

In more and more schools across Michigan, children are hooking their computers to phone lines and interacting with databases or information sources around the world.

"Computers are great to learn with," says Highmeadow's Jennifer Machesney, 10, as she started a lesson. "They're tons of fun."

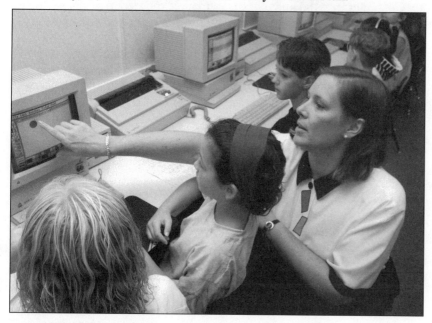

Peggy *McKinley helps fifth-graders in a class at Highmeadow Elementary School in Farmington.*

ANSWERS YOU NEED

continued ▼

Q: *What are the advantages and disadvantages of all-day kindergarten?*

A: The child-care component is probably the greatest benefit of an all-day program.

Educationally, the length of the school day does not determine the quality of instruction. A poorly designed all-day program could stress children and potentially turn them off to school at the very age they should be excited about it. However, if properly designed, an all-day kindergarten can be a boon for all.

A good all-day program can be judged by its diversity. Children should be able to work independently and in large and small groups. They should have indoor and outdoor activities, a rest period and lots of choices.

Be wary of an all-day program that has children attending school every other day to save the cost of

continued ▶

Q&A

ANSWERS YOU NEED

continued ▼

transporting two loads of kindergartners daily. Experts say children could lose more than they gain in alternate-day programs.

Q: *How much homework should my child be doing?*

A: The appropriate amount depends on the age and ability of the child and the need for the activity itself. General guidelines are: early elementary school students should receive 15 to 30 minutes of homework several times a week. Upper elementary students should receive 30 to 45 minutes on a regular basis. But other educators recommend 10 minutes per grade, so a first-grader would spend 10 minutes, a ninth-grader 90 minutes, etc.

Q: *Do I have the right to see my child's school file?*

A: Yes — if your child attends a public or private school that receives any type of

continued ▶

ABOUT COMPUTERS

Her classmate agrees.

"I like them a lot. They're cool because they're so smart," says James Kosty, 10. "You can do a lot of designs with them. They can help you out when you get into trouble."

Rob Salter expertly moves his computer mouse to draw a small sailboat, an illustration for a video biography.

"If you spell something wrong, Spell-Check tells you," Rob says. "And you don't have to erase. You just delete."

"Right," James adds. "It kind of feels like you're free, like you're flying."

For these kids, school is far from boring.

Realizing that more traditional ways of teaching children don't always work, teachers who aren't intimidated are turning to technology.

For example, in the past, an elementary student who was told to watch a nature program on a cable channel and prepare a report about a specific animal might have gone to the library and grabbed an encyclopedia for additional information before painstakingly writing the report by hand.

Today, via the computer, students can dial into an online database or glean information by asking questions of children at other schools or specialists in another country. They can type up the report, quickly make any revisions and print it out without touching a pen.

Fred D'Ignazio, a Lansing-area education consultant, says the computer is the electronic pencil of the 21st Century.

"Computers are the hub of the information knowledge media universe. With text, music and digitized pictures, the computer becomes the controller," he says.

Parents needn't worry about computers making their children more isolated or introspective. In classrooms where the machines are placed in clusters or where two students work together at one terminal, conversation and cooperation naturally occur. Teachers can use that to the students' advantage.

"Some kids may have had difficulty in spelling, others in reading. If you pull those kids together, one kid's strength helps another kid's weakness," says Jeffrey Crockett, a special education teacher consultant in the Plymouth-Canton schools.

Ten years ago, computers may have been perceived as nothing more than expensive flashcards used for teaching multiplication tables or geography. Today, much more software is available to teachers.

A state educational technology plan calls for a telephone line, computer, videodisc player, VCR and television/monitor to be in every classroom within a few years.

All school buildings, the plan says, should at least have a computer network, fiber optics, cable access and a dual-band, steerable satellite dish, which would enable the school to bring in text and video information

Techno teaching tips

Don't know a laser disc from a satellite dish? Don't worry. But don't dismiss it, either. There's no getting around the rapidly changing technologies. Besides, once you get comfortable with them, you'll find they really can make your life easier and make learning more fun.

Sometimes children know more than adults about this stuff because they're growing up with it. If you're a parent, don't be shy about asking the kids to help you understand something. They'll get a kick out of showing mom or dad the ropes, and you'll learn something in the process.

To help, here is a summary of advice from "The Parent's Guide to Technology for Children" by Fred D'Ignazio, a Lansing-area education consultant:

☆ **START YOUNG**. Many computers, video cameras, tape recorders and CD players are rugged enough to be safely operated by toddlers — with some supervision.

☆ **DO IT TOGETHER**. Whenever you have the chance, sit down with the kids, play alongside them or plop them in your lap. Your interest, your attention and your physical presence add a social dimension that enriches the experience immeasurably.

☆ **MAKE THE EXPERIENCE ACTIVE**. Children rarely use technology to create, think or work. Mostly they use it to consume. Encourage your children to use technology as authors, detectives, artists and musicians. Let them capture images and sounds with your family video camera and edit the family's home movies into film or tape scrapbooks. Teach them how to use a word processor and encourage them to write journals, letters and reports on computers.

☆ **BE PLAYFUL**. Children need to learn how to be uninhibited using technology, to be experimental. Expose your children to all sorts of creative applications of technology — even video games — and let them decide what they like most.

☆ **BE COLLABORATIVE.** Technology should never be an end, but a means to an end. And what better end could there be than to bring people together — to help them communicate, solve problems and improve the quality of their lives. Look for opportunities for your children to use technology to connect them to other people. For example, there are hundreds of children's computer networks that can inexpensively link your child via telephone modem to other children across town or around the world.

☆ **GET THEM A COMPUTER**. Powerful computers are getting more affordable. More importantly, there is a radical transformation going on in technology. All media — television, radio, books, music, paintings, movies, even newspapers — are now on computers. ○

from anywhere in the world and then retrieve it in each classroom.

The problem is finding the money to purchase the equipment and the time and money to learn how to master the rapidly changing technology. Some educators and others fear that technology adds to the already vast disparity between rich and poor districts.

Q&A

ANSWERS YOU NEED

continued ▼

federal money. That right is guaranteed to parents by an amendment to the federal Family Educational Rights and Privacy Act. Every public school in Michigan receives some federal money and many private schools do as well.

A parent of a child under age 18 should be able to examine those records at any time. However, a school officer could remove confidential reports filed by the school counselor before sharing the file with a parent.

Your child's school file will include information on the subjects taken, semester exam results, final grades earned, state test scores, immunization and attendance.

If your child attends a private school, look carefully at the contract you sign. There should be language there regarding access to your child's records.

Once a student

continued ▶

reaches age 18, parents lose their right to see the school files. But the student, who is now an adult, gains that right.

Q: *How can I say unwelcome things to the school without it having a negative impact on my child?*

A: As a parent, you are your child's chief advocate. Your guiding principle should be your child's best interest.

If you disagree with a teacher's evaluation of your child, make an appointment to discuss it. Approach the meeting positively. Listen to the teacher. Explain your view. Work together toward a resolution.

If you have a concern about a school policy or about curriculum, talk to other parents or the parent-teacher organization. Others may share your feelings. As part of a group, you may feel more comfortable meeting with the school administrator.

continued ▶

School programs need shaping up

Out of shape.
That's how you could describe the condition of physical education in Michigan elementary schools.

"Kids aren't getting the workouts they need," says third-grade teacher Devra Wagner — even now, in the fitness-conscious '90s.

Wagner, who isn't even the gym teacher, took the situation into her own hands at Avery Elementary in Oak Park two years ago. She conducted after-school aerobics classes for 25-30 students — and some of their parents — two or three times a week. She wasn't paid to do it.

She also promoted a classroom program called Growing Healthy, which integrates teaching about good eating habits and body structure.

Michigan is one of eight states that have not spelled out physical education requirements.

"The requirement we do have has no teeth," says Charles Kuntzleman, a University of Michigan fitness education expert. The law says only that each child shall have physical education. Each school district determines what that means and how it will be provided.

Where there is a physical education class, it's often offered only once a week. And, Kuntzleman adds: "The emphasis in schools is on acquisition of sports skills rather than health-related fitness education."

Programs in health, fitness and physical education have been eroding steadily since the 1960s, cut because of economics and what Kuntzleman calls "a general malaise about physical education."

"Whenever there's a reduction in class time, it always seems to affect physical education," says Vern Seefeldt, who directs the Institute for the Study of Youth Sports at Michigan State University.

"There seems to be the impression that children will learn the fundamental skills and become physically fit without any intervention on the part of the school. Those children who have the money and parents who can get them into good programs will benefit and the others will be short-changed," he says.

This decidedly un-pumped situation is puzzling in the fitness-crazed '90s, when so many adults are running, aerobicizing, working out, dieting and generally shaping up.

But kids are more likely to be playing video games or watching television rather than kicking a ball around or bicycling. They're also likely to be eating a higher-fat diet. In Michigan, kids weigh nearly four pounds more than the national average.

Elementary school teachers such as Wagner see one reason for this:

Start by getting up

Busy, budget-strapped parents of elementary school children can have an impact on the health and fitness education of their kids. Here are some ideas:

A T H O M E :

☆ Set a good example by being active. As third-grade teacher and aerobics instructor Devra Wagner says, "If parents sit, their kids are going to sit. If they go out and do, their kids are going to go out and do."

☆ Family activities like walking, running, hiking, biking, swimming, shooting baskets and dancing to the radio are cheap and uncomplicated. And the togetherness factor is a big bonus.

☆ Nutrition is an essential element of health and fitness. Set an example with your own habits. Be sure your kids are following healthy patterns of low-fat, low-junk eating.

☆ Don't let your child sit in front of the TV set when he or she could be out and about, playing, engaged in vigorous physical activity.

☆ Try making charts for daily exercise, with rewards when your child reaches goals.

A T S C H O O L :

☆ Know what your child's physical education curriculum will be each year.

☆ Know what the school's fitness education objectives are, and ask for evidence that the goals are being met.

☆ Take an active role. Let teachers and administrators know you want quality physical education for your child. University of Michigan fitness education expert Charles Kuntzleman says, "Administrators will tell you they take care of the squeaky wheel. We have clout as parents."

☆ Check into ways you might participate in school programs. If you run or do aerobics, maybe you could be a guest lecturer or demonstrator at school.

☆ Check with the gym teacher about activities outside school, such as gymnastics, dance, soccer or tee ball. The teacher can help make contacts to get your child signed up.

☆ Watch out for these warning signs: If the physical education teacher is a smoker, is obese or is not involved with fitness or if the emphasis is placed on winning rather than cooperation and fun, that's a bad situation for your children. ○

Adults who proclaim the joys of fitness often are financially comfortable or have no children.

Parents of young children, many of whom are working full time or are single parents, often just don't have a lot of time — or money — for family fitness activities.

Q&A

ANSWERS YOU NEED

continued ▼

Q: *How can I get low- or no-cost tutoring for my child?*

A: Look for an older child in the school or community who is doing well in a subject in which your child is weak. Another source for tutors is colleges and universities. And, of course, check with the teacher or district to find out what kind of tutorial services are offered.

Q: *Are there things I can do to help my child have a good relationship with his teacher and improve his chances of getting along and doing well in the classroom?*

A: You mean how to be a "teacher pleaser." That's what Marty and Barbara Nemko, authors of "How to Get Your Child a Private School Education in a Public School" (Acropolis Books, $12.95), call it. The book lists suggestions such as:
☆ Wear clothes that show respect (no rock T-shirts, dirty jeans).

continued ▶

Q&A

ANSWERS YOU NEED

continued ▼

☆ Sit in a "power seat" in front of the classroom. You get called on more and you're more likely to pay attention.

☆ Sit up straight and look interested. Teachers hate looking at bored faces.

☆ Raise your hand as much as possible, especially if no one else does.

☆ Avoid being the last student to follow a direction.

☆ Volunteer occasionally for the jobs no one likes, such as classroom cleanup.

In a way, these are manipulative, but they work.

Q: *What should I do if I don't think my child and her teacher are a good fit?*

A: Follow a series of steps that require open communication. Talk directly with the teacher. Often the concerns arise early in the year before the child has had an opportunity to settle in. Ask questions, observe the classroom and allow

continued ▶

ABOUT FITNESS

So what should schools be doing?

Maybe something similar to what Avery Elementary does. There, gym teacher Faye Frye coordinates her activities with what's going on in other classes.

"If we're studying a certain country, she'll see if she can find some native dances from that country," Wagner says. "If we're studying the abdominal muscle system, she'll do exercises that concentrate there. If we're studying cooperative learning, she'll work with games."

The U.S. Department of Health and Human Services' "Healthy People 2000" program recommends these objectives:

■ 50 percent of children should be involved in daily physical education.

■ The physical education activity should be a lifetime activity, such as walking, running, swimming, bicycling, aerobics.

■ Children should be moving at least 50 percent of the time in gym class. (Studies have shown that in a 30-minute class period, only a few minutes are spent in vigorous movement).

Seefeldt believes we're at the beginning of a nationwide movement toward a standardized physical education curriculum with objectives in four main areas:

■ Physical fitness.

■ Fundamental motor skill development.

■ Lifetime activities.

■ Personal and social development.

"We have gone about as far as we can afford to go in ignoring the health of the student population," Seefeldt says.

Devra *Wagner leads Rhonda Spector, Chris Durant, Ryan Becker and Julie Becker in aerobics at Avery Elementary School in Oak Park.*

PROBLEM LEARNERS

Unchecked difficulties won't just disappear

t may be just an inkling.

Or it may be temper tantrums, poor report cards and constant discipline problems telling you that your child is having trouble in school. Whatever it is, don't ignore it.

Experts say about one child in five has trouble learning. Maybe it's for only a year. Maybe in only one subject. Maybe with only one teacher.

A problem learning doesn't mean the child has a learning disability or needs to be in special education.

But a learning difficulty left unchecked can ruin a child's attitude about school or, at worst, can put him or her hopelessly behind peers and require serious intervention later. And in today's competitive world, later may be too late.

"Time is of the essence," says Diane Russell, a past president of the Michigan Association of School Psychologists and a psychologist for elementary and middle school children in the Chippewa Valley School District.

Until about third grade, children master skills such as reading, writing and basic math at different times. That's normal.

Parents shouldn't worry if a sibling learned faster or if other children are ahead or behind their child — as long as the child is interested in learning and excited about school.

But excitement alone won't ensure a child passes tests or help a child who is hopelessly behind catch up.

The child who doesn't learn how to read by about second grade simply will not be able to handle the reading and writing activities of third grade.

Don't panic if you think your child is having trouble. And don't pressure him or her. That will just set the child up for failure.

Just pay attention.

"The child at home really needs a lot of support and understanding, not pressure," Russell says.

And don't forget to have a professional rule out emotional or physical roots to the problems, such as a recent divorce or death in the family or difficulty hearing or seeing.

Here are some common signs of trouble outlined by educators and spelled out in the book "Why is My Child Having Trouble at School?" by Barbara Novick and Maureen Arnold:

■ Difficulty focusing on tasks; moves often from one activity to another.

ANSWERS YOU NEED

continued ▼

the teacher time to work on the relationship if there appears to be a problem.

The next step would be to talk to the principal. The parent needs to be able to describe the concerns objectively and state specifically that it's the child's issue and not the parent's. Sometimes the parent may feel the fit isn't good when the child actually is happy and doesn't perceive a problem.

The message being conveyed to the child needs to be considered.

Once a parent and an administrator talk, the parent needs to be willing to look at different alternatives before moving the child from the classroom. That should be the last option to consider. Solutions would vary depending on the situation: sessions with teachers, meetings that involve teacher, principal, student and parent to decide what might be tried to

continued ▶

continued ▼

improve the relationship. Perhaps the problem is where the child is seated, how the child is treated by other children, the teacher's voice.

Once the principal decides that the best thing to do is remove the child from the class-room, it has to be han-dled sensitively. The child in no way should be the decision maker.

Q: *What do I do if my child says some other kid is always picking on him? I don't want to fight his battles, but I want it to stop.*

A: Generally, counselors agree it's better to let children work out their differences. They often blow over and are more easily handled without adult interference. Encourage your child to tell you everything that happened. Make sure you understand what is going on.

Then, with your child, brainstorm all the things he could do, from

continued ▶

PROBLEM LEARNERS

■ Mishearing or misreading directions.
■ Careless errors.
■ Disorganized; sloppy home-work.
■ Impulsive acts and getting into trouble.
■ Forgetting to do assignments or taking too long to complete them.
■ Trouble expressing own ideas.
■ Not reading unassisted by mid-second grade.
■ Speaking in fragmented or jumbled sen-tences.
■ Inability to retell a story or recount an event.
■ Low self-esteem.

Every school will differ in its approach to chil-dren who are having difficulty. A fraction of those children will wind up in special education programs; others may turn out to be gifted, but

The source could be physical

All too often, what some parents and educators think are learning difficulties turn out to be vision or hearing problems.

Those possibilities should be eliminated before a pupil is regarded as a slow learner.

Experts say about seven out of every 1,000 school-age children have hearing disorders. Here are some signs that can indicate trouble, according to audiologist Michelle Hagy of Children's Hospital of Michigan:

☆ Strains to listen to speakers. Appears to be reading lips instead of hearing speech.

☆ Doesn't seem to pay attention when name is called. Doesn't answer when called from another room.

☆ Often asks people to repeat things or appears confused by what is said.

☆ Gives wrong answers to simple questions. Example: Says "No" to the question, "What time is it?"

☆ Has trouble pronouncing many words, especially ones with the letters "S" or "TH."

☆ Often distracted; appears to daydream. May misbehave.

☆ Does poorly in school.

☆ Frequent ear or upper respiratory infections.

☆ Turns up volume of TV or radio.

☆ Can't pinpoint where sounds are coming from.

About one in six children ages 5 to 12 has vision problems that can result in a learning disability. Typical school screenings detect only 20 to 30 percent of problems, according to the Better Vision Institute. If you notice any of these signs, the institute recommends your child have a professional eye exam:

☆ Squinting, closing or covering one eye, excessive blinking or rubbing of the eyes.

☆ Dislike or avoidance of close work, short attention span, frequent daydreaming.

☆ Placing the head close to a book when reading; losing place while reading.

☆ Complaints of headaches, nausea and dizziness; excessive clumsiness.

☆ Turning or tilting the head to one side. ○

PROBLEM LEARNERS

suffering from hyperactivity or attention deficit disorder.

Whatever the diagnosis, educators agree that communication is the best way to ensure progress.

If you find yourself battling to get help for your child, remember, the law is on your side. All children, including those with learning problems, have a right to a free and appropriate education that addresses any special needs they have.

Here is some advice for helping a child who's having trouble:

■ Talk to your child's teacher frequently. Establish a rapport that enables you to discuss problems openly.

■ Get to know other professionals at your child's school and in the district, including the principal, counselors and specialists such as a reading or speech specialist. They can be great resources.

■ Ask teachers, counselors and others to recommend tutors.

■ Don't make your home another school. Additional stress may compound your child's problem. Plan activities that involve learning, but make sure they are fun, relaxing and relevant, such as a family story hour or trip to the zoo.

■ A child who is struggling may have low self-esteem. Don't worsen the problem by calling him or her stupid, slow or lazy. Encourage your child.

■ Make sure your child has a complete physical.

■ If your physician suggests further testing, seek a psychologist or other professional who specializes in learning disabilities.

■ If your child has a learning disability such as dyslexia, or attention deficit disorder, contact a support group. Counselors, psychologists and doctors can connect you with such groups.

■ Most of all, keep on top of the situation. Gifted and special-education students get special attention. But if your child is generally among the average students, he or she could be most at risk of falling through the cracks when a problem arises.

ANSWERS YOU NEED

continued ▼

punching the child out to ignoring the behavior. Then decide together what is the best action.

The best, most effective way will always be a peaceful way.

If that doesn't work, talk with the teacher, counselor or principal at the school about the problem.

Q: *I keep hearing about developmentally appropriate education. What is that?*

A: Developmentally appropriate practices are sweeping through Michigan's early education programs.

Nicknamed DAP, the approach encourages children to make choices and do hands-on work that is appropriate for their physical and social maturity and interests. Children learn to walk and talk at different ages. They also learn to read and work with numbers at different times.

For about the first

continued ▶

ANSWERS YOU NEED

continued ▼

eight years, children should be allowed to learn academic skills at their own pace, through guided play, dramatics and problem solving — not through drills, workbooks or lectures. They are not ready for abstract thinking yet and need to see, touch and experience things rather than just hear or read about them.

Beginning in about third grade, children tend to adjust well to more structure.

Q: *My neighbor's child hasn't even started kindergarten, but she already reads well. My same-age child doesn't read. Will she be behind?*

A: Don't worry. Yet. As long as your child is interested in books and likes to be read to, she probably is fine. Children learn to read at different times, some as late as second grade.

Some studies show that some children who learn to read as preschoolers lose their

continued ▶

Don't sit on sidelines when children aren't challenged

Matthew Turner was a straight-A student, teacher's helper and peer tutor. But he was often bored.

"His teachers were telling me he was very, very smart; they were using him to assist other kids with computer skills and other functions in class to keep him interested," says Matthew's father, Tim Turner of Detroit.

At age 9, Matthew would come home occasionally and tell his parents he wasn't interested in school.

"I'd asked him what's wrong," his father says. "He says 'I don't know,' and won't say. That's the first signal that you need to give him another book. … If he says he's having fun, that means they've found something for him to do. If he says he's not, that means he's bored again."

Matthew is like thousands of academically bright students who pose a challenge to teachers trying to meet the needs of the gifted along with those of average and remedial students.

Schools seek to accommodate gifted and talented students in a variety of ways, with enrichment programs, mentorships, accelerated classes, self-contained classrooms and magnet schools, and by allowing them to skip grades, individualizing educational programs and clustering groups within regular classrooms.

There are two schools of thought on how to best educate bright students. One says separating gifted students deprives them and others of "interaction with and toleration for the range of students with whom they'll eventually attend middle and high school," says Mary Bailey-Hengesh, a consultant for gifted education with the Michigan Department of Education.

The other school argues that separate programs enable gifted students to work consistently at their own level and feel comfortable because they are surrounded by similarly talented children.

The trend nationally has been to move away from specialized programs.

Regardless of what school districts offer, it's incumbent upon parents to help teachers identify and nurture their child's gifts.

"Parents need to be very proactive in seeking out enrichment activities outside of the classroom," says Sandra Trosien, a consultant for gifted and talented children for the Washtenaw Intermediate School District.

Failure to do so can result in children who are bored and disruptive in class or, worse, children who drop out of school. An estimated 38 percent of the nation's dropouts are gifted and talented children, Trosien says.

GIFTED CHILDREN

Nine-*year-old Matthew Turner, left, with brother Ryan, 7.*

Signs of a gifted child

☆ Typically learns to read earlier and with better comprehension.

☆ Commonly learns basic skills better, more quickly and with less practice.

☆ Commonly takes less for granted, wanting to know how and why.

☆ Frequently seems to have endless energy, which is often misdiagnosed as hyperactivity.

☆ Often prefers the company of older children and adults.

☆ Shows keen powers of observation.

☆ Often reads a great deal on own.

☆ Often appears to be daydreaming.

☆ May show an intense interest in a particular area.

☆ Will have widely varied interests and be knowledgeable about many things.

☆ Has well-developed powers of abstraction, conceptualization and synthesizing.

☆ Has well-developed sense of humor.

☆ Has highly developed moral and ethical sense.

☆ Has well-developed sense of self and a realistic idea of capabilities and potential. ○

ANSWERS YOU NEED

continued ▼

edge shortly after entering school. That's because many early readers tend to learn only to decode words, rather than to understand them. To read well, a child must decode, comprehend and enjoy.

Worry only if your child isn't interested or doesn't understand stories or if she isn't reading by about second grade.

Q: *Every school day morning, my child says she has a stomachache and needs to stay home. I think she's faking. If I keep her home, she's always feeling better by afternoon and she's never sick on weekends. What should I do?*

A: Find out what's going on at school that your daughter is trying to avoid. There may be a problem between her and her teacher, with a classmate or with a subject. Tell her that you want to help solve whatever problem she's

continued ▶

ANSWERS YOU NEED

continued ▼

facing. Get her to talk about it. After you learn her version of what's troubling her, make an appointment to talk with her teacher. Depending on what you learn there, you may also need to see the principal.

Don't be afraid to advocate on behalf of your daughter. The school is probably as interested as you are in solving the problem.

Q: *A major debate in our house is whether our fifth-grader should play football. I say no way, it's too easy for kids to get hurt. My husband insists that our son join the school team.*

A: You don't mention what your son wants to do. Is he athletically inclined? Does he want to play football? If so, talk to the coach to determine what precautions are taken to prevent injury. Learn the advantages and disadvantages of playing this particular organized sport. Chat with other

continued ▶

GIFTED CHILDREN

Parents also are best able to determine if their child is gifted.

"Putting a child through a rigorous test to affirm a parent's instincts is unnecessary. Follow that child's interest, support their interest and sustain their interest," says Trosien, a past president of the Michigan Alliance for Gifted Education.

"One of the first things we would recommend is that parents keep real good charts, notes and references as to what they observe their child doing at home and what their child says about the work they bring home from school," says Bailey-Hengesh.

Observe language skills and curiosity.

"A lot of them enter school already reading; their questions are more in-depth," Bailey-Hengesh says.

Other signs of giftedness include writing and painting at an early age.

Once parents have gathered information, they should contact the school.

"Share this information with the teacher and school principal so together they can develop a program that would best meet the child's needs," Bailey-Hengesh says.

Trosien suggests providing information-rich literature for students to absorb and pairing gifted students with mentors in areas that interest them.

Trips to the library, bookstores, museums and other cultural activities should be part of the family routine, experts say.

"All parents should be doing this. These are the students that need more," she says. "They may be learning in social studies, but they need to get to that library to find out more. Their thirst is so great for knowledge."

Immediate attention is needed before a child begins hiding his or her talent.

"If those talents are not supported, they do diminish over time and the child learns how to hide it and how to cope in other ways," Trosien says.

Sometimes coping is displayed as disruptive classroom behavior, such as talking out of turn or bothering other children.

As many school districts move away from separating students with academic talents, parents will have an even greater responsibility.

"They can no longer put that young person on that little yellow school bus and assume things are going to happen," Trosien says. "They must be part of that learning. They must volunteer to help the teacher, or go on a field trip. Does that mean a parent must take a sick day or vacation day to do it? Yes, you need to assume that responsibility."

Programs to enrich your child's education

☆ Intermediate school districts in each county have lists of gifted and talented activities offered after school, on weekends and in the summer in their districts.

☆ Intermediate school districts in each county have lists of gifted and talented activities offered after school, on weekends and in the summer in their districts.

☆ The Center for Creative Studies in Detroit offers many enrichment programs in music, art, dance and other areas. Detroit's Children's Museum regularly offers workshops and other programs.

☆ Several Michigan colleges and universities have programs for the academically talented, both in the summer and during the school year. Check particularly with Wayne State University, Eastern Michigan University, Michigan State University, the University of Detroit Mercy and Marygrove College.

☆ Encourage your children to participate in academic tournaments such as Odyssey of the Mind, Future Problem Solvers of America, Science Olympiad, Math Counts, Math Pentathlon and Academic Games. All are programs that make learning fun and challenging. Students compete locally and nationally. If your school doesn't offer such programs, find out why. Maybe a team sponsor is needed, or administrators simply need to know you're interested.

☆ For more information, write: Michigan Alliance for Gifted Education, Box 1732, Warren 48090. ○

ANSWERS YOU NEED

continued ▼

parents about how they deal with their anxiety.

But if your son doesn't want to play football, tell dad to find out what junior is interested in and encourage him in that endeavor.

Q: *I'm almost ashamed to admit this, but my biggest fear as my child gets older is I won't be able to help him with his math homework. Math was never a good subject for me. How can I help myself get more comfortable so I won't freeze up when he comes my way with a math question?*

A: Many adults are uncomfortable with numbers. Sheila Tobias, author of the popular book "Overcoming Math Anxiety," (Houghton Mifflin, $6.95), recommends parents take a course designed to help them feel more comfortable with math at a community college or university extension program. Oakland Community College and

continued ▶

Q&A

ANSWERS YOU NEED

continued ▼

Schoolcraft College are among those in the Detroit area with such classes or seminars.

In Michigan, the state is promoting a family math program, says Charles Allan, math specialist for the state education department. The program encourages schools to set up evenings when parents come into the school to learn or relearn math, sometimes right alongside their children. Encourage your school to set up a similar program.

The University of California program resulted in a book that parents may find helpful regardless of whether they take the family math course or not. The book, titled, "Family Math" (University of California, $15) introduces parents and children to practical ideas to help them improve their math skills. It's aimed toward parents and children in grades kindergarten

continued ▶

60

Kids can keep culture while learning English

In a world where seemingly everyone speaks English, living in a home where only Spanish, Arabic or one of many other languages is spoken can be overwhelming.

That's true not just for children but for parents, too.

Where can parents whose first language isn't English go for help? What can they do to help their children be successful in English-speaking schools without losing their cultural identity?

"The main thing parents need to do is to help children feel comfortable," says Hattie Baker, education coordinator for Vistas Nuevas, a bilingual Head Start preschool program in Detroit.

"Kids need to hold on to their culture and feel good about it," Baker says. "As long as they do that, they won't feel like second-class citizens."

For years, educators and parents alike have been at opposite ends of bilingual education's spectrum, Baker says. Some parents only speak their native tongue at home, making school and home seem worlds apart.

Other parents and teachers discourage children from speaking their native language, relying on the adage: "You're in America now, speak English."

Yet that approach also hurts children because it makes them feel their native culture is inferior, says Lydia Lopez Engel, a bilingual specialist for Detroit Public Schools.

"You can't separate language and culture," Engel says. If children are in a setting that tends to downgrade their native culture, "they're not going to do well academically," Engel says.

Parents can help by encouraging English use at home while continuing to speak their native language and taking pride in their heritage, says Maura Sedgeman, a bilingual resource teacher for Dearborn Public Schools.

Not only will that improve their children's self-esteem, but their children will be more marketable when job-hunting later in life, she says.

"Third-generation people often grow up and say, 'Why didn't I learn it when I could?' " says Sedgeman. "In the long run, bilingual kids have an advantage from developing the language from birth."

Helping children feel comfortable with their language during their early school years — preschool to fifth-grade — is imperative for later academic success, says Shereen Arraf, an education learning specialist for the Arab Community Center for Economic and Social Services in Dearborn.

By fifth grade, problems in language development will lead to problems in other areas because the child will have difficulty reading, Arraf says.

There are ways parents can help. Before children enter preschool, Baker says, they should be exposed to people of different races and languages.

Reading to children at home in both their native language and English will help them build lifelong skills, Sedgeman says.

If parents aren't able to read or speak English, Sedgeman suggests reading books in the family's native language. Or parents can take children to story hours at libraries or community centers, so they can hear stories read in English.

Fatama *Alkhateeb, a parent-teacher, helps students at the Arab Community Center for Economic and Social Services in Dearborn.*

If that's not practical, parents can organize story hours of their own with other parents. Find a high school or college student, preferably a bilingual one, who's willing to read regularly to children in the group.

Also, parents should find out what services their school district offers and take advantage of them, says Miguel Ruiz, chief of state bilingual and migrant education programs.

The main thing for parents and educators to remember, Ruiz says, is that districts are required to provide the services every child needs to be successful in school.

Under Michigan law, districts must provide bilingual services if there are 20 or more tested bilingual children in one language.

In districts where there are fewer than 20 non-English-speaking children, federal law requires "appropriate" services. Each school district is able to define what that means. If a parent does not feel a child is getting needed services, the parent can call the state office of bilingual education.

"School districts need to be responsive to these children because their parents may not know how to ask questions and find out how to handle the system," Ruiz says. "Language should not be a detractor from having a good education."

ANSWERS YOU NEED

continued ▼

through eight. The book was written by Jean Kerr Stenmark, Virginia Thompson and Ruth Cossey.

Q: *One teacher in our school is a screamer and cannot control more aggressive children. As a result, all suffer. What should parents do?*

A: The first step is to talk to the teacher in person. Let him or her know that you are aware of the situation and that you would like to see changes. You will have a much better idea how to proceed from there.

On the teacher's behalf, you might need to insist that the administration provide counseling and additional training.

Q: *The teacher recommends my child repeat a grade. Is this good advice? I've heard kids held back are more likely to become dropouts.*

A: Research shows there are few good reasons to have an elementary

continued ▶

continued ▼

school child repeat a grade, according to Carol Payne Smith of Western Michigan University's College of Education. She says the child forced to repeat a grade often feels ostracized and loses self-esteem. In addition, the child usually gains little by going over the same material the same way a second time.

Talk not only to the teacher but the school principal and counselors — and your child. Consider having the child repeat the grade only if the school offers a way to preserve the student's self-esteem and offers a very different learning experience.

Q: *I'm displeased with the latchkey program at my child's school. It's just a baby-sitting service. I've heard that some districts offer academic or arts classes and even hire college students or teachers to help tutor kids. How do you judge a good program and what can I*

continued ▶

ADVICE TO PARENTS

Don't be shy about talking to teachers

Heart pounding, palms clammy, your time has come to face the teacher.

The parent-teacher conference can invoke bittersweet flashbacks to the time when you were the student, even if that was decades ago. Whatever your memories, put them aside for now.

As the parent, you are meeting the teacher as an equal in a high-stakes game — your child's school success. Be positive and be prepared.

Start well before the conference by listening to what your child says about school. In the first few weeks of September, all students have questions, concerns, apprehensions. Ask your child what he or she likes and doesn't like about the class. Make notes of topics to discuss with the teacher and take them when you go to the meeting.

Be ready to talk, but also listen.

"The most important thing is to keep the communication going," says Judy Greenbaum, an Ann Arbor consultant who works with parents and teachers. The goal is to exchange information and work together, keeping up the dialogue, even if you don't always agree.

■ Set the tone. Be cordial and businesslike. In a two-parent family, both should attend. A single parent may want to invite a relative or friend who can listen in and be available as a sounding board afterward.

■ Talk about the teacher's and your expectations about course work and testing. Ask the teacher what you can do to help your child at home but be realistic about how much time you can spend each day as a tutor. If you have several children, a job and other demands, you may not be able to provide regular homework help. In that case, your limited time may be best spent being "the loving person who thinks yours is the best child on Earth." Greenbaum says. "Homework help is second."

■ Share insights about your child. Perhaps he has a special talent for music or drama. Maybe she is a budding car buff. As the school year progresses, the teacher may be able to incorporate that interest in the classroom.

■ Let the teacher know if there is any special circumstance — a pending move, job change, divorce, a serious illness or recent death — that might affect the child's performance or attitude toward school.

Here are some questions parents of elementary students may want to ask at a parent-teacher conference:

■ What reading and math group is my child in?

ADVICE TO PARENTS

- How does my child get along with other students?
- Does my child participate in group discussions?
- What do you think my child likes most and is best at in school?

If the teacher says something you don't understand, ask for a clarification in a nonconfrontational way: "Do I understand this correctly? I heard you say … "

If a question or concern arises during the year, don't wait for the next formal conference. Contact the teacher and ask for a meeting.

On their part, school administrators and teachers have the job of making parents comfortable in school, whatever the parents' educational background.

Perhaps the parent dropped out. Perhaps the parent speaks a language other than English at home. Making all parents feel welcome is a big but important job.

"Making the schools user friendly for the students and the parents is really critical," says David Gross of the Michigan Parent-Teacher Association.

You may not always agree with the teacher, but it is far preferable to work out differences between the two of you. Teachers may understandably resent parents (and, perhaps, their children) who bypass them and go to the principal or other administrator. Parents should go that route only as a last resort when the situation merits that action.

ANSWERS YOU NEED

continued ▼

do to improve ours?

A: An ideal latchkey program offers the best of what a parent could provide at home: time for children to play outside and get exercise, guided homework study if needed, enrichment opportunities and a chance to talk with interested, caring adults.

Latchkey workers should be experienced and understand children's needs, says Marlynn Levin, coordinator of the work and family life program at the Merrill-Palmer Institute of Wayne State University.

Parents who think their latchkey programs could improve must take the initiative. Work with other parents, the principal and latchkey staff. Enlist volunteers — perhaps retired teachers or college students — to provide enrichment. Talk to community leaders and businesses that might sponsor field trips or speakers for the latchkey students.

Levin suggested parents periodically visit

the latchkey program unannounced. As an alternative to an unacceptable latchkey program, parents might join and hire someone to supervise children at home.

Q. *How important is music or art education in a child's overall development? Should I seek out private lessons to build up these skills?*

A. The arts are essential in helping children grow up to be imaginative thinkers, problem solvers and leaders with creative, inventive minds.

The arts give children a wonderful way to communicate and express themselves.

But if your child is in a shortsighted school district, one that has cut music and arts education programs to save a few dollars, you might protest vehemently and, in the interim, consider private lessons and other enrichment activities.

continued ▼

64

ADVICE TO PARENTS

Working parents can share part of school experience

These days, many parents simply don't have time to be part of their child's school experience in the traditional ways — working at bake sales, assisting at holiday classroom parties, chauffeuring field trips.

Those things usually occur during the school day, when many parents are working. Educators and others say schools and businesses must rethink their policies to accommodate parents who work outside the home.

No matter what the situation, there are ways working parents can put their at-school time to maximum effect — even if it's minutes rather than hours.

Here are some ideas:

■ Parents who work outside the home must explain to the child before school starts that he or she may not be at school as much as some other parents. Tell the child that doesn't decrease your interest in what happens at school.

■ Pay attention to the curriculum and set aside time for your child to talk about school. Reassure your son or daughter that you will attend everything you can, including at least one special event, such as a field trip. Then make good on your promise.

"Children will understand the fact that mom or dad can't always be there as frequently as some other parents during the day. But they certainly expect and hope their parents are going to be there when there are programs at night or when they can," says David Gross of the Michigan PTA.

■ Give highest priority to activities where your child is performing or otherwise involved in the program, recommends Percy Bates, professor of education at the University of Michigan.

■ Tell the teacher about your work schedule and ask for the teacher's help. Do it right away; don't wait until the parent-teacher conference. Some teachers may even be willing to send home weekly written progress reports.

Schools can also help in various ways, including:

■ Scheduling events such as holiday concerts in the evening so more parents can attend. Some schools may also be able to hold events for parents first thing in the morning, or from 4-6 p.m. A field trip could be on a Saturday.

If your school doesn't do such scheduling, discuss the situation with

ADVICE TO PARENTS

the administration or parent organization.

"As school people, we work for the parent. I don't know of any other business that can stay in business without paying attention to the changing needs of the clientele," Bates said.

■ Rather than assume the only way parents can participate is at bake sales or field trips, schools should create more meaningful involvement that doesn't exclude parents with outside employment, says Patricia Edwards, an associate professor of education at Michigan State University.

For example, a Lansing elementary school held monthly discussions for parents on literacy, including topics such as the whole language approach to teaching reading and new ways to teach spelling. Parents decided the most convenient time to meet.

■ Ask parents about such things as the number of children they have and their ages, marital status, employment and work hours. That way school officials will have a better idea how to accommodate parents.

A growing number of companies recognize that allowing employees time off to attend parent-teacher conferences or volunteer at school is good business. Approach your employer or union about creative ways to be active in your child's school without being less productive at work.

For example, you might want to volunteer to lead the story hour at school one morning a week and seek your employer's permission to work an hour later that day or skip your lunch hour.

ANSWERS YOU NEED

continued ▼

A lot of communities have arts centers where you can find a private teacher or seek low-cost alternatives, including group lessons.

Q. *I took piano lessons as a child but got bored and didn't stick with it. I deeply regret it. Now, my child who's been taking lessons for two years seems bored. Should I force him to stick with it, hoping he'll appreciate it later?*

A. There is no reason for music to be boring. It's hard work sometimes, but if a child is saying "I'm bored" or is frustrated for a week or month, encourage him to go on. If the complaint is ongoing, listen. Maybe you just need to find a more exciting teacher. If that doesn't work, back off and try again in a year. Or perhaps consider a group learning experience. ○

CHAPTER 2

THE KIDS IN THE MIDDLE

Khary Hobbs, an aspiring artist, with some of his favorite possessions.

Kids in 'tween years have unique needs

The kids in the middle:

They're caught between big kids and little kids. High school and elementary school. Parents and peers.

You may think of them as the wonder years, but the quirky, unpredictable time between ages 11 and 14 might better be called "the range of the strange."

Kids are in flux physically, emotionally, socially. They are tall, short, giddy, weepy, cruel, sweet. Their highs are lofty; their lows are desperate.

Just making it through a day without a crisis — a broken nail, a fight, bad hair — can be an accomplishment. The kids in the middle are so absorbed by what is happening to them and where they fit into the world that learning often is the last thing on their minds.

Blame it on puberty. But don't expect to change it.

"We used to try to put a round peg into a square hole and it just didn't work," says Ronald Johnson, principal of L'Anse Creuse South Middle School in Harrison Township. "What we're doing in the middle schools now is making room for differences — not making excuses, just recognizing who these young people are."

Middle schoolers are not short high schoolers. They don't have the attention span or discipline to handle the rigors of high school.

They aren't tall grade schoolers, either. They don't need the hand-holding and coddling they used to get.

Their schools need to coax them into stretching, making choices, taking risks, figuring out who they are.

Middle school students thrive socially and academically when educators — and parents — accept their quirks.

"They are the range of the strange," Johnson says. "The only thing consistent about them is their inconsistency. When that doesn't bother you, you're over the first hurdle."

This section on middle schools looks not only at what makes the kids in the middle tick but at the reforms that are changing their schools. The reports take a close look at some of Michigan's best middle school programs and show how new teaching methods are changing a wide range of subjects. ○

THE TYPICAL
11-YEAR-OLD

☆ Full of energy, fidgety, restless, constantly on the go.

☆ Critical, demanding, aggressive, rebellious, easily angered.

☆ Somewhat rude and discourteous.

☆ Has mood swings, uncontrolled emotional outbursts.

☆ Is more apt to cry than 10-year-olds.

☆ Sometimes feels as if nobody likes him or her.

☆ Puts no effort into cooperating with others. Once-adored parents lose their halos, especially moms.

☆ Gets along badly with siblings, but remains a staunch friend if one is in trouble.

☆ Argues about everything.

☆ Must be reminded about chores.

☆ Mainly has same-sex

continued ▶

EMOTIONAL ROLLER COASTER

Moods are part of middle years

Parents, if your middle schooler is moody, forgetful, secretive — don't panic.

That's normal.

"This is one of the highest stress periods in human development," says Peggy Gaskill, a Central Michigan University professor who is an expert on middle schools and adolescent development. "They worry about physical development, friendships, who they're going to be when they grow up, all kinds of things."

From ages 11 to 14, parents often feel as though their child has been replaced by an alien being.

They start to burst out of their clothes. Acne becomes a nightmare. They can grow up to 20 inches and add 40 pounds from the time they enter middle school until they leave.

Their bodies begin to develop sexually, and they struggle with negative attitudes as they compare themselves to peers, older siblings and parents.

Hormonal changes make them energetic but moody.

"They're irritable," Gaskill says. "The moods are real, they're sometimes physically draining and they're unpredictable. They come and go very quickly."

The middle school years are referred to as a time of "storm and stress." Many children think something is wrong with them, because their friends are developing at faster or slower rates.

"They go from ecstasy to despair in brief periods of time," says Paula Wood, dean of the Wayne State University College of Education. "They're on an emotional roller coaster."

Many districts begin conflict resolution in middle school because children become so physical. They are constantly poking, hugging, punching, tapping, flapping, twirling.

Stress and physical interaction can be an explosive combination. It can bring on severe depression. Thirteen-year-olds are the largest group of children who commit suicide.

Middle schoolers' edginess also makes them prone to fight more than younger and older children.

Dr. Rosalind Griffin, a Southfield psychiatrist who specializes in adolescents, says it sometimes takes only a small gesture to anger an early teen.

"A slight touch or a wrong look can lead to a fight," she says. "Someone violated someone's personal space, touched them, looked at them the wrong way, sent a verbal threat — that's all it takes."

EMOTIONAL ROLLER COASTER

Yet their reasoning skills are maturing.

"They have a heightened sense of what's fair," Gaskill says. "They're constantly looking at their relationships with each other. Physical contact is helping them establish who they are. But we also need to work with them to control their tempers."

Socially, they are extremely self-conscious. They think everyone is looking at them. They perform as though they're on stage. That's why they stay in front of the mirror so long before going to school, forgetting their lunch money and gym bag.

"They're terrible with responsibility," Gaskill says, "because they're too busy thinking about everything else."

One day, they may be best friends with someone; the next, they're not speaking. They aren't ready for one-on-one relationships with the opposite sex.

"They're extremely egocentric," Wood says. "Though they care for each other, they're establishing their own identity. They need activities where they interact socially, so they'll know they're socially acceptable to their peers."

David Lesar flips at East Middle School in Plymouth, aided by Cheron Rice, right , and Kelly Holbel.

Schools can play a role by providing coed activities that give kids a chance to interact.

Many kids who begin dating and sexual activity at this stage use it to mark their impending maturity, Wood says.

"They use it to say, 'I'm not a virgin, I'm a grown-up,' " she says.

Experts say it's too soon for sex and are alarmed about the growing number of pregnancies among girls younger than 15.

"I think they're overexposed to the world," Wood says. "They're less sheltered than they probably need to be. They're exposed through life to so many adult things at an early age and they're forced to make decisions much ahead of when they're ready."

THE TYPICAL 11-YEAR-OLD

continued ▼

friends, but girls talk about boys and enjoy joking and teasing from boys. Boys show little interest in girls.

☆ Rarely chooses to be alone; clusters in groups.

☆ Likes teachers if they're fair and not too strict.

☆ Takes care of self better than his or her room. ○

THE TYPICAL 12-YEAR-OLD

☆ Has a big appetite.

☆ Is more tolerant, sympathetic, friendly and calm.

☆ Has a strong sense of humor and likes making insulting remarks to friends.

☆ Tries to avoid showing feelings.

☆ Is more detached from mom; jealous of older siblings.

☆ Is less resistant to bedtime.

☆ Admits doing things wrong; can accept blame and tends to tell the truth.

☆ Becomes more aware of appearance. Is especially aware of what the crowd is wearing and never goes against it. Girls try to look glamorous. Boys are concerned about not looking like girls.

☆ Girls are more mature; develop a strong interest in menstruation.

continued ▶

Don't get rattled by things kids say

If you want your budding teenagers to keep talking to you, don't faint at the sometimes hair-raising stuff that comes out of their mouths, parents say.

Even the brave can be rattled by the world of adolescence, where hormones are leaping out of control, bodies are changing and worries about life, friends, clothes and social status seem likely to swallow kids.

"Some of the things they say knock your socks off," says Gloria Williams of Detroit. She recalls that when her son, Shaphan Williams, was 13, he sometimes started discussions with: " 'Mom, I'm going to tell you something, but I don't want you to get upset.' "

Says his mother: "I have to brace myself. Sometimes I have to take a deep breath."

It's best to keep a poker face, parents say.

"You can't let kids tell you what they want to tell you and be squeamish," says Roschelle Wilson of Detroit, who has a teenage son and daughter. "My daughter tells me what's going on to shock me. I hear it all."

When Wilson's son, Charles Wilson III, was an eighth-grader, he wanted a high-priced pair of sneakers. His parents didn't automatically deny his request. His father, Charles Wilson Jr., explained how companies use advertising to entice buyers.

"I paint a picture, he analyzes what I'm telling him and decides whether what he's buying is worth it," says Charles Wilson.

Experts say — and parents attest — that 13-year-olds can be the most challenging. The Wilsons' daughter, Charlezetta — who is a year older than their son — helped them cope by assuring them that her brother would soon pass through this stage.

"I understand his need for acceptance in the group," says Roschelle Wilson. "You fight with a lot of independent thinking."

Negotiating with middle schoolers on flexible areas such as bedtime, going out with friends and playing video games will make them more responsive on nonnegotiable issues such as homework and school attendance, the parents say.

"A lot of times parents don't think kids will understand the reasoning," Roschelle Wilson says. "Explanations work better. Dictating doesn't work. They can outlast you."

The Wilsons often make deals with their kids. If the kids mess up during the week, they lose video game privileges on the weekend.

Families set different parameters about a topic that can dominate the

THE PARENTS' SIDE

middle school years — dating. Many parents don't allow it, saying their children are too young. But they do let them exchange phone calls with kids of the opposite sex.

"I don't know why people think that 12-, 13- and 14-year-olds are supposed to do what 17- and 18-year-olds do," Roschelle Wilson says. "Let them grow up."

Charles *Wilson Jr. and his wife, Roschelle, daughter Charlezetta and son Charles III.*

Often, middle schoolers and their parents clash over friends. Roschelle Wilson says it's usually a mistake to forbid a friendship, though it may be appropriate to discourage certain companions. "I'll explain why I'm not fond of that child," she says. "Each time that child does something of a negative nature, I ask them what would've happened if they were there."

Neither Williams nor Wilson allow their children to hang out at malls with friends. But they will take them to the mall and stay with them.

Williams and the Wilsons allow their children to listen only to a minimal amount of rap music. They don't try to pick their children's friends, but they do point out unacceptable behavior of the friends.

Providing meaningful activities is important, the parents say.

"The old 'I'm bored' line irks you," Charles Wilson Jr. says. "The more time they have to do something positive, the less opportunity they'll have to get into trouble."

Williams' son sings in a choir. The Wilson children are avid musicians,

THE TYPICAL 12-YEAR-OLD

continued ▼

☆ Boys may have sessions in which they talk about sex.

☆ Is concerned about how his or her body compares with others'.

☆ Is friendly toward opposite sex. Girls know what boys their friends like; boys know what girls their friends like. But girls and boys don't expect the opposite sex to say they like them. Girls are more interested in boys than vice versa.

☆ Is happy about success in schoolwork and worried about report cards, exams.

☆ Still has to be reminded to clean up his or her room. ○

THE TYPICAL 13-YEAR-OLD

☆ Likes to snack, but not as ravenously as 12-year-olds.

☆ Is still energetic and busy, but more thoughtful.

☆ Feels and acts more independently.

☆ Is nicer away than at home.

☆ Except at meals, is hard to find around the house.

☆ Often unfriendly, withdrawn, uncertain about self, uncommunicative, sensitive, suspicious, feelings easily hurt.

☆ Overcome with worry.

☆ Not often seen crying, but will do so privately.

☆ Is drawn to the mirror like a magnet, worrying about body, features, personality.

☆ Considers everything mom does or says as "ridiculous" and doesn't want to be seen with

continued ▶

THE PARENTS' SIDE

Lending a hand

Some advice for parents:

☆ Listen, but don't poke or pry.

☆ Don't argue. Let irritable middle schoolers cool off, which often happens quickly, then try to talk. Remain calm.

☆ Don't be offended if your middle schooler doesn't want to be your friend. It's part of the independence they're developing. It's no longer socially acceptable to pal around with parents. They believe that as young adults, they don't need supervision.

☆ Be available for them, but don't be offended if they push you away. They need closeness, but it's more acceptable to receive it from peers.

☆ Don't criticize; they're doing enough criticizing of themselves.

☆ Help middle schoolers feel better: If they feel dumb, help them feel smart. If they feel ugly, help them feel beautiful.

☆ Refrain from asking too many questions because you won't get any answers.

☆ Stand by them in crises, such as losing a longtime friend.

☆ Listen to their conversations with friends for clues to what's happening in their lives.

☆ Drive them places with friends.

☆ Even though they don't want you hanging around, make your home a place where they feel comfortable inviting friends.

☆ When reprimanding, deal only with the precise problem. Don't bring up other issues.

☆ Don't give in to manipulation.

☆ Break down big chores into small parts.

☆ Discuss and negotiate rules with them.

☆ Write lists of things to do so they don't forget.

☆ Explain the wide range of sexual development and assure them they are normal. Give them data to support what you say.

☆ Encourage group activities; discourage dating.

☆ Seek support from friends who are in the same position as you.

so lessons and practice take up much of their free time. Both play the piano; Charles also plays the drums and Charlezetta the flute.

Single parents have an added responsibility because they don't have a partner to back them up.

"You have to teach them that for every action, there's an equal and opposite consequence," says Williams, a single parent.

Same is good, different isn't

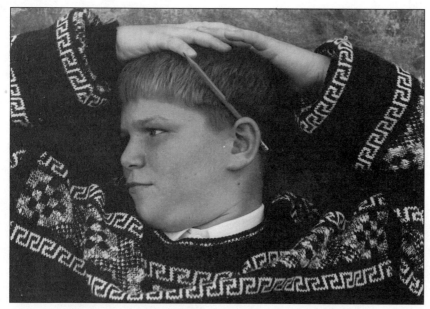

Once *ostracized for wearing suits to school, Kevin VonHolten, 13, switched to sweaters like the other kids at East Middle School in Plymouth.*

Kevin VonHolten was used to getting picked on. About his name. His lisp. His preference for wearing suits to school.

Throughout elementary school, Kevin usually just took a deep breath and put up with the taunts. But when he reached middle school, things changed.

"Now, it gets me so upset that people don't seem to think of me as a real person," Kevin said as a 13-year-old seventh-grader at East Middle School in Plymouth. "All I want is for them to think I'm normal."

At first, Kevin fought back with his fists when other children pestered him. After that didn't do anything but get him in trouble, he decided to listen to his mother and turn the other cheek — and stop doing things other kids considered geeky.

"I stopped wearing suits, even though I liked to. I guess I don't need to act like I'm all grown up," he says. "And kids called me a mama's boy when I wore them. They're treating me better now, but they'll never let me live it down."

Kevin now wears what the other kids wear.

her; less rebellious with dad.

☆ Wants to get away from siblings; quarrels over trivial things.

☆ Complains that people don't understand him or her.

☆ Has fewer friends but considers them their only bright spot.

☆ Is firmly focused on the opposite sex. Many begin dating.

☆ Boys begin a height spurt.

☆ Hair care is important for both boys and girls.

☆ Still influenced by group preferences in clothing, but surer of likes and dislikes.

☆ Girls are more concerned about attractiveness, popularity, future.

☆ Boys are more concerned about school,

continued ▶

THE TYPICAL 13-YEAR-OLD

continued ▼

money matters.

☆ Both think about careers.

☆ May experiment with alcohol.

☆ Still has to be reminded to clean up his or her room. ○

FITTING IN

Normalcy. It's everything to preadolescents. Individuality is a curse. Middle schoolers usually try to hide any hint of it by dressing the same, talking the same, walking the same — and, yes, thinking the same.

"You can't even pick your kid out of a group anymore," says Mary Barrett of Grosse Pointe.

Fitting in is crucial for self-esteem as children go through the natural process of figuring out what is socially acceptable, says Jeffrey Parker, a University of Michigan professor who studies adolescent peer relationships.

Good friends can keep each other from making fools of themselves and boost each other when they're down.

"They'll validate you, stick up for you, make you feel good about yourself. … That's a lot more compelling and meaningful when it comes from friends than from parents," Parker says.

Strong, supportive friendships also help children develop social poise and traits such as leadership and cooperation. Clumsy peer relationships can make life miserable — and may signal troubled times ahead.

In 29 out of 31 major studies about peer relationships, children who are rejected by their peers early on — and often — are eight times more likely to drop out of school or become delinquent, Parker says.

Children who have trouble fitting in aren't doomed to be outcasts forever. A thick skin is often the only protection. But with a little help and a lot of support, children with weak social skills can overcome problems.

Search for acceptance

INDICATORS OF PROBLEMS
Signs that can indicate a child is struggling socially:

☆ Has no regular companions.

☆ Isn't invited to slumber parties or other social activities.

☆ Avoids social situations. Says things such as: "Nobody would like me there anyway."

☆ Makes up excuses to stay home from school.

☆ Teachers complain about inappropriate behaviors, such as fighting, crying or moping.

☆ Comes home from school angry or hostile. Picks fights with siblings.

WHAT YOU CAN DO ABOUT IT

☆ Take your child's concerns seriously. Dismissing or minimizing them tells your child the problems aren't important.

☆ Try to pinpoint problem behaviors by talking to your child's teacher and watching your child interact at school.

☆ Once you've determined what triggers negative behavior, suggest alternate ways of responding and practice them in hypothetical situations.

☆ Remind your child that she's not going to like everybody, and everybody isn't going to like her. And that's OK.

☆ Get help from school counselors or private psychologists if you don't feel you can help your child cope, or if your child's behavior is dangerous. ○

Academic preparation can't start too early

College may seem a long way from middle school, but nearly all educators agree that preparation for higher education needs to start then. Despite years of steering lower-achieving middle schoolers away from college track classes, educators now say all students in grades six through eight should be placed in academic classes that will ease their entry into college, should they decide to go.

"The middle school becomes the pivotal part of whether kids get the access to the right courses and information, particularly if they are first-generation college students," says Phyllis Hart, executive director of Achievement Council. The 10-year-old national organization, based in Los Angeles, is designed to steer younger students toward college.

With access to higher-level courses in math, foreign language, science and English, all students will be equipped to make educational choices after high school.

The College Board, a New York testing organization, recommends that college-bound students take algebra and geometry in high school. That means they need pre-algebra instruction in middle school, says Jean Llewellyn, coordinator of the College Board's Equity 2000, a national educational reform project designed to increase the number of college-bound minority students.

"Everybody should have high standards and a rigorous curriculum," Llewellyn says. "If they're not having demanding courses, they're not being prepared for college."

Math proficiency, for example, opens the door to numerous careers, says Paula Wood, dean of Wayne State University's College of Education. "Math is the language of all sciences. Children who don't master that can't go on to the study of science," she says. "It's absolutely critical that advanced math skills be part of every middle school child's curriculum; they should master beginning algebra by the end of middle school."

Critics argue that all students aren't capable of taking upper-level math and including them only harms the higher-achieving students.

Research, however, shows that high-achieving students do just as well when joined by lower-achieving peers in accelerated classes. And lower-achieving students do better when placed with accelerated students and worse when grouped only with low-achieving students.

Even if students are not thinking about college, the skills they get from rigorous academics — responsibility, goal-setting, problem-solving and teamwork — will help them enter the job market, says Charlene Pike, a L'Anse Creuse South Middle School teacher and president of the National

THE TYPICAL 14-YEAR-OLD

☆ Has verve, vigor, energy.

☆ Loves life; has many friends of both sexes.

☆ Is offended if not provided all the luxuries he or she wants.

☆ Is critical of the way people look, dress, act.

☆ Walks far behind or in front of parents if forced to go somewhere with them.

☆ Talks frankly about thoughts.

☆ Feels nagged by parents; doesn't want advice.

☆ Has debates about dating, homework, curfews.

☆ Is outgoing, bouncy and bubbly outside of the home.

☆ Has incredibly full schedule.

☆ Girls talk about boys constantly.

continued ▶

THE TYPICAL
14-YEAR-OLD

continued ▼

☆ Boys are less interested in girls and the less mature ones like everybody but girls.

☆ Couples change constantly; lots of quarreling and making up.

☆ Nearly all have done some drinking or know someone who has.

☆ Girls are focused on their bodies and cleanliness.

☆ Boys have more marked growth; may have nocturnal emissions.

☆ Spends most free time in social gatherings.

☆ Schoolwork is often a minor part of school life.

☆ Neatness starts to set in; most keep rooms passably clean. ○

COLLEGE PLANNING

Middle Schools Association.

"They should be learning critical thinking," Pike says. "My students set their own learning goals and criteria for success. Then they keep accurate data on 'How am I doing?' … They're taking responsibility."

Educators agree that middle school students also need to know how to prepare for careers.

"Parents need … to push schools in the direction of 'my child needs to be in these courses because my child is going to go to college to have a better life than I had,' " Hart says.

Looking ahead

To help prepare middle school-age children for college, experts recommend that parents:

☆ Visit the school and talk to teachers, counselors and the principal; ask that your child be placed in college prep courses.

☆ Get information from counselors about the middle school courses needed to prepare for college prep courses and the high school courses needed for college.

☆ Spend at least a half hour a day helping your child with homework and offering encouragement.

☆ Encourage study groups to help students digest information and pick up information they may not have grasped individually.

☆ Monitor your child's time at home after school, including the amount and kinds of television watched.

☆ Inquire about after-school, Saturday and summer education programs that might help your child. ○

Teachers also wear advisers' hats

Rusty Towers spends 25 minutes a day listening and looking for clues from her first batch of students at Ann Arbor's Clague Middle School.

Are any of them at risk for suicide? Having trouble at home? Experimenting with drugs? In the heat of a major crush?

"My eyes and ears are open for every little hint," Towers says. "I may spot someone pretending to smoke a joint, or catch that knowing look between two students when someone cracks a joke about sex."

Sometimes she searches for signs by watching how students get along during a volleyball match or an impromptu game. Other times she puts students into discussion groups and listens to the chatter, which can range from homelessness to the hottest new video game.

Afterward, she teaches them U.S. history.

"We're here to teach them, but we also need to be listening to them and helping them through this time in their life," Towers says. "Every student has a story and they really want to be able to tell it to somebody."

As a teacher, Towers says she has always been part instructor, part

Clague *students Jason Burton, left, and George Blevins – both 14 – huddle with teacher Rusty Towers.*

K E Y S   T O   A

GREAT SCHOOL

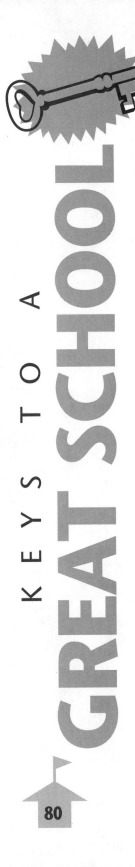

ADVISING

mother and part counselor. The adviser-advisee program at Clague doesn't change the job much; it just gives her more time to do it.

"This legitimizes the extra time that teachers would love to take with their students but can never seem to find," Towers says. "And it really allows you to get into a kid's life — not that they always want that."

All academic subject teachers at Clague have an advisory period first thing in the morning with groups of 24 to 29 students. The teachers follow the students from seventh to eighth grade, returning to seventh-graders at the end of the two-year cycle.

Teachers use the time in various ways, but the goal is to develop bonds with the students and offer them stability.

Advisers — also called anchors or mentors — work with counselors, sharing information, consulting with parents and disciplining students. But counselors still do most scheduling, career planning and organizing of support groups.

"You can talk to your friends, but they can't solve your problems," says Nina Lysloff, who was in Towers' class in seventh grade. "But the teachers are there to help you solve your problems. … And you know you can always go to them and they'll be there for you."

During one advisory session, Towers watches her students play volleyball with other groups. But a couple of boys try to sabotage the game by purposely missing the ball.

"Those boys see themselves as on the outside looking in right now," Towers says, after they give each other high fives for losing a point. "They resist group activities and they frustrate other students here and in the classroom."

Towers puts the boys on separate teams and later talks with them.

The advisory period helped Towers identify the problem and address it earlier than she otherwise would have.

Over the 20 years that Clague has had the adviser programs, Towers has helped settle countless student struggles with parents. She also has helped students who used drugs or experimented with sex.

"It's a lot of work; it can be emotionally taxing," Towers says. "But we'd lose so many of these kids without it."

Sharing sharpens students and staff

Melissa *Beck, left, Jennifer Jefferson and Sarah Rock – and St. Clair Middle School classmates – earned a scavenger hunt on the St. Clair River.*

Nancy Motte stands in front of 100 squirming seventh-graders in the St. Clair Middle School auditorium, microphone in hand, and announces their long-awaited final project:

They are to pick a Michigan region and use graphs, brochures, pictures and prose to promote it as a tourist destination.

Then Motte, a math teacher at the school south of Port Huron, explains what math concepts they should use.

"Tell me what it would it cost for a luxury trip there. How about an economy excursion? How cold is it in December compared to February or April? Graph it."

Ken Mareski, a social studies teacher, grabs the microphone and asks the students to think about what ethnic groups settled in the region, what major industries located there and what the topography looks like.

And finally, English teacher Vern Albrecht urges the students to get poetic and use lots of description: "Is it pristine, cosmopolitan, industrial?"

After about 20 minutes, when the students can sit still no longer, Motte instructs them to pick two or three teammates and spend four periods a day for the next week working on the project. As an incentive, the stu-

KEYS TO A

GREAT SCHOOL

TEAM TEACHING

dents are told they'll get a boat tour and scavenger hunt along the St. Clair River after finishing.

Grouping students and teachers in teams has gotten hurrahs from middle school educators since it started taking hold a decade ago. It appears to be getting results, too.

It helps schools keep better track of students' progress and problems. Teachers meet daily in planning periods to compare notes on the students they share. They also have team conferences with parents.

If a student is having trouble in more than one class, teachers learn about it sooner and work together to solve it. Under the old approach, teachers rarely compared notes and sometimes even undermined each other.

"The kids know now that they can't pit us against one another or tell us that so-and-so is giving a test tomorrow when they aren't," Motte says. "We're nipping things in the bud now."

In the five years that St. Clair has used teaming, student attendance has gone up, along with grades and test scores, Motte says.

Middle school teaming doesn't necessarily mean that teachers teach simultaneously, although sometimes they do. But it does mean that three to five teachers share the same 80-100 students. They also can lengthen or shorten class periods to accommodate various lessons.

At St. Clair, sixth- and seventh-graders are divided into two teams per grade. Eighth-graders do not work in teams, because the school believes they need a year to get used to what high school will be like.

Teaming helps Motte, Mareski and Albrecht coordinate many lessons throughout the year. Now, when students are learning about weather in geography, they study the metric conversion of temperatures in math.

"I take the geography book home; Ken takes the math book home," Motte says. "Then we come back and say, 'Why would I do this or that unit in the spring, when you're doing something that would relate to it in the fall?' "

The approach energizes teachers and makes learning more fun for students.

"It's more exciting when we do things together," says Aaron Ross, 13, of St. Clair. "You get to put your heads together and see how much more you can accomplish together and what kind of grade you can pull off together."

Dabbling in lessons produces a musical

Years ago, Pierce Middle School in Grosse Pointe Park never would have tackled a full-scale musical production:

Three acts. Eleven speaking parts. A chorus of 30. Thirty student musicians in the pit orchestra. Seven on the stage crew. Dozens of students building sets, selling tickets, passing out programs, applying make-up. Nearly one-third of the school's 500 students involved.

But it did in spring 1993, and by accepting $2 donations from theater-goers, its production of "Cinderella" broke even.

Pulling it together was no overnight phenomenon. In fact, Pierce's first step toward its major production had been taken nine years before, when the school created an exploratory curriculum for sixth-graders.

Known as Encore, it requires sixth-graders to enroll in five eight-week courses in foreign language, technology, life skills, keyboarding and art.

Just as grade schools focus on giving students the basics — primarily math and reading — experts say middle school is the time for kids to sample nonacademic courses to prepare them to make good choices in high school.

"It's slam, bang, a quick taste," says art teacher Betsy Bangs.

In Tom Pachera's introduction to technology class, for example, students touch on drafting, woodworking and using computers to design a product.

Life skills teacher Val Moran's class includes lectures on baby-sitting skills. But, while she's telling them how to be responsible baby-sitters, Moran also teaches a little bit about cooking, disciplining children, even what to do if confronted by a drunken parent.

By seventh grade, the school asks students to pick four of the options to pursue in greater depth. The same holds for eighth grade.

The second stage in Pierce's evolution of its exploratory program came two years ago when Pachera proposed doing a musical. His Encore colleagues quickly agreed to help — and to have their students participate.

"We could not do that unless we had a team that was already pulled together," Moran says. "This kind of stuff didn't happen before."

So while Pachera doubled as drama coach, gym teacher Suzanne Snyder handled publicity and worked on the set. Bangs designed the programs. Moran worked with parents to pull together costumes. Instrumental music teacher Elizabeth Pamerleau directed the orchestra.

The teachers tied classroom lessons to the after-school production. In keyboarding, two students put together the program. Woodworking stu-

KEYS TO A

GREAT SCHOOL

EXPLORING

dents cut parts for the set; art students painted. Technology classes took an in-school field trip to learn how weights and pulleys raise and lower stage curtains.

"At this point in their lives, you can't give these kids enough knowledge or enough ideas," Pachera says. "I like to see their skills develop in math, science and English. But I also want to see their skills develop in technology and communications. This is the best way to do that."

Folders chart student progress

Teacher *Diana Kennedy goes over student portfolios with youths at Detroit Open School.*

Michele Szpunar's eighth-graders at Detroit Open School giggle when they look through folders at the self-portraits they drew and poems they wrote two years ago.

They giggle because they can see how they've matured.

Inside the folders are the milestones of their middle school careers.

Each year, Szpunar's students develop academic goals. Then they select their best work — work that shows how they're meeting those goals — and place it in the special folder, known as a portfolio. It follows them throughout their time at the school and is used for grading.

At the end of the year, teachers assess each student's progress and pass that information on to the next teacher. Students, meanwhile, can see how well they've met their goals.

"It shows students how much they've changed," Szpunar says. "It shows parents how children develop. It's a visual for parents and students to look at and see how much they've learned. They realize how far

K E Y S   T O   A

GREAT SCHOOL

they've come."

Portfolio assessments, which have gained popularity in some schools, are considered a more accurate measure of skills and knowledge than the snapshots provided by test scores and grades.

Standardized tests occur only once or twice a year, while portfolio assessments are ongoing, says Bob Williams, who heads the Portfolio Project for the Macomb County Intermediate School District, a program to establish portfolio assessments in elementary schools. More than a dozen Macomb districts are using portfolios.

"Standardized tests are not assessing the things that teachers want to know," Williams says.

Teachers want to know what thinking skills students display and how well they express themselves in writing. Portfolios provide a measure of growth because they contain the students' actual work — homework, projects, photographs, letters, lab experiments and other work.

One student's portfolio told Detroit Open social studies teacher Diana Kennedy that she could identify only four countries on a map in September. By June, the student knew 24 countries.

Vermont has adopted statewide portfolio assessments, but nationally the movement has been held back because it requires not only storage space but more teacher time.

"There's no question that it takes more time than maybe other means of assessment, so if it's added on to what teachers normally do, it won't go very far," Williams says. "We find that it takes a very long time for teachers to refine it and to become comfortable with it."

Most schools that use it also have a traditional grading system. The two systems complement one another.

Portfolio assessment is easier for elementary teachers because they usually meet with the same students all day for a variety of subjects.

"The departmentalization of the middle school means you have a number of teachers to confer with," Williams says.

The biggest strength of portfolios, teachers say, is that students can evaluate themselves. "It's a student's evaluation of 'how much I've grown,'" Kennedy says. "They're definitely aware that this is part of their lifelong resume."

Time-outs curb class disruptions

When Jason's already droopy jeans slip down to his thighs, his teacher just has to say something.

"Jason, you're sagging," Sharon Mazurek tells the eighth-grader at Oakwood Middle School in East Detroit Public Schools. "Pull up your pants."

Jason grumbles and complains and finally yanks them up — *waaaayyy* up. And as the other students giggle, Jason unabashedly passes gas.

The students roar.

But Mazurek isn't amused and orders Jason to the school's time-out room so he can ponder his behavior and come up with a plan to improve it.

The time-out concept, called reality therapy at Oakwood, is a disciplinary program that can be used with any student. Most often, it is used to help troublemakers or students at risk of dropping out figure out how to resolve their problems.

"We are saying that the teachers don't control the students, the students must control themselves," says Mary Bisciaio, co-coordinator of Oakwood's reality therapy program. "Without this approach, we just punish and put Band-Aids on the problems. Now, whatever the problem, it gets resolved in here."

Reality therapy starts in the regular classrooms, where teachers and students draft rules. In theory, middle school students are more willing to comply with rules that they help write.

As a last resort, teachers can send students to the time-out room, a converted office with several desks. Time-out sessions are based on the number of times students have been sent out of class for misbehaving and the seriousness of the infraction.

Two teachers staff the time-out room on a rotating basis throughout the day. They keep busy working with students or checking with teachers and parents.

In the room, students discuss the problem and agree on a plan to resolve it. They must either put their plan in writing or record it and have it approved by a teacher.

If they don't improve on their own, students may have to plot a course of action with their parents. If students are suspended, they must come up with a plan to change their behavior.

"Sometimes the kids would rather you just yell at them or send them home," Bisciaio says. "It's easier than taking responsibility for their actions."

KEYS TO A GREAT SCHOOL

DISCIPLINE

In the first five years Oakwood used reality therapy, discipline problems decreased from about 25 to 30 to less than a dozen a day at the 870-student school, Bisciaio says.

After giving Jason several warnings in a week, Mazurek has had it. She sends him to the time-out room — his third trip.

"Come on, Jason, it's your turn," says Mary McKiernan, co-coordinator of the time-out program. "Tell me what happened."

Jason describes and then writes an account of what happened. But he isn't quite sure why he got in trouble.

"Do you think that maybe you're trying to be the class clown?" McKiernan asks.

"Yes, I like to make people laugh," he says. "But I guess the way I did it was wrong because it caused commotion."

So what is his plan?

He'll try to make his friends laugh only at appropriate times — outside class and after school — wear a belt to keep his pants up, leave the room when he needs to pass gas and, he jokes, get some Beano.

McKiernan gives him a stern look, then laughs with him.

SOCIALIZING

Peer pressure put to good use

Jessica *Paschke and Sean Thornton, both 12, participate in a three-legged race at East Hills Middle School in Bloomfield Hills.*

B etsy Caskey was visiting a friend's home when her friend tried to entice her to sample the peach schnapps in her parents' liquor cabinet.

"I thought that was disgusting. I went home," says Betsy, tossing out the kind of disgusted look that seems to belong only to teenagers.

At age 13, Betsy has never had a drink of alcohol, taken illegal drugs or smoked a cigarette. "I don't want to. I could if I wanted to, but I don't. I'm proud that I haven't," she says.

Much of that attitude comes from her parents. But what she hears at home is reinforced by messages she gets at school through a network of kids who participate in Youth-to-Youth, a national program aimed at discouraging teenagers from using drugs and alcohol.

Youth-to-Youth dominates the culture at Betsy's school, East Hills Middle School in Bloomfield Hills, which enrolls about 400 students. A hundred kids showed up for the first meeting of the organization in 1991.

SOCIALIZING

By the next year, nearly 300 students were involved.

Simply put, at East Hills, it is cool to do Youth-to-Youth.

Instead of using words to preach its message, Youth-to-Youth uses positive peer pressure. The program focuses on showing kids that they can have fun with their friends without drugs or alcohol.

"Kids are bored. There just aren't places around here for kids to just hang out without getting in trouble. So they turn to other things," says faculty sponsor Jan Luedtke. "We wanted to spread a message that it's OK to be drug-free."

The almost teens and early teens who populate middle schools have a powerful need to be part of a group and to be social. Youth-to-Youth tries to build on that. The key is getting the group to endorse the idea that being drug- and alcohol-free is cool. That way, positive peer support replaces negative peer pressure.

At East Hills, Youth-to-Youth has created dozens of activities to prevent bored kids from looking at dangerous alternatives. It has sponsored volleyball tournaments and a talent show. It has sent middle school students to elementary schools to spread the word.

"Some of the stuff we do is silly," admits Betsy. Like Hippie Day, for example. East Hills students dug into their parents' closets and dressed up in bell bottoms, Indian print skirts, tie-dyed T-shirts, sandals with socks, granny glasses.

The most popular activity, by far, was a Youth-to-Youth camp-out at the school when 170 kids were "locked in" overnight. They were saturated with activity from 7 p.m. Friday until 8 a.m. Saturday.

Experiment lets kids open arms to peers

Hand in hand, Sydney Golden and Stephanie Field head into a carpeted hall at Bloomfield Hills Middle School.

In black stretch pants and colorful cotton tops, they look like typical 12-year-olds.

Once in the hallway, however, Stephanie yanks off her glasses and lurches away from Sydney.

"Stephanie, you must put your glasses back on," Sydney says firmly. Stephanie resists, but finally lets Sydney do it for her.

"She's really good. She just doesn't like to wear these glasses," says Sydney apologetically as she takes Stephanie's hand and continues their walk.

Stephanie is one of nine developmentally disabled students from Wing Lake Developmental Center who attend classes at the middle school.

Chronologically and physically, the Wing Lake students are the same

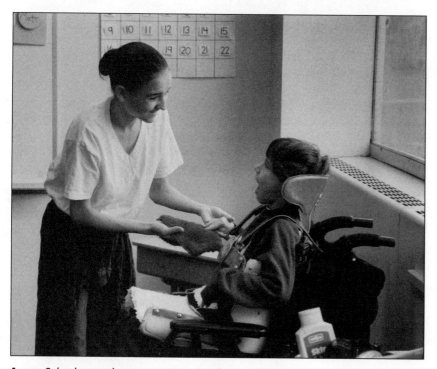

Lara *Scherba works on sensory stimulation with Matthew McDonald at Bloomfield Hills Middle School.*

KEYS TO A GREAT SCHOOL

VOLUNTEERING

age as their middle school counterparts, but the Wing Lake students range in intellectual ability from about 10 months to three years. They attend separate classes that focus on improving their ability to care for themselves and handle simple tasks.

Sydney is one of the 52 students who volunteered to work with the Wing Lake students, greeting them at their buses, helping them find their lockers and hang up their coats, assisting with their lunches, working with them in special activities and generally making them feel welcomed.

The pair are part of an experiment at the middle school, where service is considered a crucial component of learning. Student volunteers earn course credit for participating.

"We have to realize that a life is more than book learning. Balance is what's important. If it was all work and no service, no play, it wouldn't be worth living," says Diane Koehler, a resource room teacher at the school.

If there is time for one-on-one work, volunteers look first at the education plan that has been prepared for each student. Activities are listed there with information on which cupboard contains the appropriate materials.

Stephanie's plan called for focusing on fine motor skills. A student volunteer might work with her on stacking plastic plates or filling an egg carton with objects.

For special education teacher Gladys Herrle, the service program has meant a renewal.

"These kids are amazing," she says repeatedly. "In the beginning, they only see the handicap. But later they see the child."

As the volunteers become more comfortable with their companions, other students also become more accepting. As Stephanie walks through the hall with Sydney, she's frequently greeted with cheery hellos from other students.

In the hallway, Stephanie once again begins pulling off her glasses. Then, in frustration, she starts to walk away.

Sydney calmly strides up, places her hands on Stephanie's shoulders and says: "We are going back to the room. ... Kids are in classes; you can't run in the halls or they can't study."

Sydney takes Stephanie's hand, and the two walk calmly back to class.

CO–TEACHING

Special kids fit in, learn more

Teachers *Charlene Pike, left, and Michele Makarewicz, right, work with a group of regular and special education students.*

Charlene Pike dances around her fourth-hour class at L'Anse Creuse South Middle School, singing a song as many of her geography students roll their eyes.

"Longitude slices the long way around," sings Pike, gesturing to the eighth-graders to join in.

"I know you think this is stupid, but I hear you humming it in the halls all the time," Pike shouts. "Sing it!"

"Latitude dices climb up or down," they sing.

As the chorus grows, special education teacher Michele Makarewicz keeps her eyes on eight students with learning problems, making sure they, too, are in sync. She points to the horizontal stripes on a student's shirt to illustrate latitude and uses a Styrofoam ball to demonstrate longitude.

"These children would never be learning longitude and latitude in special education," says Makarewicz, who is with the students full time. "They'd be lucky to learn north and south."

As co-teachers, Pike and Makarewicz work together to make sure that each of their 31 students keeps up. They team up on teaching strategies

KEYS TO A GREAT SCHOOL

CO–TEACHING

and ideas for lessons.

Makarewicz tutors special education students and modifies materials to meet their needs. But she also helps out with the other students.

"We have four eyes, four ears and two heads working together," says Pike. "It's very hard for a kid to fall through the cracks in this class."

Makarewicz also co-teaches in math, English and other subjects.

Putting children with learning problems — especially middle schoolers — in regular classrooms instead of segregated resource rooms is a key part of helping all students learn to tolerate diversity.

The approach helps special education students see that they can fit in and tackle mainstream lessons. And it helps regular students learn to work with others.

In one of Pike's lessons, groups of students list songs that include geographic names. Some special education students have trouble coming up with any; others come up with dozens.

"At first, they just wanted to copy my work or make me do it all," says Robin Gurjack, 13, of the special education students in her group. "But I don't let that happen. Instead, I teach them what they're supposed to be doing or I give them a job they can do in the group. I learn more that way and so do they. Sometimes they just need another kid to explain it to them."

Focused students explore professions

I n a classroom cluttered with anatomical models of human bodies, 30 premed students in white lab coats check their friends' heartbeats with stethoscopes and test each other's reflexes with rubber mallets.

In addition to a medical dictionary, each student has, as required reading, a book about Ben Carson — the famous black neurosurgeon from Detroit who heads pediatric neurosurgery at Baltimore's Johns Hopkins Hospital.

The Pre-Medical Career Exploration program at Detroit's Beaubien Middle School is among five career programs of choice at the school, which includes grades seven through nine. The northwest side school's 1,000 students also can preview careers in engineering, law, journalism and aeronautics.

"It's important to allow youngsters to learn what's out there for them," says Principal David Porter. Otherwise, "how will they make decisions about what path their lives should take?"

Each Beaubien career program is connected to a Detroit vocational high school that specializes in that area. Aeronautics students, for example, visit Davis Aerospace High School weekly to learn about fixing and

Beaubien *Middle School students Paris Wells and Maurice Hill, both 13, investigate the human chest and abdomen.*

K E Y S T O A

GREAT SCHOOL

CAREERS

flying planes. Engineering students visit Breithaupt Vocational Technical Center to learn about car design.

Students must write letters explaining why they want to enroll in a particular program. "It's important to tap students' interests and involve them in hands-on activities," says science teacher Charline Coats.

Each career program is closely guided by a committee of educators and outside professionals. Together, they devise a program that meets academic requirements and provides real-life experiences.

For example, premedical students take related classes two periods a day, including a laboratory. They also study algebra, English, Latin and civics. Their days are extended to allow time for career-related activities. Premed students can volunteer at Henry Ford Hospital.

Extracurricular activities in 1992 included completing a booklet on AIDS for the NAACP that was published and distributed nationwide. And in 1993, some premed students visited Meharry Medical College in Nashville, Tenn.

"They showed us everything — patients with broken jaws, Down's syndrome," says Beaubien student Michelle Yancy, 14.

"There's so much to explore. It will help us determine which part of the medical field we want to go into."

Touching, feeling make language live

Carmella Briggs sits at her desk at Steele Middle School in Muskegon, scratching her ankle vigorously, then her elbow, then her knee.

"We went out there, saw everything, got mosquito bites and now we have to write about it," Briggs, 12, says as she works on a journal entry about her visit to a swamp behind the school.

Briggs didn't expect mosquito bites to be a big part of language arts. But at her school, they can be. So can birds, weeds and just about everything else associated with the nearby wetland.

Like the teachers at Steele, middle school language arts teachers across the state are chucking traditional approaches for the chance to let their students dodge bugs, get dirty and, most of all, get out of the classroom.

Old-fashioned rote approaches increasingly are looked on by educators as ineffective — especially for temperamental middle school students.

A startling 1985 report from the U.S. Commission on Reading, "Becoming a Nation of Readers," drove home just how badly language arts lessons were failing students: nearly 40 percent of the 13-year-olds who took a national test could not locate information within a paragraph or make simple generalizations based on what they read.

The 1992 report card on student reading achievement from the National Assessment of Educational Progress showed that most eighth-graders don't read for pleasure, talk about what they read or visit the library. But 64 percent of them watch three or more hours of television a day.

Writing skills also were weak. A 1992 National Assessment study of 2,000 fourth- and eighth-graders asked students to submit their best piece of writing. The study concluded that the compositions were not well-developed and showed little evidence of planning or revising.

Exploring a swamp won't cure the problems. But it is the type of activity that generates enthusiasm for learning and puts lessons about commas and composition in a framework that excites middle schoolers.

Because they are developing so dramatically, children in this age group need to move around, explore and talk about what they are learning. And they need to see that what's going on in their lives connects to what they're learning in class.

Turning out literate middle schoolers starts with turning them on, educators conclude.

GOOD STUFF TO READ

For books of interest to sixth-graders, see Pages 35-41.

Grades 7 and 8

☆ "I Know Why the Caged Bird Sings," *Maya Angelou*

☆ "The Voyage of the Lucky Dragon," *Jack Bennett*

☆ "A Gathering of Days: A New England Girl's Journal, 1830-32," *Joan W. Blos*

☆ "Alice's Adventures in Wonderland" and "Through the Looking Glass," *Lewis Carroll*

☆ "Neighbor Rosicky," *Willa Cather*

☆ "The Dark is Rising," *Susan Cooper*

☆ "The Red Badge of Courage," *Stephen Crane*

☆ "Madame Curie: A Biography," *Eva Curie*

☆ "Robinson Crusoe,"

continued ▼

GOOD STUFF TO READ

continued ▶

98

READING

"They need to know, 'What good is this going to do me?' " says Dianne TerVree, an eighth-grade language arts teacher at Steele. "They need to get out of textbooks and into the real world more."

That idea grew on teachers at Steele, who came up with the three-week Green Gully Environmental Project. Virtually all of the school's 825 sixth- through eighth-graders traipsed through the woods next to Ryerson Creek. Their teachers worked as a team.

Math teachers reinforced spelling and grammar in lessons they did about graphing the trash collected and the animals spotted in the swamp. Math teachers also worked with students on field guides they were producing for language arts and science classes.

In language arts classes, spelling words were taken from science lessons on birds, insects and the environment — *thrasher, mosquito, reservoir*. Students wrote in journals after exploring the wetland, penned legends such as "How Beavers Got Their Flat Tails" and wrote letters to President Bill Clinton on environmental issues they were learning about in science and social studies.

Kelly *Doyle picks up trash in the wetland behind Steele Middle School in Muskegon.*

READING

The emphasis in middle school shifts from getting a grasp on basic skills, such as punctuation, grammar, sentence structure and reading strategies, to using them with ease in various situations and across subjects.

In addition to learning about the creek, students made daily treks there to collect trash as a community service project. They hauled out an old box spring, curtain rods, bikes, hundreds of bottles and cans and even a dead dog.

"Look at this mess," says Shawnta Donahue, 13, a seventh-grader, as she carts a plastic bag full of trash collected during her excursion. "We need our wetlands. And it scares me what we're doing to them. I'm not about to sit back and watch us destroy them. ... I'm going to write to the president."

Like a tennis player who has mastered the serve, volley and ground stroke and is ready to put them together in a game, middle school students should be producing more complex projects with greater ease.

"You don't expect it to be perfect the first time," says Sheila Potter, a language arts consultant with the Michigan Department of Education.

"I like to compare teachers to coaches. They set the playing field, outline the conditions and then work with players to make them winners."

GOOD STUFF TO READ

continued ▼

☆ "Diary of a Young Girl,"
Anne Frank

☆ "You Come Too,"
Robert Frost

☆ "Spin a Soft Black Song,"
Nikki Giovanni

☆ "A Raisin in the Sun,"
Lorraine Hansberry

☆ "The House of the Seven Gables,"
Nathaniel Hawthorne

☆ "The Old Man and the Sea,"
Ernest Hemingway

☆ "The Gift of the Magi and Other Stories,"
O. Henry

☆ "Kon-Tiki,"
Thor Heyerdahl

☆ "Legend Days,"
Jamake Highwater

☆ "Thunder of the Gods,"
Dorothy Hosford

continued ▶

MATH

Problem solving replaces memorizing

Kalvin is a typical 12-year-old. On the cusp of becoming a teenager, he reasons that he ought to be able to stay up until 11 p.m. during the summer. His mom disagrees: He'll be less crabby if he goes to bed earlier.

Kalvin proposes an experiment, hoping his mom will let him use it to determine his bedtime. He makes a pie-shaped spinner and puts three 9 p.m. and three 10 p.m. slots on it. Only two spaces are allotted for 11 p.m., but one of the 11 p.m. spaces is larger than the rest.

Kalvin figures he's got it made.

Portland Middle School teacher Debby Flate's sixth-grade math students are pondering Kalvin's plight.

"I think his chance of going to bed at 11 o'clock is better than his chance of going to bed at 10 o'clock," says Tom Densmore.

Matthew Smith disagrees. "The probability of Kalvin staying up until 11 p.m. is about 35 percent," he says, rising to announce his conclusion.

Flate's eyebrows arch and a smile creeps across her face. "You've been thinking about that word 'probability,' haven't you?" she asks.

Matthew shrugs, grins with pride and sits down.

Before the year is over, Flate's sixth-graders will calculate the value of pi on their own, discover the definitions of mean and median, and learn how to calculate the area of various geometric shapes. That's hardly the kind of arithmetic their parents studied in the classrooms of the 1960s and '70s.

Flate has a traditional background in elementary education, and that didn't include much mathematics. But that didn't stop her from becoming part of an innovative math project at Portland Middle School, west of Lansing, that was recognized in 1992 by the U.S. Department of Education with its "A+ for Breaking the Mold" award.

"This is meatier. There is quality here, not quantity. That's what children respond to. It's not watered-down soup," says Flate, a teacher for more than 24 years. "This is the best program I have ever seen."

Portland's math reforms have boosted the district's scores in the annual Michigan Educational Assessment Program tests dramatically at a time when most school districts are experiencing declines.

The Portland program was created by teachers who focused on the latest thinking about how kids learn math. Traditionally, teachers had spoon-fed information through lectures and by offering rules.

"I was programmed to teach out of a textbook. There was a right answer and there was a wrong answer. There was really no comprehen-

MATH

Portland *Middle School teacher Debby Flate explains a probability experiment.*

sion of what went into it. It was strictly memorization of a rule and a formula," Flate says.

The crux of the new system is the belief that math is a science full of exploration and discovery. Instead of giving students answers, teachers guide them so they discover the answers, either alone or with others.

In Flate's class, students made nearly 100 measurements of circles to discover an equation for finding the circumference of a circle. In repeated calculations, they kept coming up with an equation that required multiplying the diameter times "three plus a little bit more."

Flate finally told them about the mystery of pi, that handy figure that is needed to calculate numerous mathematical formulas.

Because the students discovered the value of pi themselves, they probably will remember it longer than students who are told what it is and how to use it, Portland's teachers say.

Developed by former Portland math teacher Mary Bouck, the new math program is far from a quick fix. If anything, it proves what many educators have been saying for years: Reform takes time.

Bouck says she was a very traditional teacher who had grown tired of facing eighth-graders who couldn't recall what they'd learned the previous year.

By the early 1980s, she no longer believed the old methods worked.

GOOD STUFF TO READ

continued ▼

☆ "The Yearling,"
Marjorie Kinnan Rawlings

☆ "The Light in the Forest,"
Conrad Richter

☆ "The Little Prince,"
Antoine de Saint-Exupery

☆ "Early Moon,"
Carl Sandburg

☆ "Shane,"
Jack Schaefer

☆ "Ivanhoe,"
Sir Walter Scott

☆ Plays and sonnets,
William Shakespeare

☆ "Frankenstein,"
Mary Shelley

☆ "Upon the Head of the Goat,"
Aranka Siegal

☆ "The Red Pony" and "The Pearl,"
John Steinbeck

☆ "The Strange Case of Dr. Jekyll and Mr. Hyde,"
Robert Louis Stevenson

continued ▶

GOOD STUFF TO READ

continued ▼

MATH

The math revolution at Portland began when Bouck was tapped by nearby Michigan State University to join a project aimed at experimenting with teaching methods and developing new math curriculum for middle schools. As part of that project, MSU professor Perry Lanier coached Bouck for more than 10 weeks, showing her how to change how she was teaching.

Then, Bouck continued the tradition by coaching another Portland math teacher. The two later coached other teachers, and so on.

Bouck left the district in 1989 to work on a doctorate at MSU but has returned often to visit classes and coach teachers.

The hallmark of Portland's math project may be the amount of time teachers have devoted to learning new methods and materials.

Bouck estimates Portland teachers spend 20 to 25 days a year improving their skills and learning new material. "These teachers volunteer a lot of their time," she says. "The union won't like that, but that is a reality. And they've done that for a long time."

Let's Make A Deal

Kalvin is out of school for the summer. He just turned 12, so he thinks he should be allowed to stay up as late as he wants because he is almost a teenager and he doesn't have to get up for school. His mom disagrees. She thinks he is less crabby if he goes to bed earlier. Kalvin decides to try to make a deal with his mom. He makes a spinner and wonders whether his mom will let him use it to determine his bedtime each night. He puts three 9 p.m. and three 10 p.m. spaces on the spinner to try to make his mom like it. He puts only two 11 p.m. spaces on the spinner, but he makes one of them the biggest space of all — and he hopes he will land on that space most often.

Question:

If Kalvin spins the spinner, what are his chances that he will go to bed at 11 p.m. most of the time?

Make your own version of the spinner. Spin it and keep track of the data you collect. Continue spinning until you are confident of your answers to Kalvin's question.

MATH

To help Kalvin with his challenge, Flate's students assemble their own pie-shaped spinners. With virtually no direction from Flate, the students agree they should flick the spinner once for each of the 90 days of summer vacation.

But how should they record the data?

Coaching helps

☆ Don't panic if your child's teacher isn't using a textbook. Many teachers believe they can create a more dynamic curriculum by making selections from several texts and developing their own problems.

☆ Homework is great — as long as it's not routine computation. Students should be thinking, not simply drilling on the same equations again and again. Studies have shown that one to three hours per night of homework can make low-achieving students perform as well as average students who do no homework.

☆ Monitor your child's homework. Studies have shown that students complete more assignments, have higher test scores and higher math grades when their parents are more attentive to their homework. But parents should never use math homework as punishment.

☆ Calculators should be evident in the classroom and used freely in doing homework. The National Council of Teachers of Mathematics believes the calculator is a powerful instructional tool at all grade levels.

☆ Ask your child's math teacher if he or she observes other math teachers — in other schools — in their classrooms. If not, let the principal know you'd like to see more such opportunities created.

☆ Play math games in your home. Card games and chess are great. ○

In traditional classes, the teacher would have given students instructions. Not in Portland. For nearly a quarter of the class, Flate's students debate the question.

Flate's colleague, Yvonne Grant, says that kind of exchange is essential: "We're trying to develop a community of learners, including the teacher. We don't want to be the ones who stand up there with all the answers."

Flate and Bouck work at the chalkboard, responding to ideas about how the data should be recorded. In the end, they agree to create a simple chart, listing bedtimes on one side and the result of the spins on another.

"I don't think you'd find many sixth-grade classes that talk on the level that was in there today," Bouck brags later.

THE RESULTS

These are the results of the Kalvin experiment:

Each team of two students flicked the spinner 90 times. They collected results from 1,260 spins. This is how they looked:

9 p.m. — 491 hits, or 39 percent
10 p.m. — 327 hits, or 26 percent
11 p.m. — 442 hits, or 35 percent

"Middle school is, like, wow, I'm learning something."

CURT TITUS, 13, seventh-grader at St. Clair Middle School in St. Clair

SCIENCE

Studies come alive in you-touch method

U p first on science teacher Dwight Sieggreen's classroom show-and-tell menu is a Nile monitor, an armored lizard that is distinctly unhappy about being taken out of his aquarium and paraded before two dozen sixth-graders at Cooke Middle School in Northville.

"The first thing he likes to do when he's handled is what?" Sieggreen asks.

"Go to the bathroom," the students chorus back.

"That's right. On who?"

"ON *YOU!!!!!*" they shout.

Sieggreen laughs heartily. "That's right. Every suit I own has his mark on it."

For his first 15 years of teaching, Sieggreen, 48, was a traditional science teacher who taught science straight out of a textbook. He lectured; students listened.

If he wanted students to learn about reptiles, he'd point to a picture in a book instead of handing them one. Perhaps he'd use a film strip, but he had no critters in aquariums in his classroom, no crickets chirping from barrels at the front of the room, no cases filled with rocks from Alaska or nets from deep-sea fishing trips.

That changed in the mid-1980s, when Sieggreen became convinced that he would be a better teacher and that his students would learn more if he did more hands-on work. Now, he believes more than anything that students — especially rambunctious middle school students — need to touch, feel, try, explore and question.

That, he says, is the essence of learning science.

Unfortunately, Sieggreen is by no means a typical middle school science teacher. But his touch-and-explore approach epitomizes current thinking that investigation, not lecture, is the best way to teach the subject.

"What we're trying to do is shift from teacher-centered learning to more learning by doing, more student-centered learning," says Mozell Lang, science specialist with the Michigan Department of Education.

"For the first time, science educators are all speaking the same language in the same voice," Lang says.

Why change? Because no one can learn everything there is to know about science. But it is feasible for students to appreciate science and learn how to investigate scientific questions.

Middle school students are at an ideal age to blossom in this discovery: still enthusiastic yet mature enough to refine some of the essential

SCIENCE

skills for becoming good scientific observers and thinkers.

Dale Rosene, one of the state's top middle school science teachers, says that means experiments and mini-research projects should dominate science classes. Rosene teaches eighth-grade science at Marshall Middle School in Marshall and writes a guide for teachers for Scholastic's Science World magazine.

In his class, Rosene might have students design a package strong enough to ensure an injury-free, three-story drop for a raw egg.

He's also asked eighth-graders to design cars that will go up ramps and to create nontraditional one-minute timers. In that project, one student designed a timer that measured 60 seconds by determining how much Coca-Cola had to be poured into a bottle to create foam that took one minute to dissipate.

In situations like that, students learn to rely on themselves and their partners for the answers. "They pursue the answers in a way that means they're truly performing like little scientists," Lang says.

Norm Hannewald, who teaches seventh-grade science at Northville's Meads Mill Middle School, suggests another reason the new approach is smarter than the old stand-and-lecture style: "We're not going to make scientists out of every one of these students. But we need to make all of them literate citizens. This interest will set the stage to keep them interested in science all through their adult life."

Sieggreen subscribes to the learning-by-doing approach. But doing science in the classroom doesn't mean he favors a free-for-all, especially not when animals are in the mix. Part of what his students must learn is how to observe.

So, as he brings out each animal, he repeats the instructions: Be quiet. Be still. Be respectful. Look and listen. When you're done, make notes on your observations.

He peppers the show-and-tell sessions with suggestions and questions.

"Look at the air pockets on each side. Look how bloated he is right now. Do you see that?" he asks while they observe a 2.2-pound African ridgeback frog.

"Do you expect this frog to come from a wet or a dry or a medium environment?" he asks.

They guess he's from a wet environment. Actually, his home is a desert. How can that be? Sieggreen asks.

There is a pause before Jenna Eads says slowly: "He must burrow into the ground? To stay wet? Is that right?"

Sieggreen beams his approval and peppers them with more questions.

QUOTES FROM KIDS!

"I worry that we won't be able to keep up with technology. And I worry about getting a job and a good education. If you don't go to college, you can't get a job."

DANNY STEINERT, 13, eighth-grader, East Middle School in Plymouth

GENDER GAP

Science, math aren't just for guys

Math teacher Jenny Melkvik stands before 30 eighth-graders at East Middle School and shuffles a deck of cards as she outlines the day's lesson: making, flying and measuring the flight of a paper airplane.

Back and forth, back and forth, she shuffles the cards. Finally, she deals one card to each student.

"The ones over here, the twos here, the threes there," she says. The students collect their books and scurry to their assigned groups.

With a deck of cards, Melkvik has taken one small step toward trying to help girls maintain an interest in math.

"If they were allowed to choose, they would sit with their friends," Melkvik says. That means girls with girls and boys with boys.

Then Melkvik takes another step: Within each small group, students draw another card. Their assignment is keyed to the card. It's a way of further ensuring that boys don't end up flying the planes while girls record the information.

In the late 1980s, educators in the Plymouth-Canton school district were alarmed when they looked at the small number of girls in high school math and science classes. There were roughly the same number of boys as girls in the school, but girls made up less than half of the students in biology, chemistry, algebra, geometry, trigonometry and calculus.

Particularly disturbing was the fact that girls with high potential were no more likely to take upper-level math classes than other students, says Ellison Franklin, math-science curriculum coordinator.

Plymouth-Canton educators knew the district needed to reach girls during middle school.

"The erosion begins there and they never rebound," Franklin says.

The gender gap stretches far beyond Plymouth-Canton. In 1990, a national report by the American Association of University Women showed there was a strong relationship between math and science and preadolescent self-esteem: As girls "learn" they are not good at math and science, their sense of self-worth and aspirations deteriorate.

In the year 2000, women are expected to make up nearly half of those entering the workforce for the first time. Female students must get an adequate background in math and science to keep the job force competitive.

Waiting until high school to encourage girls to pursue math or science is too late. "They are making their decisions about high school curriculum in eighth grade," Franklin says.

GENDER GAP

Plymouth-Canton tackled the problem head-on, talking to teachers about classroom methods, holding conferences for girls and parents, and talking to counselors.

"We asked counselors, 'Are you encouraging girls or are you sitting back and saying, 'What would you like to take?' Teachers have become much more assertive in saying, 'You have ability in this area, you should pursue this course,' " she says.

After five years, Plymouth-Canton could see some results:

■ In 1988, only one-third of students in high school chemistry were girls. By 1992, nearly half were.

■ In 1988, 36 percent of calculus students were girls. In 1992, it was 42 percent.

■ The percentage of girls taking physics jumped from 36 in 1988 to 43 in 1992.

■ Half the students in algebra were girls in 1988; in 1992, for the first

☆ Do you call on girls as often as boys?

☆ In class discussions, are girls interrupted more often than boys?

☆ Do you make as much eye contact with girls as with boys?

☆ Do you expect girls to solve difficult problems?

☆ Do you give girls specific feedback on problem solving?

☆ Are you angry with girls when they break the rules, but assume "boys will be boys"?

☆ Do you expect girls to have better reading skills than math skills?

☆ Do you compliment girls for assertiveness? Or do you resent "pushy" girls?

☆ Do you encourage both boys and girls to try harder?

☆ Are boys criticized for not trying hard enough while girls are criticized for lack of ability?

☆ Do you use bias-free language? (Instead of saying, "When your mother cooks dinner," say, "When you cook dinner.") ○

Sarah Carson, 14, cheers after becoming a math quiz finalist in Jenny Melkvik's class at East Middle School in Plymouth.

GENDER GAP

time, girls were a majority in trigonometry and precalculus.

In spite of the efforts, challenges remain, largely because boys and girls are still boys and girls.

Science teacher Jan Coratti is a leader in trying to solve the gender gap. For example, in an eighth grade general science class in 1992, she carefully divided students so no single group was dominated by boys.

But in one group, Ryan Kelley, the only boy, immediately took charge of assembling an electrical circuit. Three girls sat back and watched.

When asked about it, Ryan was chagrined: "Did I do that, really?"

Putting a spin on global subjects

Barbra Harte's eighth-graders made Indian jewelry, researched and performed ceremonial dances from Plains and Southwest tribes, and listened to songs and stories from a visiting American Indian who spoke about his life and the trials his people faced through history.

Then, the students at Birmingham's Derby Middle School turned to newspapers and magazines to learn about Indians today. They found articles on reservation life, powwows, casino gambling, fetal alcohol syndrome and other topics.

"We're trying to learn about Indians by becoming them," says Harte from a classroom decorated with totem poles, face masks and tribal costumes. "I want them to understand historically what has happened, but I want them to look at today."

Native Americans are not the Indians we're used to seeing in John Wayne movies," Harte says.

One student saw parallels in the signing of Middle East peace initiatives and the peace treaties signed by the U.S. government and Indian tribes in the last century.

"I like them to draw their own correlations between history, the pre-

QUOTES FROM KIDS!

"I love when I get my locker open on the first try every time. That's a good day to me."

KAREN DUTHIE, 11, sixth-grader at East Middle School in Plymouth

Former Detroit Superintendent Deborah McGriff has said: "Children who learn about themselves, their families and their ancestors will be inspired to achieve excellence."

"My mother treats me more like an adult than she used to. She's slowly blending from treating me like a child to treating me like an adult. It's a privilege. I depend on myself more."

SHAPHAN WILLIAMS, 13, eighth-grader, Ann Arbor Trail Middle School, Detroit

SOCIAL STUDIES

sent and future," Harte says.

Almost none of Harte's lessons come from a textbook. So much history has been made in the last few years — the fall of the Berlin Wall, the Persian Gulf War, the breakup of the Soviet Union — that publishing companies can't make revisions fast enough.

"The textbooks are being written as they're sitting in class," Harte says. The historic changes in the world place a tremendous burden on social studies teachers, who "feel responsible for so much information."

Dave Harris, social studies specialist for the Oakland County Intermediate School District, says, "It's impossible to cover it all."

But experts are pleased that the pace and complexity of current events are forcing teachers to step away from traditional methods stressing a chronological approach and memorization. Instead of heaping information on students, teachers are concentrating more on a few areas.

"We can't fall into the trap of trying to make these kids miniature geographers or historians," Harris says.

Traditionally, social studies mixes history, geography, economics, civics, government and the environment — each taught separately. Now, teachers are merging those subjects into a collective discipline. The goal is to mold responsible citizens.

"If a child graduates and doesn't care about religious persecution, race bigotry or police brutality, we have failed," Harris says.

There is a recommended state social studies curriculum, but there is no universal approach in Michigan middle schools.

"There seems to be a gap between elementary school and what they get in the ninth grade. Some say we're doing geography, others say we're helping them learn study skills," says John Chapman, social studies consultant for the Michigan Department of Education.

Chapman would like middle school social studies classes to spend more time exploring careers and the world. "It should get away from the academic stressing of history and move toward meeting people and finding out what they're doing ... That's important."

Another area of disagreement involves multicultural lessons. Some experts say teaching youngsters about cultural diversity is necessary to create adults who are receptive to living and working alongside different people. Others fear that focusing on a culture could lead to indoctrination or stereotyped impressions.

As those issues are debated, social studies teachers continue to fight for recognition. Many say that because Michigan has no statewide social studies skills test, the subject often gets pushed aside by schools in favor of math, science and reading programs.

"It causes local school people to invest their resources in the subjects that are tested," Chapman says.

Technology blends in — when it's there

Thea Ermalovich learned about polygons in eighth-grade math at Royal Oak's Churchill Junior High School.

Working with a computer program about the multisided geometric figures, she pressed keys to answer questions posed on the screen. The computer beeped.

"You only get two chances" for a right answer, Thea explains. "It's easier to understand it on the computer."

Earlier that year, Thea had used computers in English and science classes. What she was doing wasn't unusual — at Churchill. By several accounts, the school is one of the more progressive middle or junior high schools in integrating computers and telecommunications in the classroom.

Students spend dozens of hours a year in front of the screen, learning that the computer is a tool with a wide variety of uses. They don't take

"This school seems like an elementary school, like they're treating us like we're little kids – like we're in the fourth grade or something."

BREE CAMPBELL, 13, seventh-grader at St. Clair Middle School in St. Clair

Johari *Smith designs a butterfly in art class using a computer at Birney Middle School in Southfiield.*

"I like com-ing to school because I like spend-ing time with my friends. At first I didn't know if I would like middle school, because I didn't know if the kids coming from other schools would be nice."

ANGELA MOORE, 12, seventh-grader at Miller Middle School in Detroit

COMPUTERS

computer classes — they take regular classes and use computers.

"We were teaching them how to use them, but never used them for anything worthwhile," says Mike Quinn, computer lab coordinator.

But when the machines were integrated into lessons, students got much more time with them than before.

Royal Oak appears to be ahead of the pack. Several experts say Michigan's middle schools aren't paying as much attention to technology as grade and high schools.

"The technology is where the money is," says Dan Schultz, assistant superintendent for grants and technology at the state Department of Education. "The federal and state funds for technology tend to be ear-marked for specific uses" that leave out middle schools.

"At the elementary level, there are a lot of state and federal programs geared toward reading, writing, math and science," he says. "High schools are at the other end, where you're preparing either for vocational education or college prep."

Schultz says the need is equally great for middle schoolers, though dis-tricts don't tend to spend the money there. Schools are "dealing with a population that's going through lots of physical and emotional changes that are particularly challenging for schools," he says. It's also a time when technology can be effective as a learning tool.

Some middle schools are pointing the way. Moreover, as technology improves and prices drop, an explosion of computer-assisted learning may be just around the corner, particularly when multimedia, the interac-tive combination of computers and video, becomes the force that every-one expects.

School districts are installing high-speed networks that connect all school buildings. Over time, educators say, students will gain enormous advantages by having connections to each other and the rest of the world.

Lamphere Middle School in Madison Heights, for example, is one of several in the Detroit area where students and faculty have been connect-ed to the Internet for over a year. The Internet is an international collec-tion of computer networks, mostly at universities, government facilities and companies.

It's time to get personal and to get kids thinking

Linda Brill passes out a ditto with dozens of tiny drawings of high school students.

"It's going to be a lot like the 'Where's Waldo?' cartoons," Brill tells her seventh-grade human relations class at Chatterton Middle School in Warren. "Only in this game, you're going to have to search even harder to find the main character. … You're looking for who spread AIDS."

At first, the students giggle and fidget and joke about the silly names and funny cartoon characters. But then, the laughter fades and they get serious.

"There are so many people in this picture," one student blurts out. "Does AIDS mean they'll all die?"

Maybe, Brill explains. She tells the students there are still many unknowns about AIDS, but one thing is certain: "It's like the common cold. We just can't seem to find a cure."

Brill then talks about the dangers of unprotected sex, the long incubation period of the virus that causes AIDS and risky behaviors.

"Think about a lot of the parties you go to," Brill says. "Think about the things that happen at those parties. Isn't it possible that people your age could end up in bed with people they don't know? … That's dangerous."

Youths *study the symptoms of sexually transmitted diseases in Linda Brill's class at Chatterton Middle School in Warren.*

QUOTES FROM KIDS!

"I feel really good if a girl I like notices me. But I don't ask them out or anything. I'm not up to that yet."

PAUL RUSSETTE, 12, seventh-grader at East Middle School in Plymouth

"**Making boys notice you is important. I flirt a lot. Usually I hang around them and joke with them or tell them secrets that I wouldn't tell other people. I giggle a lot, too.**"

CHERON RICE, 12, seventh-grader at East Middle School in Plymouth

Here are some tips for talking about sexuality with your child:

☆ Both parents should be involved in teaching children about sex and instilling the family's values about it. If only one parent is at home, find a trusted adult of the opposite sex to whom your child can turn with questions.

☆ If parents have conflicting values, discuss the differences and make sure the child has lots of books and other resources to make his or her own decisions.

☆ Continue to talk to children about child abuse and inappropriate touching, and introduce the subject of date rape: Alert girls to the dangers and teach boys that "No" means "No."

☆ Begin sex education as soon as your child begins exploring his or her own body. Call all body parts, including genitals, by their proper names so youngsters will learn that there is nothing wrong, silly or dirty about them.

☆ Answer your child's questions about sex honestly and simply. Don't ignore them and don't send him or her to someone else for answers unless you do not have the information. That would condition your child not to turn to you for help.

☆ If you feel insecure about facts, ask your doctor for information about reproduction, AIDS and other sexually transmitted diseases.

☆ Talk to your child about your own experiences with puberty and relationships. Discuss your fears and how you handled them.

☆ Don't focus on the inconvenience or pain of menstruation. Girls and boys will develop a better attitude about it if parents emphasize the biological role it plays.

☆ Use television and books to find opportunities to bring up the subjects of sex, relationships and peer pressure. For example, ads that use sex to promote jeans or soft drinks could provide a good opportunity to discuss the media pressure to have sex.

☆ Talk about sex as something natural between people who love each other. But emphasize that it is a private act.

☆ Teach your children to respect your privacy. In turn, respect theirs. ○

The students look at each other in silence.

Brill knows that several of her seventh-graders are sexually active and that simply giving them facts and statistics about sexually transmitted diseases and teen pregnancy probably isn't enough to make them think twice. She has to get personal — and get them thinking about their own lifestyles and relationships.

"A lot of kids just think it's normal to be having sex now," says Danita Buchholtz, 14, an eighth-grader at Chatterton. "And definitely by the time you're 16 years old. Everybody thinks everybody is doing it by then."

Middle schoolers are experiencing a range of new emotions, and sexual urges are growing

SEX EDUCATION

stronger as they simultaneously are pulling away from their families and making more decisions — good and bad — for themselves.

Without support or explanations for what's happening to them, adolescents easily can have trouble.

"They absolutely need an explanation of what's happening to them and how they can deal with their feelings," says Helene Mills, a sex education expert and principal of Seaholm High School in Birmingham.

Few middle schools have special programs like Chatterton's. Many just include a lesson or two about human reproduction in science class. Most intensive health and sex education begins in ninth grade, if at all.

That, many experts agree, is too late. While others argue that sex education doesn't belong in schools, many experts and some studies say schools need to teach it because too many parents avoid the topic.

"I hear 'better you than me' from parents all the time," Brill says.

Middle schoolers should get basic lessons in human reproduction, and they also should be taught how to combat peer pressure and develop healthy relationships, she says.

Often, educators work on those skills through self-esteem-building lessons and discussions about emotions, relationships and the struggles of being a teenager.

"If you don't reach them by middle school, high school is too late," says Pat Nichols, a consultant with the Michigan Department of Education.

Children generally decide as early as sixth or seventh grade whether they will be sexually active during their teens, Nichols says. And teenagers are among the groups at highest risk for AIDS.

"They may not have intercourse tomorrow, but they are making up their minds then that this is something they're going to do," Nichols says. "After that, it's just a matter of when they have the first opportunity. This is, after all, the age of experimentation."

QUOTES FROM KIDS!

"I've had about 10 to 15 girlfriends. But it's not like we go out to dinner or anything. In middle school, you just kind of call each other boyfriend and girlfriend."

ZACH BORNE-MEIER, 13, eighth-grader at East Middle School in Plymouth

"**How I look is important to me. But as long as I look nice to me, that's all I'm worried about. Sometimes I like to stand out and sometimes I like to blend in.**"

NATALIE
WOOD, 13,
eighth-grader at
East Middle
School in
Plymouth

A little creativity keeps kids moving

Holmes Middle School in Livonia is no country club, yet kids there are driving the fairways and honing tennis backhands on school time.

They can thank an innovative gym program that highlights individual and lifelong sports, balancing the traditional school emphasis — some say over-emphasis — on team sports.

"At the end of our tennis unit, one kid came up and said, 'I've always wanted to play tennis and I never knew who I could play with.'

"I said, 'Look around you, Joe. Now you know 40 people your age who play tennis,'" says physical education teacher Doug Curry.

Curry's aim is to build skill and interest in tennis, golf, bowling, archery and other individual sports, to help spawn a generation of active adults — a crucial goal if our nation is to lower health care costs by reducing its 56 percent level of sedentary people.

Middle school is a prime time to reach kids through phys ed, experts say, because students are ripe to apply motor skills they learned in elementary school. But too many become fitness dropouts when they can't qualify for team sports or don't want to.

They turn into bench warmers, sometimes for the rest of their lives, says Dr. Charles Kuntzleman, director of Fitness for Youth, a joint program of the University of Michigan and Blue Cross and Blue Shield of Michigan to test fitness innovations on thousands of children statewide.

Says Kuntzleman: "At age 10, about half of today's kids are involved in sports. By the time they're 18, it drops to about one-fifth. Middle school seems to be the tough spot" when kids drop out of sports.

"With girls, maybe a father or society says, 'Don't be a tomboy.' That's changing, but the old attitudes are still pretty pervasive," Kuntzleman says.

"With guys, it's more of an ego thing. 'I can't keep up. I don't have the moves.' They don't want to be embarrassed" by competition, he says.

The high fitness dropout rate, coupled with diets increasingly high in fat, is fattening up Michigan middle schoolers, raising their cholesterol levels and pumping up blood pressures above those of students a generation or two ago.

Middle school fitness has mental health effects, too, Kuntzleman says.

"This is the time when kids are at greatest risk for being lost to society. Fitness teaches about delayed gratification, about setting goals and reaching them and getting satisfaction from that. That's very powerful to young people.

116

FITNESS

"It's also been shown that fitness programs have been a deterrent to drug use and that kids of this age miss less school if they're involved in fitness programs."

With school cutbacks the norm, improving phys ed has taken a low priority, says Dr. Paul Vogel, associate professor of physical education at Michigan State University.

But good programs don't have to be costly, says Vogel, who heads an MSU-based, statewide research effort to improve physical education. One example? That country club at Holmes Middle School. It runs on a shoestring.

Curry scavenged cast-off golf clubs from local courses, then purchased an inexpensive kit of flags, tee markers and restricted-flight golf balls that won't sail beyond the tidy nine-hole course he sets up each day on the school athletic field. (The kit that makes the course, First Swing, is sold by the Professional Golfers Association; in Michigan, call 1-313-522-2323, weekdays 9-5.)

For tennis on a budget, Curry saved balls that tennis coaches had discarded, bought 40 inexpensive rackets, then turned a blacktop parking lot into a mini-Wimbledon.

The court "cost me maybe 50 bucks," he says. "I set up standards I made out of two-by-twos that I stuck into coffee cans filled with cement. Then I ran a rope across the top. The rope becomes the net," creating the equivalent of 10 side-by-side courts.

"It was amazing how quickly these kids learned, many who'd never played before," he says.

Curry doesn't ignore team sports but he improvises to get everyone in play.

"In football, we rarely go with more than three or four players on a team. The idea is, you don't improve by standing in line. You improve by touching the ball and participating," he says.

Another focus is fitness testing, a gauge that Curry's students use not for comparing themselves to others but instead for setting personal goals. To meet those goals, Curry requires his kids to exercise at home.

"They keep a log and their parents sign it. We have to break away from the idea that the only time you're active is at school."

Fitness standards

Middle schoolers should be able to pass these tests:

ENDURANCE: Run a mile in under 10 minutes; 37 percent of Michigan middle schoolers can't, usually because they are overweight and lack heart-and-lung stamina.

FLEXIBILITY: Sit with head, back, shoulders and buttocks flush against a wall while extending legs completely; 16 percent of middle schoolers lack the flexibility to do this.

STRENGTH: Do 10 push-ups; 39 percent can't. And do 10 bent-leg curl-ups; 39 percent can't. (Curl-ups are modified sit-ups: Sit with knees bent, feet flat on floor and curl forward raising shoulder blades off floor.)

"I can't believe I did it, but I dared one of my friends to crawl on his hands and knees around the teacher's desk and bark like a dog. Then I told him to ask the teacher if he could be her pet. He was smart. He didn't do it."

DAVID LESAR, 12, sixth-grader at East Middle School in Plymouth

---

Here's how to stop the moaning and groaning

"It's good to be my age. You don't get treated like such a kid anymore. My mom is trusting me more to do things like baby-sit, go to the mall."

KRISTIN WALSH, 11, sixth-grader at East Middle School

Never on a Monday. Or a Friday. Or, for that matter, a Wednesday. As far as middle schoolers are concerned, there's never a good time for homework.

"If it's on a Monday, we usually say, 'Aw, come on, you can't give us homework on Monday. It's the first day of the week,' " says Chris Stockwell, 14, of Eastpointe. "It's not OK on Friday, either. Everybody will be quite upset to be sitting home on the weekend. … Really, I guess we moan and groan whenever we get homework."

Middle schoolers gripe that there's too much of it. It's boring. It's meaningless.

Too often, they're right.

Teachers tend to assign homework more as a ritual than a learning tool.

"Homework can be a tremendous advantage or a tremendous trap," says Thomas Gwaltney, an education professor at Eastern Michigan University.

Sometimes teachers sabotage the process by doling out homework before teaching the skills necessary to complete it or by giving busy work. That can frustrate everyone.

"Homework is not supposed to drive a wedge between parents and teachers or parents and students," Gwaltney says. "It is supposed to create a bond."

Ideally, homework should show parents what — and how — students are learning.

But today's homework looks a lot different than it did when today's parents were in school. Traditional assignments, such as end-of-chapter questions and math and grammar worksheets, still are used. But more teachers are trying more creative and interesting assignments. They want students to use technology, work in teams and learn to solve complex problems.

"I hate the boring, five-pages-of-questions kind of assignments," says Bree Campbell, 13, a seventh-grader at St. Clair Middle School in St. Clair. "I do them, but I don't learn anything. I'd take a project any day."

Middle schoolers generally are bursting with energy and literally can change their minds minute to minute. To be meaningful, homework assignments must include choices, variety, creativity and fun.

The best homework for middle schoolers includes a balance of rote exercises and activities youngsters would want to do even if they weren't required: videotaping an interview, visiting a museum exhibit, collecting

118

information in a mall or calculating batting averages of baseball stars.

Those activities help make education come alive.

"Unfortunately, that's not usually the kind of homework they get," says Harris Cooper, a psychology professor at the University of Missouri and a leading homework expert.

There are no hard-and-fast rules about homework — except that it's effective when the assignment is right. Few dispute the notion that practice makes perfect. But many experts agree that homework should not be used only to practice already learned skills; it also should help students prepare and get excited about future lessons.

There are a lot of questions about how much and what kind of homework to give, and how much weight it should carry. Finding the right formula requires creativity, sensitivity and trial and error, Cooper says.

"It all depends on the topic, the time of year, the group of students," says Charlene Pike, a social studies teacher at L'Anse Creuse South Middle School in Harrison Township.

Pike prefers to assign projects that require students to manage their time, work in groups and get out in the community.

Making it work at home

☆ Provide a quiet, well-lit area that is always available for homework.

☆ Plan a homework schedule around your child's activities, habits and learning style. Some students need a break after school. That's OK; pick another time for homework.

☆ Monitor your child's homework to make sure it gets done.

☆ Mark important project due dates on a calendar.

☆ Watch for signs in your child that may suggest homework is missing the mark: anger, staying up late to finish it, refusing to do it, doing it in front of the television. Consult with your child and your child's teacher to find out what the problem is.

☆ Children in middle school should spend anywhere from 30 to 90 minutes a night on homework. But even if your child doesn't have homework, set aside at least an hour a night to read or do other educational activities.

☆ Try doing your own homework during your child's homework time — pay bills, balance checkbook, wash dishes, read a book.

☆ Ask the teacher for ways to help your child with confusing lessons. If you don't understand the work, offer your child what you can: tips about how to study, manage time and get organized.

☆ Take your child on educational outings — to museums, festivals, zoos, planetariums. Such experiences enhance what children are learning in school and make schoolwork more relevant to the real world. ○

"**Sometimes my mother makes me really mad, but I know she only does the things she does because she's looking out for my best interests.**"

LORA CANTY, 14, ninth-grader at Beaubien Middle School in Detroit

Educators need parents' input

Parent-teacher conferences are a ritual more widely practiced than understood. And the ritual can become more tense, confusing and frustrating as children move into middle school.

Suddenly, parents accustomed to private, 20-minute, one-on-one meetings with teachers who have 25-30 pupils may find themselves struggling through a crowded gym to capture a few minutes with each of their child's six or seven teachers. Each teacher may have more than 100 other students to remember and evaluate.

Some schools are working harder at scheduling conferences to minimize waiting times. Others are trying new ways of organizing conferences, such as having parents meet with a team of their child's key teachers, or student-led conferences aimed at improving parent-child communication.

Whatever the format, experts say, parents who take a little time to prepare can become much more comfortable with the process and make the conference a useful tool in managing their child's education.

The preparation need not be elaborate. Relaxed, but regular, chats about school between parent and child can keep the parent in touch and provide a basis for asking useful questions at conference time.

One problem with parent-teacher conferences in middle schools is that there are no consistent models, says Patricia Edwards, an associate education professor at Michigan State University. Most teachers are never trained on what should be covered in conferences or how to communicate effectively with parents, she says.

As a result, conferences can vary dramatically from school to school and teacher to teacher. One may focus heavily on behavioral issues; another may concentrate on academic weaknesses, still another may emphasize academic strengths.

Preparing a few specific questions for the teacher in advance can ensure that all aspects of the child's development are covered. Jotting them down on paper also helps make sure the questions are not forgotten in the frenzy of a conference arena.

Many middle schools are looking for ways to make conferences more effective. For some, it's simply a matter of scheduling them more efficiently.

A few schools, such as Algonquin Middle School in Macomb County's Chippewa Valley District, have begun using team conferences that let parents talk to several teachers at once.

Principal John Savel says parents meet with the two-teacher team that

120

TEACHER CONFERENCES

instructs their children in the main academic subjects — science, math, language arts and social studies. Teachers of specialized subjects, such as art and music, are available in the school's media center before or after parents' scheduled appointment.

Talking with the teacher

☆ Know what classes your child is taking and generally what he or she is studying.

☆ Meet briefly with or call your child's teachers early in the year. That will lay the groundwork for further communication. Don't wait until the conference if your child is having a problem.

☆ Talk regularly to your child about what is happening in school so you'll be able to spot problems and know what issues need attention at the conference.

☆ Think about what you want to explore at the conference before you go. Is there anything you should tell the teachers to help them understand your child better? What questions do you have about your child's schoolwork? Jot notes to yourself so you'll remember all the points.

☆ Make sure the conference covers academics and behavior.

☆ Ask the teacher to suggest objectives for your child and things you can do to help your child, even if your child gets top grades.

☆ If there is anything you are uncomfortable about or do not understand, ask the teacher to explain until it is clear. If you are still unsatisfied or confused, ask a counselor or the principal for help. ○

A few other schools, such as Steele Middle School in Muskegon, are experimenting with student-led conferences, in which the child explains to the parent what has been covered in class and why the student's grades are as they are. Parents like the format, says sixth-grade teacher Denise Bray.

"They said, 'We never realized how much our children did,'" Bray says. "I think for some of these people, it was the first time they've actually sat down and had a conversation about school with their children."

Communication is what parent-teacher conferences are all about. But teachers, principals and counselors say parents will be more satisfied with the conferences if they start preparing from the first day of school and come with specific objectives in mind.

"I want to be an actor and I want to teach calculus. In the future we're going to need people who can do a lot of different things, not just one thing."

CHRISTOPHER FLEMING, 13, eighth-grader at Beaubien Middle School in Detroit

INVOLVEMENT

Parents become key players

Sharon Ferrara used to believe that bake sales and gymnasium fund-raisers were the best ways to improve her son's Northville school. But as she learned more, she began to realize how much more complicated it was — and that millage votes, state politics, special-interest lobbying and legislative wheeling and dealing could have far more impact on school quality.

As Ferrara's perspective changed, she realized parents need to get more involved — and not just at bake sales.

"People are tired of special-interest groups and politicians with an agenda deciding their children's fate, and they often don't trust school boards," says Ferrara, one of many parents working with Advocates, a nonpartisan school reform group in Northville. "They want to get back to what's important, and that's the kids."

Parents nationwide are organizing to become important players in schools.

"Very often, parents banding together will produce change," says Pat Nichols, a state Department of Education supervisor who works on drug and sex education and health programming. "Maybe not in 24 hours, but they will see change."

Experts say parental involvement is fundamental during middle school, a time when children are establishing who they are and need guidance. It's also when educators often track teens into college prep versus job-training courses.

Ironically, it's when parental involvement often begins dropping off.

"When our kids didn't do well in a class, we'd say, 'You've got to try harder,'" says Roger Parlett of Redford Township. "We woke up when my son was a sophomore when his college entrance scores were low."

Like many other parents, Parlett at first felt frustrated and intimidated when he began working on school reform with other parents at Thurston High School in the South Redford Schools.

As parents consider how to increase their involvement, or to press for school improvements, they should first assess their school and district.

Start with your child, who best knows what's going on in school, Nichols suggests. "Ask your child every single day, 'How was school?' Listen and look at their facial expressions. … If you get the usual, 'Fine,' be more specific: 'What went well, what went poorly?'"

Get to know the school's teachers and administrators through volunteering and attending school board and parent/teacher/student association meetings.

INVOLVEMENT

"You'll get a feel for what is going on with the district curriculum-wise, money-wise and problem-wise," Nichols says. "And administrators will be more likely to ask for your help if they know you're interested."

Parents can obtain their school's overall Michigan Educational Assessment Program scores, dropout and parental involvement rates and other information usually by requesting the school's annual education report.

Under Michigan Public Act 25, if a school doesn't make such reports available, the entire district could lose $25 per student in state aid. The 1990 law also requires districts to develop school improvement teams that include employees, parents, citizens and students.

Parents may want to form their own group to press for change.

In 1992, the Advocates was formed in Northville to research school issues in a nonpartisan way. Members study issues, write research papers and present their findings to the school board and community.

The group tries to present all sides of an issue without taking a stand, but may take a position if one side is clearly perceived as best.

Another approach is to join existing groups, some of which may be well-established.

> ## QUOTES FROM KIDS!
>
> **"I don't think the world gives me freedom. A lot of things going on these days make me unable to do the things I would like to do — like go out and have fun."**
>
> CHARLES WILSON, 13, eighth-grader at Ann Arbor Trail Middle School in Detroit

---

Resources for reform

Parents who want to work on school improvements can use these resources:

☆ Join the parent-teacher organization at your school, or the Michigan Parent Teacher Association, 1-517-485-4345 anytime. In Detroit, parents can find out about their parent organization by calling their child's school or the Detroit Public Schools' community and family relations office.

☆ If you've gone through the chain of command in your district and haven't gotten results, call the Michigan Department of Education in Lansing at 1-517-373-3900, weekdays 8-5. Their specialists can offer advice and act as mediators.

☆ The U.S. Department of Education's Goals 2000 program is designed to help parents organize their communities and reform their schools. For free, step-by-step information by phone and mail, call 1-800-USA-LEARN anytime. ○

"Every time we see a problem, a lot of people want to start a new program," says Dan Jarvis, public policy coordinator for the Lansing-based Michigan Family Forum.

"The problem is, with so many groups not working together, they don't know what each other are doing. It's better to work within statewide, organized groups to connect across the state rather than within just a school district."

Jarvis' conservative group has lobbied school districts successfully on issues such as sex education and homosexuality.

INVOLVEMENT

Jarvis advises parents to "pick their battles carefully."

"It's essential to be reasonable and rational," he says. "Parents need to be willing to compromise on certain areas that won't give up their principles."

Reforming public schools has a lot to do with politics. And the way parents play the game has a lot to do with a reform's success, experts agree.

Parents should put their observations or complaints in writing and go through the chain of command: teacher, principal, superintendent, school board.

Ultimately, if parents feel the school board isn't listening, they can hold members accountable at election time, Parlett and others say.

Credibility also is key, Jarvis adds.

"Be accurate on the facts you present," he says. "We figure, 'Somebody may not agree with our position. Let's not give them reason to disagree with us because of poor research.'"

Children *stand at attention during a presentation by Michael Deren at Meads Mill Middle School, Northville. Parents have helped provide the middle schools with funding to invite speakers to hold programs on topics the children are working on.*

CHAPTER 3

HIGH SCHOOL, HIGH STAKES

Maysan *Haydar with one of her favorite possessions. For more on Maysan's busy high school life, see page 132.*

Cutting through the complications

High school has always been about trigonometry and transcripts, pep rallies and proms, goofing off and getting serious.

Today, it's also is about dodging violence, coping with stress and dealing with depression. It's about resisting peer pressure and booze and drugs. It's about getting along in a diverse world. Hey — it's about learning to survive.

And it isn't easy.

Good grades are more important than ever. Making the right decisions seems harder than ever. And the stakes are higher than ever.

Nobody's holding your hand — not that you'd want them to, anyway. After all, you're almost an adult.

The years between 14 and 18 are a time to test your mettle, to explore and experiment. In fact, figuring out who you are is one of your top assignments in high school.

Spend these years trying interesting classes, learning a new language, playing a sport, getting to know people of different cultures.

You'll make some mistakes. Flame out. Fall down and be forced to get back up.

Kids do it all the time, but they don't always share their expertise. This section features high school kids of all kinds who have learned how to maneuver through the maze. Some have beaten big odds; some have turned weaknesses into strengths and mistakes into lessons. All have interesting stories to tell.

They represent the range of students who attend the typical high school, which still looks a lot like the one your mom and dad attended.

Also, look for a Survival Guide full of advice and encouragement from other teenagers and experts on coping with everything from managing time to getting along with teachers.

Finally, there's a guide to the hot jobs of the future, articles on getting ready for college (and completing the applications) and tips on extracurricular activities and after-school jobs. ○

HIGH SCHOOLERS: WHAT THEY'RE LIKE

One day you may think there is no such thing as a typical high school student. The next day you may think they're all alike — rebellious and difficult.

One thing is certain, high school students are all going about the same task — figuring out who they are, where they're going and how to get there.

They'll pass through different stages at different times, but here's a glimpse of what to expect along the way:

THE TYPICAL 9TH-GRADER

☆ May show symptoms of loss — shock, denial, anger and blame. Leaving behind middle school is like losing childhood. It takes time to adjust.

☆ Can be confused. Habits and attitudes developed in middle school don't often work in high school and freshmen often learn that lesson painfully. May flunk a class.

☆ Experiments with everything from positive activities such as dance or a sport to harmful ones such as alcohol, marijuana and sex. Tests values and interests, trying to determine where he or she stands.

☆ Is unsure of a lot — what to do in life, where to go to college, what opinions to hold. May debate social issues constantly or ignore them.

☆ Often acts silly. May throw things at others, pull hair, giggle a lot.

☆ Talks about getting driver's license and more freedom.

☆ Is fascinated by upperclass students. May imitate their actions, dress and talk.

☆ May deny that there are problems at school or socially. Feels invincible.

☆ Is fixated on the body and appearances; often thinks everyone is looking at him or her.

☆ Girls are physically, mentally and socially more mature than boys. They may be attracted to older boys and older boys may pursue them.

☆ Many boys may just begin to show signs of puberty; voices change, body hair grows. ○

THE TYPICAL 10TH-GRADER

☆ Begins homing in on specific friends and activities; develops a better sense of self.

☆ Values and habits become clearer. Alcohol or drug use patterns may set in. Peer group influence is stronger than ever.

☆ May show signs of depression, eating disorders; talk of suicide can show up.

☆ May express self in wild and wonderful ways. Green hair, pierced navels and Madonna-esque styles show up more as students experiment with their identities. Some kids take this method of expression to the extreme because it's one of the most visible ways to say: "I'm not like you."

☆ Can be giddy with the freedom and high expectations unleashed after learning to drive.

☆ Starts thinking about and considering career choices. May take classes oriented toward a career.

☆ Likes hanging out at malls and going to weekend parties. ○

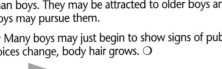

THE TYPICAL  **-GRADER**

☆ Acts an awful lot like a 10th-grader.

☆ Good and bad habits will be well established — and hard to break.

☆ Narrows interests and goals; focuses on the future, particularly post-graduation plans.

☆ Anguishes over decisions.

☆ Is often stressed out.

☆ Boys begin to catch up to girls sexually, emotionally and behaviorally. They may stop pulling girls' hair to get their attention and actually ask them out on dates.

☆ Because students begin taking college entrance exams and grades begin to count more than ever, students may re-evaluate goals. They may realize they're not likely to get into an Ivy League school and begin looking at more realistic options. ○

THE TYPICAL  **-GRADER**

☆ Can be very emotional — super happy one day, weepy or melancholy the next. Anxious and nervous.

☆ Becomes more reflective and analytical about self and life.

☆ May express appreciation and love for friends and family.

☆ Often is panicked: "Oh my God! I've blown off the last three years and now I'm graduating! What am I going to do?!"

☆ May cram in too many activities, trying to make up for lost time. Reality hits that this is it for high school.

☆ Can't focus well. "Senioritis" sets in and students may blow off assignments or classes.

☆ Begins to feel like an adult and eagerly anticipates that stage of life. May seem super confident. ○

She wants to be everywhere and try everything

Maysan Haydar wants to do *everything.*

Learn karate and Arabic. Be on the student council. Host "Teen Talk" on Sunday mornings on Flint's WSMH-TV (Channel 66). Ride horses. Lead an environmental action group. Write a teen column for the Flint Journal.

Her weekly schedule may be more jam-packed than Hillary Clinton's — and Maysan is trying to maintain a 3.3 grade point average.

Most of the time she does it all, even if it means getting fewer A's and less sleep.

"I'm not happy about getting C's in trig or anything," says the 17-year-old senior at Carman-Ainsworth High School in Flint Township. "But when I think about all the things I do, I think it's worth it. I have more fun."

Balancing grades and extracurriculars has been a challenge for Maysan — as it is for many high school students.

Maysan lives on Mountain Dew, chugging a can every few hours. She sleeps about four hours a night. And when it comes to studying — well, she fits it in when she can.

Her mother, Basima Haydar, often worries about Maysan's health and says she would have better grades if she wasn't involved in so many other things.

"She says, 'You cross the line; you do too many things.' "

But, Maysan — swigging her second Mountain Dew of the morning — says: "There are so many interesting things to do! If I was doing one thing, I'd get bored."

Educators, businesspeople and college recruiters agree that there are benefits to stretching oneself beyond the expected.

Trying a variety of things helps students figure out their interests and skills early on. And school and job recruiters like to see a range of activities on applications, says Lisa Chavis, Michigan State University associate admissions director.

"They want students who are well-rounded, who have good communication skills from being in different organizations, leadership positions and working part-time jobs," Chavis says. "It helps the student interact with different kinds of people."

Yet colleges base their admissions on grades and test scores ahead of extracurriculars, Chavis says. That worries Maysan.

She'd like to have straight A's when she applies to the University of Michigan in Ann Arbor or Georgetown University in Washington, D.C. —

STRATEGIES FOR SUCCESS

MAYSAN HAYDAR

Maysan *at Carman-Ainsworth High School.*

☆ **Age:** 17

☆ **School:** Flint Carman-Ainsworth High School, senior

☆ **Educational goal:** Wants to attend the University of Michigan or Georgetown University in Washington, D.C., to pursue a career in politics or journalism.

☆ **Likes:** Talking, Mountain Dew and the color black ("I don't know why. Maybe it's a rebellious thing against the color pink and femininity or something").

☆ **Dislikes:** Snapple ("It's too good for you") and deadlines ("I'm a procrastinator.")

☆ **Quote:** "I don't like sitting in the same place for more than five minutes. I have so much energy; I don't know why. Maybe it's the Mountain Dew. It's the way I've always been … I need 26 hours a day, at least." ○

continued ▼

Eat healthily. Avoid caffeine, alcohol and drugs. Get seven to eight hours of sleep a night. Give yourself time to chill out. Even superteens need to recuperate.

☆ When you're in class, focus on the lesson, not your after-school schedule. Use strategies to help discipline yourself, such as highlighting your notes or outlining your reading. The more you concentrate during class, the less study time you'll have to make up later.

☆ If possible, look over your notes right after school, before you head to the next thing. The sooner you review your notes, the better your retention.

☆ If you're just entering high school, wait until after the first semester to join a slew of groups. You'll know better how much time you'll have after studying, and you'll have a better idea of which ones interest you more.

continued ▶

her top choices.

Setting priorities is tough. She tries to reserve 7 to 8 p.m. as her study period, and usually keeps the commitment. But it's typically not enough time to study to maintain a B average. "I usually study during fourth hour," she says. "I'm an office aide and there's not a lot to do."

This year, though, Maysan won't have a "blow-off" hour in which she

continued ▼

☆ Having trouble deciding what not to do? Make a priority list, then eliminate what's at the bottom.

☆ Consider your interests when choosing a college. Smaller ones probably won't offer the same or as varied a number of clubs and activities as larger ones. Likewise, urban colleges will offer a different set of extracurriculars than a college in a rural setting.

☆ Don't stress out if you can't figure out what you're most interested in. Many college students change their majors five to eight times, counselors say. Keep trying out different jobs, clubs and internships that are career-related. Career choice often is by process of elimination; you won't know unless you try it. ○

STRATEGIES FOR SUCCESS

can study or catch up on her sleep, as she regularly did in math class. So she's showing some restraint: she decided against becoming a Big Sister and taking advanced placement calculus. And she lost her run for class treasurer, almost to her relief.

"It's probably better I didn't win," she says. "I want to do so much this year, but I need to work on my grades, too."

Maysan has been thinking a lot about which of her many interests she enjoys the most. Her decision will help her decide what her college major will be and which college she should apply to. So far, she's torn between journalism and politics. "I like to argue and I love to talk," she says.

Juggling everything may be challenging but it's good preparation for life after college, says Pat Shipp May, an educational counselor at Oakland Community College in Auburn Hills.

"So much of life is a balancing act," May says. "If they learn to do it now, they'll do better in college and in life and work."

May says the key is discipline, setting priorities and managing time well. A simple formula: Figure out the grades needed for the college you want to attend and budget enough study time to make those grades. Schedule extracurriculars around that — and stick to the plan.

Bruce Davis, Maysan's counselor at Carman-Ainsworth, says students also need to think over why they are signing up for an activity. If the interest comes from themselves, that's cool, he says. But if it's being driven by parents' wishes, there's something wrong. Let your parents know why you're not interested and make the best decision for yourself.

Parents, meanwhile, should ask their kids what they enjoy doing.

"When your kid quits something, accept it. Don't push it," Davis says.

For Maysan, the drive definitely comes from within.

"It'd be nice to be really, really good at one thing," she says. "But I'd get bored. … The world just ain't one thing."

High school years almost slipped away

Matt Oldes was a fairly typical "average" student at Lake Orion High School. He coasted through classes, studied little, worked more and had lots of friends who loved to hang out with him.

Then the bell tolled: senior year. Suddenly, Matt, 18, looked around and his friends, who had been working methodically while he breezed, were headed off to universities with big names. And Matt wasn't.

"That first week of senior year, when everybody was filling out college applications … I was like, 'What am I going to do?' " Matt says. Then, "Everybody's getting accepted and I'm like, 'Great.'

"I felt left out."

What happened to Matt didn't surprise adults at the school. They watched the highly likable student change during his three years at Lake Orion High, which starts with 10th grade, from a reluctant student to one with his eyes on the prize.

They saw a student with above-average ability and below-average motivation. Matt was never one to skip class, but he would do his homework just before the bell rang. He took college prep courses and could participate intelligently in class discussions, but he often hadn't done all the work.

"He's a bright kid," says humanities teacher Aileen Cronin, who taught Matt all three years. "He just didn't have a clear view of what he wanted to accomplish."

Kathleen Ferguson, his counselor, says, "Matt had a tendency to be a little lazy, a little procrastinating. His way was to just kind of smile and say, 'Everything'll be OK' … but then it hit him, 'Wow, I've got to plan.' "

What Matt went through isn't unusual for kids starting high school. Graduation seems pretty far off and waiting is difficult, Ferguson says. Plus, students are expected to stay focused and act responsibly in the face of overwhelmingly negative messages about the future.

"Young people like Matt can't see and touch the future; it's too abstract. And before he could get there, there were these hours of study, hours of boring classes — that stuff's the last thing he's going to do because the interest isn't there and the reward is so far off," Ferguson says.

When reality hit senior year, Ferguson saw a maturing Matt, who became concerned about his grade point average and more engaged in the process. All the pieces began to fit together.

"He began looking at his options and saw he didn't have a lot … so he began to grow up and exhibit some adult-like qualities," Ferguson says.

If you're what might be called an average student, you'll have to fight the odds to get what you want out of high school — and life. You'll probably have to force yourself to do things you don't want to do — such as studying extra hard. To succeed, look for ways to enhance and build on your strengths and consider these suggestions:

☆ Focus on subjects you like early in your high school career, and concentrate on them. When things get boring in school, as they almost surely will, it's your interest in art, languages, wood shop, computer-aided design or whatever, that'll get you through.

☆ If you work, don't overdo it on the hours. You must maintain balance with school, which, believe it or not, is the *real* No. 1 job in terms of your future. If your time on the job creeps up from just weekends to weekends *and* after school, look at your priorities. Remember: There are

continued ▶

continued ▼

only so many hours in a day and if work at the mall is taking up much of that time, what attention are you giving your books?

☆ Don't let yourself slip through the cracks at school. Get to know your guidance counselor, let him or her know who you are and what you're interested in. They're aware of special programs and activities that could benefit you and keep you focused. Likewise, if you do your best to make sure your teachers know you — especially if yours is a big, big high school — you won't feel like just a face in the crowd.

☆ Get involved in extracurricular activities. That's one of the best ways to find people with interests similar to yours, who want to get the most out of high school. Working with them can help you get the most out of things, too.

☆ Don't float through easy classes. Take classes that will challenge you, get your mind

continued ▶

STRATEGIES FOR SUCCESS

Matt listened in class. He studied with serious intent, often with those very classmates who were heading to top-flight colleges. He cut out dating and cut back on hanging out. And he made what for him was a big step: He emphasized school as much as he did work at the Paint Creek Country Club in Lake Orion, where he has worked for two years.

That will happen with most students as they mature, educators say. It also helps to have, as Matt did, a tight bond with good parents — "His dad kept kicking him in the butt," Ferguson says — good role models in two older sisters, a nurturing school environment and longtime friends who were motivated and cared about him.

Matt has decided to enroll part-time at Oakland Community College's Auburn Hills campus, to ease himself into the college scene and allow himself breathing room to pull up his 2.5 grade point average enough to get into a four-year college.

He hasn't decided what he'll major in — his mother wants him to try acting because of his engaging, outgoing personality. He is thinking about law or criminal justice because he says he likes trying to crack unsolved mysteries.

"I was stupid for not working harder in high school, for not taking the time to study. I was more concerned with making money and going out with friends and girls — I really got caught up in that," Matt says. "I didn't say 'screw school' or anything like that, but my priorities have been mixed up.

"That's what makes me so mad: I wouldn't have to struggle with work if I'd just *do* the work, if I'd just studied and done my homework. But I'm telling you right now, that's what I'm going to do from now on."

STRATEGIES FOR SUCCESS

Matt *sits on his new (used) Mustang near his Lake Orion home.*

☆ **Age:** 18

☆ **School:** Lake Orion High School, Class of '94

☆ **Educational goal:** Attend Oakland Community College in Auburn Hills part-time to bring up grades, then transfer to a four-year state school. Interested in drama, building and construction, law and criminal justice.

☆ **Likes:** Going out with friends, talking to his two sisters, his new white 1989 Mustang 5.0.

☆ **Dislikes:** Boring teachers, students making out in the halls, not doing better in high school because he knows he was capable.

☆ **Quote:** "I liked high school. I wanted to be there. All the things I like, all the people I like were there. … Only problem was, I wasn't doing what I should've been doing while I was there." ○

continued ▼

percolating. Often, the best teachers who have a knack for inspiring students are in the most stimulating classes. A good teacher will teach you something as long as you come to class awake, interested and prepared for the lesson. Step up to the challenge! It'll make classwork more fun and homework easier to do.

☆ It's never too late to change. If your habits have been holding you back, you can change them. It may take a while to get the hang of it, but it's possible. Your life and your future are at stake. ○

Friends enjoyed battle of wits

Tips

A few pointers for high school students who want to land a coveted admission ticket to an exclusive university:

☆ Keep up your grades. If your transcript glistens, it's worth its weight in gold. You'll be surprised how much you can earn with a summer job at a Fortune 500 company.

☆ Speaking of summer, make sure you find something interesting to do during those long vacations. Consider trying to spend a few weeks away from home, either working or exploring the world.

☆ Take tests such as the PSAT, SAT and ACT early. If you do well, prestigious universities will deluge you with information. That can help focus your thinking about where to apply. Consider a test-taking course such as those offered by Kaplan Education Centers.

☆ Volunteer for leadership positions in your school and community. Run for president of the club.

continued ▶

Courtney Lake and Kikuyu Matthews weren't the best students in the Class of '94 at Detroit's King High School. But they were close to the best, and close friends, too.

For months, they vied for the title of salutatorian, comparing scores after every test. Then a transfer student from a Catholic school in Redford Township beat them out for the No. 2 title.

Kikuyu and Courtney cooled their competition and rekindled the friendship they had built by trading information about summer jobs and after-school opportunities.

Now, the pair are settling into separate lives at exclusive private universities at opposite ends of the country. Courtney plans to study management, psychology and Japanese at Stanford University in Stanford, Calif. Kikuyu is a budding engineer at the Massachusetts Institute of Technology in Cambridge, Mass.

"We're like yin and yang," Courtney says. "We were No. 1 and No. 2 at everything we tried out for. We strove to be each other. What she didn't do, I did. What I didn't do, she did. I start a sentence; she finishes it."

Courtney's grade point average was 3.91 out of a possible 4.0. He was vice president of the National Honor Society chapter at King. Kikuyu's GPA was 3.92. She was the society's president.

"We sort of followed each other around," Kikuyu says. "Not consciously. We were involved in a lot of the same activities, but we're also very different. He's not into arts. I am. I'm not the kind of person who wants to take the center stage all the time. He likes a lot of attention."

How did these two become part of the *creme de la creme*? What set them apart from other classmates who had the brains but not that something extra required to win an invitation to one of the nation's most elite schools?

Self-confidence is one ingredient to their success, Kikuyu and Courtney agree. Family support also helped. So did a dynamic counselor, Deborah Harley, who opened their eyes to a world of scholarships and loans.

"I have representatives of different schools come in to talk, hundreds of them," Harley says. "I try to expose the kids to as much as I possibly can."

But most of all, Kikuyu and Courtney say that what made the difference for them was developing a strong sense of adventure, a willingness to move far away from home and explore the world.

"I'm not afraid to get out of Michigan," Kikuyu says. "It's all part of tak-

138

STRATEGIES FOR SUCCESS

COURTNEY LAKE & KIKUYU MATTHEWS

☆ **Age:** 18

☆ **School:** Detroit's King High School, Class of '94

☆ **Educational goal:** To graduate from Stanford University with a bachelor's degree in psychology, then to pursue a master's in industrial psychology and a career as a professor.

☆ **Likes:** Fine clothes. (He's a part-time model.) Dancing.

☆ **Dislikes:** People who have no sense of humor.

☆ **Quote:** "I wanted to go to Harvard, but I got rejected. So I'm going to Stanford instead. That's OK. I knew that when you went to that kind of school, there was a certain amount of respect you got back. And I knew I wanted that from other people." ○

☆ **Age:** 17

☆ **School:** King High School, Class of '94

☆ **Educational goal:** Earn a graduate degree in chemical engineering, then start her own cosmetics business.

☆ **Likes:** Drawing, painting on clothes, eating ice cream (all flavors), writing poetry.

☆ **Dislikes:** Traffic jams.

☆ **Quote:** "When I was in grade school, I remember asking my mommy why did I have to get A's when B's are also good? She didn't really push me. I basically decided on my own that I wanted to study hard. You get a lot of opportunities just by having good grades." ○

Kikuyu *(top) and Courtney in the hallway of King High School.*

continued ▼

Why not? Care about other people. Be more than a boring egghead.

☆ Develop a plan for what you want to do in life. Talking to adults you admire, even strangers who have jobs you might like, can help. Be creative. Try to take steps toward implementing your plan. Remember that it's OK — even desirable — to change your mind along the way.

☆ Be well-rounded. If you excel at science, dabble in art on the side. If you're a wizard with words, take an interest in engineering. Practice seeing the world through other people's eyes. If you live in the suburbs, don't be the kind of suburbanite who never goes to Detroit. If you live in Detroit, don't be the kind of city-dweller who has never appreciated Michigan's natural beauty. Also look beyond your home state's borders. The term "global village" is more than a cliche. If you can, get to know people from other cultures and

continued ▶

ing a risk, doing something different."

Both she and Courtney expect that moving from the largely African-American environment of Detroit to the wealthy, largely white society of

continued ▼

countries. Computer bulletin boards can help. Foreign language skills will be useful no matter what career you choose.

☆ When the time comes, fill out all the scholarship application forms you can. It's a lot of work, but it's worth it. If your school counselors don't gather information about these opportunities, be aggressive about seeking information from counselors at other schools or from universities themselves. If you can, visit college campuses to get a feel for the schools.

☆ Challenge yourself but don't force yourself to do things you really don't want to do.

☆ Keep your college and career goals in perspective. That kind of success isn't the only important thing in life. Leave time and energy to develop life skills such as cooking, doing laundry, saving money, making friends, being a good son or daughter or brother or sister. What is

continued ▶

140

STRATEGIES FOR SUCCESS

these upper-crust schools will be difficult. But they're willing, even eager, to compete in that world.

Some of their college classmates will spend about $100,000 on tuition, room, board and fees during their four years of undergraduate training.

Courtney received a full, four-year scholarship to Stanford. Kikuyu has a scholarship and loan package that probably will leave her tens of thousands of dollars in debt by the time she graduates.

"I guess they figure engineers won't have a hard time finding a job," she says.

Both Kikuyu and Courtney come from nontraditional homes. Kikuyu's parents are divorced; she grew up with her mother, Sandra Matthews, a grant administrator for the Detroit Public Schools. Courtney's parents never married; he was raised by both of them, and by his maternal grandmother. In high school, he lived with his father, St. Clair Lake, an insurance salesman, and his stepmother, Kathryn Means-Lake, a Northwest Airlines reservationist.

Kikuyu and Courtney say their experiences prove that families don't have to be storybook perfect to be supportive. Both students give their parents lots of credit for encouraging but not pressuring them to apply to big-name colleges.

"If your parents want something more than you, you're going to dislike it. I don't care who you are," Courtney says. "All the people I know who got into good schools, they had parents who basically let them make mistakes and learn from their mistakes. Guidance, yes. Pressure, no. My parents always told me, 'Do your best and we'll always be proud of you.' If I had tried my best and gotten straight D's and barely gotten into Wayne County Community College, my parents would have been proud of me regardless."

Courtney's parents never had to even imagine a scenario like that.

Before they were in high school, both Courtney and Kikuyu knew that their good grades and test scores gave them a shot at fancy colleges — and they each decided to take it. They also knew that good grades and high test scores weren't necessarily enough. They needed a hook, something to make them more interesting than the average applicant. So they lined up a series of impressive summer jobs and sought leadership roles in after-school activities. They also entered contests like crazy.

By the time she packed her bags for Cambridge, Kikuyu had spent summers working in a Ford Motor Co. material science lab, in a Dow Chemical Co. lab in Midland, at home starting her own business selling her hand-painted clothes and studying engineering, math and English composition at the University of Michigan.

She won $300 and a trip to Chicago in an NAACP poetry contest for a verse about hair weaves that spoofs Hamlet's soliloquy. She won $1,000 in a drawing contest sponsored by Perry Drug Stores and cosmetic companies. She won numerous awards for academic excellence, was King's student of the year as a junior, was president of the ski club and a member of the varsity volleyball team and the Del Sprites service club.

"Her grandmother used to complain that Kikuyu was too busy, but I believe busy kids stay out of trouble," says her mother, Sandra Matthews.

After a while, Courtney said, a packed schedule "becomes second nature. You're just always on the go."

He should know. Before he headed west to California, Courtney had spent summers working as an intern in the resources department of Citizens Insurance Co. in Howell, in a Wayne State University lab doing research on Parkinson's disease, in a lab at Louisiana State University in Baton Rouge, and in the claims department of a Cigna Insurance office in Southfield.

He also worked after school at an international law firm and attended the Hugh O'Brien Leadership Conference, an annual gathering in northern Michigan for students identified as future leaders. He won city and state oratory contests sponsored by Business Professionals of America and was a student of the month for the Exchange Club of Detroit.

Both Kikuyu and Courtney predict they'll be friends for life.

Says she: "I can't imagine that we would fall out of touch."

Says he: "Out of everyone I know, she's most like me. She's goal-oriented. And she has her eye on the finish line. Thirty or 40 years from now, she's going to be up there, and I'll be up there, too."

continued ▼

important is doing your best and being proud of whatever you're able to accomplish.

☆ If you don't get into your top choice school, it's not the end of the world. You're not alone.

☆ Tell your parents you need their support — but not heavy pressure — to excel. ○

Courtney *and Kikuyu say they'll remain friends for life.*

Sports makes everything worthwhile

continued ▶

Like many young men, 15-year-old Steve Champine dreams of being a professional basketball player. Or football player. Or baseball player.

But even if he doesn't become a pro, the Grosse Pointe North sophomore says he'll love sports. Always has. Always will.

Whether it's the crack of a bat in the blazing sun, the swish of the basketball as it sinks through the hoop, or the roar of the crowd on the final touchdown, Steve loves the sounds and smells of each game.

The honor student is a 6-foot, 160-pound, three-sport fanatic who played on two varsity teams as a freshman.

His coaches say that's a little unusual and Steve is a special athlete.

Steve says he just works hard and loves to play.

"When I'm not doing anything at home, I'll shoot hoops or think about the game," Steve says. "I just go all out, even in practice."

Last year, Steve was the varsity quarterback, a guard for varsity basketball and a shortstop and pitcher for junior varsity baseball.

Basketball is his favorite sport. He loves its intensity and constant movement.

"I find it more competitive than other sports, and you're always up and down, moving and scoring," he says. "Baseball can get a little boring sometimes when you're waiting around. Your mind can wander and stuff."

But Steve enjoyed playing JV baseball because he played with teammates his age and ability. Playing with older athletes can be intimidating, he says.

"I wasn't ready at first for the competition and how tough it was. It was a lot different than those other leagues," he says. "But when you play against better people, it makes you a better player."

Steve's basketball coach, Dave Stavale, says Steve welcomed the challenge of playing on the varsity team. He was a starting guard, too.

"He works very hard and has many leadership qualities," Stavale says. "He handles pressure way beyond his years."

But like any 15-year-old, Steve has interests outside of high school sports. He enjoys golfing, watching movies, hanging out with friends and spending time with his family. He finished driver's training and says dating is somewhere on his agenda, although he isn't sure where.

"I haven't quite figured them out yet," he says about girls.

His three sisters — two older and one younger — are athletes. His father, a former basketball coach, encouraged Steve's outside interests as

STRATEGIES FOR SUCCESS

Steve *"has many leadership qualities," one of his coaches says.*

☆ **Age:** 15

☆ **School:** Grosse Pointe North High School, sophomore

☆ **Educational goal:** To maintain a 3.6 grade point for all four years and go on to the University of Michigan.

☆ **Likes:** Challenges, all sports — especially basketball — math, movies.

☆ **Dislikes:** English classes. Being bored.

☆ **Quote:** "It's hard to fit it all in sometimes. You just have to plan really well, and sometimes you can't do everything you want to." ○

well as athletics.

"I've never tried to push him. Steve has always been motivated and works hard at sports," says Jim Champine. "Even during the winter break when I used to be coaching, Steve would set his alarm and get up for practice at 7 a.m. He just really enjoys it."

Steve is carrying a 3.6 grade point average and finds outside interests difficult to fit around studying, playing sports and working at a local construction company. But grades are a top priority.

continued ▼
even if you would like to.

☆ Take care of your body. Eat right and get enough sleep. In the rush from school to work or practice, you may not have time to eat well-balanced meals. You need those nutrients and at least eight hours of sleep every night to maintain a high energy level.

☆ Study first. Do your homework before going out with friends. You'll feel better about yourself and be able to relax more with company you enjoy.

☆ Use those in-between hours. Time often is wasted during the hour after school but before practice, or in front of the television after dinner. Take that time to plan the next day or week, or go through your class schedule and mark due dates for homework, tests and papers.

☆ Thank those who help you. When people are busy, they often forget about others around

continued ▶

continued ▼

them. Take time to appreciate and thank your family or teachers for helping and supporting you. They will remember it later, perhaps at a time when you are too busy to be friendly or thankful.

☆ Remember reality checks. In the heat of the moment, things often get blown out of proportion. Failing a test, losing a game, or fighting with a friend or parent or coach often may seem like the end of the world. Stop and think: "Will I remember this in 20 years?" Chances are, you won't — or at least it won't mean very much in the course of a lifetime. ○

STRATEGIES FOR SUCCESS

Frank Sumbera, Steve's baseball and football coach, says he stresses the importance of high grades to his players.

"We tell them from the beginning they have to keep their grades up. They know if they want to go to college, they've got to have the classes," says Sumbera, who has coached at North for 25 years. "Steve is on the right path. He's very good at decision-making. I hope he keeps making all the right ones."

Steve says he studies hard, although he may not love it. Studying often follows a hectic day of school and practice or games. Sometimes, he fights to stay awake over an open book. That's why he enjoys the problem-solving in math and science but dislikes English.

"I like math because I'm good at it and I find it more interesting. It just comes natural," he says.

Planning study time is what it takes to keep up on schoolwork, Steve says. When he knows an assignment is due the day after a big game or busy day, he'll work to get it done early.

"It's not easy — sometimes it can be kind of tough, but you know you've got to do it," he says.

Steve isn't sure yet what he wants to study in college or what career he'll enter. His dream is to play professional sports.

To do that, Steve knows he has to keep up his grades and work at his game. He plans to start lifting weights to build a stronger frame.

"I need to get stronger," he says. "Hopefully, I'm still growing."

Steve is looking forward to his sophomore year. He'll get his driver's license and possibly play varsity baseball in the spring.

After that, who knows? He says he'll keep setting goals. Coach Sumbera says that at the rate Steve is working, he'll quickly reach them.

Label doesn't limit her educational aims

Antoinette Sauro didn't need anybody to tell her that she wasn't likely to get elected president of the student senate at Pontiac Northern High School.

And she didn't need to hear that she had a slim chance of winning many cross-country races.

She knew that, as a special education student, success and popularity wouldn't come easily. She'd have to fight every step of the way.

"I can't let anybody tell me I can't do something just because I'm in special ed," says Antoinette, 15, a sophomore. "I have to at least try. … And I have to believe in myself."

In victory and defeat, Antoinette holds her head high. She lost her bid for the senate, but she is on the cross-country team.

Such self-confidence among special education students is rare. So many students with learning disabilities or physical impairments go through school known as less capable than their peers.

In their early years, they're harassed on the playground or labeled as stupid, strange or a "sped." By the time they enter high school, many special education students — students who need extra help in school because of physical, emotional or learning impairments — are used to being ignored, ridiculed and having their dreams shot down.

Students like Antoinette, whose disabilities are not obvious to others, may struggle the most, some experts say.

"People are more willing to make allowances and adapt to the person in a wheelchair than they are for the person who says, 'I can't read that' or 'I can't do that math,' " says James Nuttal, consultant with the Michigan Department of Education. "A lot of times those kids just hear, 'You're not trying hard enough,' and they spend a lot of time with low marks and low self-esteem."

Often, they never recover. About 37 percent of learning-disabled students and 55 percent of emotionally impaired students nationally drop out of school; figures vary for students with other disabilities. The dropout rate nationally among other students is about 25 percent.

Antoinette has been overcoming the odds since birth. She was born two months premature and struggled with health problems that put her physically and mentally years behind her peers.

She was labeled learning disabled in preschool and has been in special education programs ever since. She was taunted along the way, but with her father's help, she learned to ignore it. Antoinette can't recall a single disturbing incident.

Special education doesn't have to limit possibilities or close doors. But special education students often must work harder to achieve what they want. And their parents must be strong and constant advocates.

Here are some tips for students and parents on encouraging independence and self-reliance:

Students:

☆ Everybody learns differently and everybody struggles with something in life. Don't think that you're stupid just because you have a learning disability.

☆ Ask your teachers to let you try to tackle regular education work. And take classes such as art and gym and other electives with non-special education students. The more you challenge yourself, the more you will achieve. But don't take on so much that you set yourself up for failure.

☆ Try everything. Don't let others discourage you from exploring activities, classes and hobbies. You won't know what you're

continued ▶

continued ▼

good at unless you try different things. You may struggle in reading, but be great on a tennis court.

☆ Don't feel sorry for yourself or expect others to do things for you.

☆ Take advantage of any other resources that your school offers, such as tutoring.

☆ Get to know lots of students. Don't hang out with only special education students. That's how you get stigmatized.

☆ If communication skills are difficult, work as much as possible on computers. Many programs help special education students communicate, write and learn more easily.

Parents:

☆ Don't coddle your child. By sophomore year, your child should know — or be encouraged to learn — what kind of help is needed to pass classes. Let your child test the waters on his or her own. Even allow your

continued ▶

STRATEGIES FOR SUCCESS

"Obstacles simply do not deter her," says Diane Eisenberg, special education teacher at Pontiac Northern. "That is one of her strengths. She sees them as challenges and tackles them. She doesn't even care if she fails. She tries everything. She's a true exception."

Antoinette loves to crochet and do crafts and says she tries to learn from all experiences — good and bad.

Losing the bid for president of the student senate, for example, taught her that she needs to start campaigning earlier, put more posters around the school and get to know more people. But she also learned that her platform — boosting student involvement and stopping school violence — was right on the mark.

And every race she runs for the cross-country team is exhilarating. She wins sometimes, but that's not what thrills her.

"One person said to me, 'I don't know why you're on this team, you never win,'" Antoinette said. "I said, 'At least I finish. And that's a victory.' And besides, running makes me feel free. It's an escape."

Her immediate goal is to pass the Michigan Educational Assessment Program test and then figure out what it will take to graduate as a regular student.

"I've learned a lot in special education, but it seems I've never gotten ahead," she says. "I'll probably always need a tutor in some areas, but I really want to graduate from regular education."

She plans to attend Oakland Community College and eventually transfer to a four-year college and study nursing or education.

"I didn't think she'd get this far," says her father, Vincent Sauro, 44. "It's been a struggle, but I tell her she can do whatever she puts her mind to. And she puts her mind to a lot."

Vincent Sauro dropped out of school in the seventh grade and, at 17, found a good job in a General Motors Corp. factory. But he preaches the value of a good education to Antoinette. He knows he's raising her in a world where there are fewer low-skill jobs that pay well.

Antoinette knows that, too.

"The world isn't easy," she says. "There's a lot of pressure out there, and you have to learn everything you can to make it."

ANTOINETTE SAURO

Antoinette *on her dad's Harley.*

☆ **Age:** 15

☆ **School:** Pontiac Northern High School, sophomore

☆ **Educational goal:** To get out of special education, go to college and become a nurse or teacher.

☆ **Likes:** Rural areas, running, being involved in school activiites.

☆ **Dislikes:** Violence, racism, big cities.

☆ **Quote:** "I think boys are just trouble. Right now I have to concentrate on getting good grades and learning. Once I have a good job and my life is together, then I'll think about boys. But not until then." ○

continued ▼

child to fail. That will help your child learn just how far he or she can go without support.

☆ Ask questions of teachers, counselors and administrators. Get the course syllabus so you can monitor what is expected of your child.

☆ If you don't understand something about your child's program but are embarrassed or afraid to ask, contact a parent special education representative. All school districts are supposed to have parents who can advocate for special education children. If your district doesn't, contact the intermediate school district for help.

☆ Reinforce the message that everyone wrestles with difficulties. ○

'If my hands get dirty, I'll wash them'

Jodie Novick knows she's getting a good education when grease and grime are embedded under her long, frosted-pink fingernails, her blue jeans turn black and her hands turn numb from the grinding, zipping and pounding of power tools.

"I'm not a gearhead or anything like that," says Jodie, a 17-year-old senior at Warren Mott High School, using the nickname for students who are more interested in shop than Shakespeare. "I just love learning about cars."

Unlike a lot of her female counterparts, Jodie is most comfortable tinkering with tools, tires and transmissions. Too often, however, others seem most comfortable trying to steer her away from such activities.

"My counselor told me I'd be the only girl in auto class and I'd get dirty and break my nails," Jodie says. "Well, I told her, 'If my hands get dirty, I'll wash them. If my nails break, I'll put fake ones on. Just let me give it a shot.'"

After a grueling debate, her counselor gave in.

And she was right. Jodie *was* the only girl at first. She got filthy. And she went through a lot of Lee Press-On Nails.

But Jodie also learned about success, pride, overcoming fear and what route to take to become an auto mechanic.

"I was so scared I wouldn't be strong enough, or wouldn't understand stuff and everybody would say it was because I'm a girl," Jodie says. "And at first, all the guys ignored me. I was sort of an outcast. Now, the guys in class come up to me and ask me about things. And they don't think anything of it."

Jodie has always hated limitations — when friends told her she couldn't possibly enjoy football because she's a girl, or when she couldn't understand conversations her boyfriend was having about cars.

So it wasn't surprising to her family and friends that she decided to be a mechanic instead of a secretary or beautician.

"Even when she was a little kid and she'd see an old car go by, she'd stop and say, 'Wow, I like that car,'" says Norma Novick, Jodie's mother. "I told her I really didn't care what she decided to do as long as she was good at it and happy — as long as it was legal."

Norma Novick says she's proud her daughter is succeeding so far in a man's world. "I don't want her to be like her mother," she says. "I used to think the air filter was the entire engine."

More and more, teenagers — especially girls — are finding opportunities, success and happiness in jobs once dominated by the opposite gen-

continued ▶

STRATEGIES FOR SUCCESS

JODIE NOVICK

Jodie *was once ignored by the boys in shop. Now she's consulted.*

☆ **Age:** 17

☆ **School:** Warren Mott High School, senior

☆ **Educational goal:** To attend Macomb Community College's auto technology program.

☆ **Likes:** Working on cars. Her boyfriend. Cowboy boots. Her 15 pet mice.

☆ **Dislikes:** Closed-minded people. Racism, sexism. Traffic. Spiders.

☆ **Quote:** "I don't want to be a sheep. I don't want to follow and I don't want to give a damn about what people say about me. I just want to do what I want to do — and be the best at it." ○

continued ▼

you be allowed to take the classes you need.

☆ Ask your counselor or a teacher to help you find a mentor, someone who is doing what you want to do. If you're a female and want to be a mechanic, hook up with a woman who has succeeded in that field. If you're a male and want to be a nurse, find a successful male nurse and ask for advice.

☆ If you can't connect with a mentor through your school, call the local Chamber of Commerce or go directly to a business or institution that employs people who do what you want to do. Find out if there is a mentoring program that would work for you.

☆ Community colleges often provide career counseling services. Call your local community college and ask to speak to a counselor, or ask your high school counselor for a contact at the college. If you're told the service is only for students, be persistent; you may

continued ▶

continued ▼

succeed in getting help. Many community colleges are eager to talk to high school students and can offer good advice.

☆ Attend school career workshops, seminars and programs put on by outside speakers. Talk to the presenters. Ask those who are doing something you're interested in if you may contact them later about career opportunities and visit them on the job. Some may let you tour their workplace or spend a day with them.

☆ Use summer or part-time jobs to make connections in the field you're interested in. If you want to be a kindergarten teacher, baby-sit kids in your neighborhood or volunteer to read to children at a local library. If you want to work in manufacturing, accept a job sweeping floors or answering phones at a small factory.

☆ Do well in all your classes. Good grades and attendance give you options. ○

STRATEGIES FOR SUCCESS

der.

"How many girls are tired of being pushed into nail salons and low-paying steno jobs?" says Richard King, auto shop teacher at Warren Mott. "I tell them it's ridiculous to let that happen. They will go just as far as guys, maybe even farther, in auto mechanics. Companies are just hollering for us to send them more girls."

Males, too, are finding more freedom to pursue careers in nursing, elementary education and secretarial work.

Indeed, the Michigan Department of Education offers incentive money to schools that attract students to nontraditional programs.

"More and more we're saying if a person has a skill, they should be able to pursue it," says Halyna Bialczyk, a consultant with the Wayne County Regional Educational Services Agency. "That means we're doing away with the old idea that if you're male, here's what you can do and if you're female, here's what you can do."

Still, bucking the norm isn't easy. For many students, the struggle starts at home trying to win over family.

The next hurdle is convincing guidance counselors and teachers that they haven't lost their minds.

Once Jodie got past her counselor, the next obstacle was the boys in shop classes. And now, it's customers at her job at a Goodyear garage in Madison Heights. The skeptics peer over her shoulder as she tests car batteries, balances tires or changes oil.

"They want to make sure I don't do anything wrong," she says. "Not that they always know how to do it, but they just don't think that I do."

Jodie usually hears that she looks more like she should be modeling — or doing anything but crawling under a car.

She gets all A's in auto shop classes. And those classes helped her boost her grades in other classes to mostly A's and B's.

"My auto classes were the reason I got up in the morning and even came to school at all," Jodie says. "They inspired me and made me feel so proud of myself."

Jodie plans to attend Macomb Community College's auto technology program when she graduates and pursue an apprenticeship with one of the Big Three car companies.

She expects the road will always be bumpy. But that's no problem, she says. She absorbs the jolts and journeys on.

"All my life, I've hated hearing that I can't do something like sports or work on cars or whatever, because I'm a girl. All I can say is, 'Oh yeah? Just watch me.'"

Alternative setting let her begin again

Lindsay Bithell cringed when she walked the halls at Lahser High School. It felt like all eyes were on her all the time.

Most of the students didn't know her, but they knew she'd been caught selling LSD as a freshman. That was enough to poison her reputation for good.

"Drug addict," "hippie," "lost cause," her peers whispered behind her back. Some even said it to her face. The Bloomfield Hills School Board, in suspending her for three months, called her a threat to other students.

"It was downhill from there," says Lindsay, now 18. "Imagine being considered a threat to your peers."

But when Lindsay returned to Lahser her sophomore year, she was ready to get serious about her education. She had stopped using LSD. She never felt she was addicted, so she says it wasn't a hard habit to break.

"I basically just got tired of feeling sick all the time," she says.

But Lindsay soon discovered that picking up her life wasn't so easy. She turned angry and frustrated because she thought she wasn't accepted by students or teachers. She didn't like the rules, the busywork, the pressure to conform, the emphasis her peers placed on money.

"I don't get everything I want," Lindsay says. "And here were some of my friends whose parents just hand them a credit card and say, 'Here, have a good time.' The clothes you wore, the car you drove, the college you got into meant everything."

By her senior year, Lindsay, who wears big bell bottoms and sometimes styles her hair with dreadlocks, had had it trying to find her niche at Lahser.

"I called them up on the first day of class and I just said, 'You know I'm not going to be coming back to Lahser.' The secretary kept saying I couldn't do that and she wanted to talk to my mom. I had to laugh. There they were again, treating me like a child. And here I was old enough to quit school if I wanted to."

Lindsay knew better than to drop out. Counselors had mentioned that attending the Royal Oak Opportunity Center could ensure that she would graduate on time, but she wasn't convinced it was right for her until she heard other students rave about it.

They said it was a school where what she had done wouldn't matter as much as what she was capable of doing. The Opportunity Center is an alternative high school that accepts students from several Oakland County districts. It is located on the Royal Oak campus of Oakland

Rules.

Some high school students live to break them. And some teachers and administrators live to make life miserable for those who do.

The routine and rigor of many regular high schools turns some students off to education and on to rebellion. Whether you've already gotten into trouble or see yourself heading in that direction, you can salvage your education — and even learn to live with rules. Here's how:

☆ Nothing is worse than spending six hours a day, five days a week doing things you hate. That's enough to make anybody rebel. Try to find something to make attending school worthwhile. That may be a shop or art class, choir or sport. It may even be an independent study project you design.

☆ Another way to make school tolerable is to find ways to get out. That doesn't mean quit. Try getting into a work-study program or doing community service. That will take you out of

continued ▼

continued ▼

school and into a community setting for a few hours. And you'll get credit for it.

☆ It's one of the hardest things to do, but stop hanging out with students who pull you down. Find peers who challenge you to be a better person.

☆ If you're getting in trouble for resisting the authority of one or more of your teachers and you really want to solve the problem, don't confront the teacher in front of 20 other students. The teacher will always remind you who's boss in a situation like that. Discuss problems with teachers before or after class, when they are alone.

☆ If you think you're just not going to make it in your regular school, ask your counselor what options are available. You may find a range of alternatives, from full-time schools to part-time programs.

☆ Check with Don Tassie, president of the

continued ▶

STRATEGIES FOR SUCCESS

Community College and many students take college courses while working toward their high school diplomas.

Lindsay was earning C's, D's and even flunking classes at Lahser.

"I could recite the health class lessons better than the teacher," says Lindsay, who passed health with a D on the third try. "If the teacher forgot something in the lesson, I'd just chime in."

Figuring she had nothing to lose, Lindsay called the Opportunity Center, got her records from Lahser and enrolled. It was that simple.

She finished her senior year there, earning A's in all her classes both semesters. Lindsay also won a $500 scholarship from the school for her performance. She graduated in June.

Being able to make a fresh start gave Lindsay the boost she needed. At the Opportunity Center, she was just Lindsay, the teenager who loved children, sewing her own clothes and following the Grateful Dead.

"I was stereotyped at Lahser. I was that drug dealer. Kids stayed away from me and teachers never took an interest in me," Lindsay says. "All I wanted was for people to get to know me, the real me."

She's now a freshman at Western Michigan University and dreams of becoming a kindergarten teacher and midwife.

Garry Anderson, Lindsay's counselor at Lahser, says some students can't adjust to the rigors and structure of a school like Lahser, where academic competition and scrutiny are intense.

"Some kids, for whatever reason, need more flexibility," Anderson says. "They need to be able to start school later, stay later, work and go to school, whatever. They just need options."

In addition, he says, students who have gone through rehabilitation or who have returned from suspensions often come back to old habits and traps.

"It's very difficult to return to that same environment; your friends are still there and so are many of the temptations," Anderson says. "Sometimes success literally depends on going somewhere else and making a fresh start."

Lindsay says she also related much better to the teachers at the Opportunity Center. They didn't dole out busywork. Every assignment had meaning to Lindsay and she was allowed more choices in how she did her work. If she challenged teachers, they listened to what she had to say.

"They would bend over backwards for you, drop anything they were doing if you needed help," Lindsay says.

They reminded her of her third-grade teacher, who talked to Lindsay about life, made her feel special and took the class on lots of field trips.

"I loved school then," Lindsay says. "Then I get into high school and it feels like a jail. But now, now I'm free, and I'm going to do great things."

STRATEGIES FOR SUCCESS

LINDSAY BITHELL

Lindsay *has bounced back from her problems. She wants to teach.*

☆ **Age:** 18

☆ **School:** Royal Oak Opportunity Center, Class of '94.

☆ **Educational goal:** To earn a degree from Western Michigan University and become a kindergarten teacher and midwife.

☆ **Likes:** The simple things in life: children, nature, honesty. And the Grateful Dead.

☆ **Dislikes:** Greed, hatred.

☆ **Quote:** "I don't have a single regret. I call them learning experiences. I am who I am because of everything I've gone through. And I like who I am." ○

continued ▼

Michigan Alternative Education Association, 1-517-784-3144. You may find out about programs even your counselor didn't know existed.

☆ Visit some of the alternative programs to see if they would suit your style. Some programs are designed for teen parents or kids who've gotten in trouble with the law; others are geared toward students who learn better with less structure and more freedom. Talk to your counselor, parents or other trusted adults before you make a decision. Discuss the pros and cons of leaving your regular high school.

☆ If you decide to attend an alternative school, use it as a chance to start over. Take charge of your life and take responsibility. ○

Life isn't easy for teen parents and likely never will be. The stigma has softened over the years, but teen parents still must juggle adult problems while they're in a kid's world. Here are pointers for how teen parents can succeed:

☆ Make education a priority. Getting a diploma and even a college or trade school education is necessary to support yourself and your baby.

☆ Assume you're going to struggle, times are going to get tough and you're going to get down.

☆ Don't worry about graduating on time. If you miss some school, ask a counselor what your options are. Too many girls think dropping out for a time means they've lost their opportunity for a diploma. Not true. Some high schools allow students to make up work over the summer or to finish their senior year a year late. Adult and community education programs also

continued ▶

STRATEGIES FOR SUCCESS

Teen mother won't lower her expectations

No way was Angela Patterson going to settle for a General Equivalency Diploma.

She knew a GED wouldn't get her far these days. And she had dreams, including going to college and becoming an accountant. Maybe even owning her own business.

But Angela also had Christina, her daughter born in March 1993, and a lot of sleepless nights, breast-feeding and baby-sitting ahead of her.

Taking classes at Wayne Memorial High School would be too hard for her, a counselor told her. She wouldn't fit in. She'd be away from home too many hours. She'd miss her baby.

Wrong, Angela thought.

"I told him, 'I want my diploma. A GED is nothing compared to a diploma. It's my life, and I want you to let me into the regular high school.' "

He did. And that summer, Angela moved in with her boyfriend's parents in Wayne and took American History I and II in summer school so she could catch up and eventually graduate on time. She earned A's in both classes and went on to graduate with her class — and with honors — in June.

"Everybody at school was out doing their party thing and I was at home doing my mother thing," Angela says. "I feel like I'm 30 or something. But I gritted my teeth and went through everything I had to and I made it … with honors. It was low honors, but it was honors."

Angela completed school with a 3.2 grade point average, which meant she got to wear a special white tassle on her mortarboard. She earned a 4.0 her last semester — the best she'd ever done.

That's not how it usually works. Teen mothers often drop out or graduate from alternative high schools or adult education programs. Many leave high school without a diploma but return to school later in life.

But about 30 percent never get a diploma or a GED, according to the Alan Guttmacher Institute, a New York City-based nonprofit reproductive health research organization.

Today, pregnant and parenting teens have more options than ever — from child care classes offered at regular high schools to special schools that provide day care, counseling and even medical services. The teens often just need to find the right fit.

Still, that doesn't mean success or even stability will come easily.

"Out-of-wedlock childbearing doesn't carry near the stigma it used to. It is much more acceptable today, but still the peer pressures and the negative consequences are much worse for a teen parent than for a non-par-

ANGELA PATTERSON

Angela *with her daughter Christina.*

☆ **Age:** 18

☆ **School:** Wayne Memorial High School, Class of '94

☆ **Educational goal:** To become a certified public accountant.

☆ **Likes:** Working with numbers. Being productive.

☆ **Dislikes:** Ignorant people. Snooty people.

☆ **Quote:** "I want my baby to be happy and to be able to do whatever she wants to do. But she's not going to be spoiled. She's going to know how rough life can be. Hopefully, though, she won't have it as rough as I have it." ○

continued ▼

provide General Equivalency Diploma programs.

☆ Don't expect that teachers or parents or other adults will recognize your problems and rescue you. Find out if your school district has a student assistance program that offers counseling and support for students who have substance abuse problems, family struggles or other difficulties. Exchange phone numbers with peer counselors if your school has them. And go to them for help when you need it.

☆ Carve out time to study every night and do it. Some parenting teens study after others in the house have gone to sleep; some wake early and study then. Making good use of study hall and lunch hours also helps.

☆ If you're struggling in a class, ask for help. Knowing when you need assistance is a sign of maturity, not weakness.

continued ▶

ent," says Susan Tew of the Guttmacher Institute.

Child care is the most critical concern of teen mothers. Without reliable, inexpensive baby-sitting, few teenagers can keep up with their peers. And even with it, staying on track may be impossible.

Doing things in sync with peers isn't the most important thing for teen parents. Getting an education is. Good jobs — especially ones with health benefits — don't come readily to high school dropouts.

Angela relied on her fiance and his mother to help her care for Christina during the school year. Still, there were plenty of days and nights when Angela cradled her crying baby while trying to study for an accounting test or prepare a speech for public speaking.

Often she studied after everyone else had gone to bed. That meant living on four or five hours' sleep.

Angela had always done well in school, even though she had attended a different school every year since third grade. School was a refuge, a place where she could escape family problems and earn her own rewards.

Some members of Angela's family told her that "I wouldn't amount to anything, that I'd end up on welfare and unable to support myself," Angela says. "No way was I going to let that happen."

A recent trip to a welfare office to find out what kind of assistance she qualified for strengthened her resolve.

Angela took a number, sat and watched the flurry of activity and listened to people's desperate stories. She left before her number was called.

"I didn't want to be looked down upon all of my life because I was on welfare," she says. "I'm looked down upon enough because I'm a teen mom."

Angela doesn't have a job. And she isn't certain when she, Christina and her 22-year-old fiance Tom Porter, a truck driver, will be able to move out of the cramped bedroom they're sharing at his parent's home.

But she is collecting community college brochures and information on financial aid. That helps her keep a grip on her dream.

"There are some of us teen moms who can make it," Angela says. "But you can't sit and do nothing. You have to have a dream. And you have to realize that you get there day by day."

continued ▼

☆ Build a support network of adults to help you. You will need adults who know the ins and outs of your school system as well as how to maneuver through health and welfare agencies. Start to put that network together by asking counselors, teachers, social workers and others you trust for help. Don't get discouraged if many say "no." You may have to ask 10 or 15 people before you find one who says, "I understand."

☆ Get some peer coaching. Connect with successful teens who are parents and find out what's working for them. Talk to successful adults who had children when they were teenagers. Find out what lessons they learned and how they made it.

☆ Be assertive. Verbalize your needs and fight for help meeting them. Keep pushing until you get what you need. Don't give up if somebody tells you "no." Ask someone else. Persistence pays off.

continued ▶

156

STRATEGIES FOR SUCCESS

Angela *beat the odds teen mothers face. She graduated with honors.*

continued ▼

☆ Talk to your doctor on a regular basis about your baby's health — and your own. If you don't have a regular doctor, establish contact with health professionals at a teen health center in your community (look under Teen Health in the Yellow Pages) or with a family planning clinic or with your county Department of Public Health. Many agencies provide prenatal and pediatric services.

☆ Document your communication with everyone, from health care agencies to teachers. Write down the name and phone number of everyone you talk to. Make sure you know who advised you to do what and who rejected requests from you. You never know when you'll need this information.

☆ Take a parenting class at school or through community education or a hospital. Nobody is born with parenting skills. You learn them, and taking a class or reading up is a great way to start. ○

Demons on the brain mess with concentration

When other kids his age drew stick figures, Paul Wheat penciled people with muscles.

Now, they have fangs, weapons and superhuman powers. But his drawings still are far more sophisticated than the average Southfield High School sophomore.

"He's way beyond his years," says Veronica Straus, Paul's art teacher. "His awareness of shadow, composition and musculature is very advanced. … You don't see his kind of talent that often."

Paul spends every available moment drawing. Though his current subjects of choice are often gruesome and ghoulish, his talent is fresh and flourishing.

"It's a way to translate what's going on in my head … a way to communicate," Paul says. "I can't imagine being happy doing anything else."

But, like many artistically talented teenagers, 15-year-old Paul struggles to put art in perspective. He knows it isn't everything, that he needs to do well in other areas — to socialize more, get better grades and pay more attention to the world around him.

"I just want him to clean his room," says Ibbie Frazier, Paul's mother. "But all he wants to do is draw, draw, draw. He gets in trouble for it, too."

In English, math, science and at home, Paul has been called on the carpet many times for drawing when he shouldn't. But during his freshman year, he learned some important lessons about harnessing his talent.

For starters, he learned that the demons, space creatures and superheroes he loves to draw for himself and friends aren't going to get him into a good art school — and Paul has his eye on Detroit's Center for Creative Studies.

He tries to force himself to draw more still lifes, portraits and landscapes.

Paul plans to design and paint a mural on his bedroom wall, but, says his mother: "I don't want his little brother to wake up screaming. … I keep reminding him of the pretty flowers and things he used to draw for me."

Straus says many teenagers like Paul gravitate to comic-book art. "It's what they're interested in at this age, and I have to push them to more classical drawing and to get a feel for form and color and composition."

Paul also learned from Straus and his mother that computer and other academic skills will be as important to his success as his ability to draw. So much of today's commercial art — newspaper graphics, advertisements, architect's renderings — is done on computers.

Students who are aspiring painters, dancers, actors or musicians often want to pursue only those activities. But that isn't all it takes to have a successful career in the arts. Here are some tips for following your dream of becoming a famous — or at least not a starving — artist:

☆ Don't forsake academics. Get good grades in language arts, math, social studies, history. A well-rounded, well-educated artist has far more to draw on for his or her work.

☆ Speaking and writing skills are critical because artists will need to convey their ideas in many ways.

☆ Learn to work in teams. Take advantage of classroom lessons that emphasize group projects and play a team sport to learn how to depend on and support others.

☆ Learn to use computers. They figure in almost everything these days.

continued ▶

STRATEGIES FOR SUCCESS

PAUL WHEAT

Paul *spends every available moment drawing. His room looks it.*

☆ **Age:** 15

☆ **School:** Southfield High, sophomore

☆ **Educational goal:** To attend a prestigious art school and maybe become a cartoonist or animation specialist.

☆ **Likes:** Drawing demons and robots, football and going to the forest and natural places.

☆ **Dislikes:** Being grounded, stress and history.

☆**Quote:** "Sometimes it seems like I'm always grounded; and when I'm grounded, it's for the whole semester. That happens about every third semester. If my parents tell me I can't draw when I'm grounded, I write stories — horror stories." ○

From the time he was a toddler, Paul was encouraged to draw. Two of his uncles are professional artists and they spent a lot of time teaching Paul about shadows, depth and composition.

Paul's second-grade teacher gave him a book on drawing and urged him to sketch whenever he finished assignments early or had free time in class.

"It seems like somebody has always been there," he says.

continued ▼

☆ Ask teachers lots of questions. Find out if your teacher can recommend someone who gives private lessons.

☆ Draw, sculpt or create artwork from real life, not by copying pictures.

☆ Compile a portfolio of your work. Make sure you include a range and make sure it is neatly put together. Whether you draw, take pictures, sculpt or work with other media, art schools recommend that you avoid trite subjects. They've seen far too many rock stars, sunsets, unicorns, cartoon characters. Musicians need to concentrate on classical works rather than pop music.

☆ Visit art galleries and look at other people's work. But look critically, not just at how aesthetically pleasing the work is. Look at what message the author or artist is trying to convey. Step back and see the big picture.

☆ Get an internship at a

continued ▶

STRATEGIES FOR SUCCESS

continued ▼

gallery or museum, where you can learn firsthand about art, crafts, history.

☆ Study the nuances in the world around you. Observe shadows and unusual colors and placement of objects. Listen to classical music and opera; attend musicals and plays.

☆ Take community college art courses, adult education courses. Play in your school band or orchestra or join a community music group.

☆ Go to summer camps that specialize in the arts. Financial aid and scholarships often are available. About 70 percent of those who attend such programs at Interlochen and other academies get financial aid. ○

But Paul knows that won't always be the case. Two years ago he bought a book about careers in art. It got him thinking.

"I've wanted to design my own video or own my own comic book company," he says. "But now, I'm thinking architecture is possible."

To keep even more career doors open, he plans to turn the mostly B's and C's he gets in school into A's this year.

Whatever career he picks, experts agree on one thing:

"There has to be an innate ability," says Tom Bewley, admissions director of the Interlochen Arts Academy. "The other 90 percent is hard work."

Paul *on his art: "I just can't imagine being happy doing anything else."*

Weirdness was fun but misunderstood

Nat Synowiec has always stood out in a crowd.

In elementary school, his peers admired him for the mini play he wrote and directed. In junior high, kids picked on him because he used bigger words than most of them.

And at Walled Lake Central High School, students and teachers were nervous about him. He wore a rubber chicken around his neck.

"They even thought I was in with a bunch of kids they thought were in a satanic cult or something," says 18-year-old Nat, who graduated in June. "It was ridiculous. We just dressed weird and wore green hair and stuff because we could. It's not like we'll be able to get away with it when we're 21."

The chicken, nicknamed Judy, doesn't mean anything, Nat says. He just likes it.

That's Nat — offbeat, creative, always pushing the envelope. He doesn't really care what people think of him. And he doesn't really care to explain himself, either.

"I'm not on a crusade, but I have to do what I want to do," says Nat, who loves theater and was part of Central's improvisation troupe. "If I do what others want me to do, I'll be cheating myself."

His ability to shrug off others' opinions was acquired the hard way — by working through some bad feelings that nearly overwhelmed him in junior high school.

Nat was angry at the world then and "thought that anybody who didn't like me was dumb." He alternately lashed out at other kids or himself, further lowering his self-esteem.

He can't explain how exactly, but Nat says he changed direction on his own — his parents didn't nag him — long before he established himself on the wrong path.

"Here I was, this little, grumpy, mad-at-the-world kid and I thought, 'What am I going to do at 12, change the world?' " Nat says. "Being mad at the world wasn't going to change what was wrong with it. Plus, it gets really annoying to your friends."

Nat's parents told him he could do whatever he wanted — even drop out of school. But they also reminded him constantly that he had the potential to do great things. That stuck in his mind. And so did his dream of becoming a Hollywood screenwriter.

Still, Nat says he never worked up to his ability in high school. He did enough to maintain a solid B average and took some advanced placement courses.

Some high school students just have to be different. They have to dress differently, act differently and think differently. Sometimes it's a mark of distinction. Other times, it's a curse. Here's some advice for how students who live outside the mainstream can stay afloat:

☆ Don't isolate yourself. It's hard to be different, and teenagers sometimes think it's easier and smarter to be a loner. But that could lower self-esteem and hurt your reputation. Besides, you learn more by interacting with others.

☆ Determine your strengths and get involved in activities that allow you to shine and interact with others who share those interests. If you're a good musician or actor, sign up for band or try out for a play. Then you can get positive recognition.

☆ Have a life outside of high school. Get active in a church youth group, scouting, community theater or coaching

continued ▶

continued ▼

sports. You'll get feedback from a different group of people and develop different strengths and talents.

☆ The pressure to be one of the bunch is intense in high school. Many students can't buck it. Be proud that you can. And remember that many students may ridicule or tease you because they are jealous.

☆ Get to know all kinds of students, from all kinds of different groups — jocks, special education students, brains. If you're open to others, they will be more open to you — quirks and all. ○

STRATEGIES FOR SUCCESS

Busywork was his downfall, he says. He often blew it off. The rote drills in math and repetitive exercises in science seemed a waste of time. He preferred meaty projects and hands-on activities.

"It's like I'd ask my teachers, 'Why would you make me do this?' " Nat says of the drills. "And they'd say, 'It's to reinforce this or that principle.' Well, if I already knew the principle, I wouldn't do the exercise. Sure, I got in trouble for it. But it's not like it destroyed my life or anything."

Nat's grades aren't what will earn him success, says Jim McKee, Nat's guidance counselor at Central.

"It's those other characteristics he has that will really set him apart. He's the kind of kid who, instead of saying, 'Pity, pity, pity me,' says, 'I have to move forward with my life.' "

And, McKee says, Nat's ability to be open-minded and sensitive to differences, to ask questions and to take responsibility for himself will be the keys to his success.

"Nat even learned along the way that sometimes when he felt students wanted to get him or they were less than kind to him, they were real envious and uncomfortable with his ability to be his own man," McKee says.

Nat plans to attend Michigan State University beginning with the winter semester. He wants to try out for local plays in the fall and delay getting back to the academic grind. After two years, he hopes to transfer to the University of Michigan and study English. He says he'd rather take his basic humanities, general science and English courses at MSU, where he thinks they'll be easier — and a little cheaper.

Nat has always had a lot of friends. He hangs out now with some of the smartest students in his class. Many were outcasts at one point or another.

But some of Nat's most treasured friends are the doctors, engineers and lawyers he met through Eagle Scouts. He has been in scouting since elementary school and says he often connected better with the leaders than his peers. The adults guided him, encouraged him, boosted his self-esteem.

"They're my buddies," Nat says. "They've helped me get to know and accept myself."

Having lots of activities and friends outside of school made it easier when, as a freshman, Nat was called names and beaten up because he wore his hair long in back and shaved the sides.

"You really need more than one world in which to know and base yourself," Nat says. "You see how you act in different situations and if you act the same with kids as you do with adults, you really get to know and feel better about yourself."

STRATEGIES FOR SUCCESS

NAT SYNOWIEC

Nat, without the chicken, plans to be a Spartan, then a Wolverine.

☆ **Age:** 18

☆ **School:** Walled Lake Central High, Class of 1994

☆ **Educational goal:** Major in English at Michigan State University for two years, then transfer to University of Michigan. Hopes to be a screenwriter.

☆ **Likes:** Performing — acting, playing his violin, singing. Eagle Scouts, his girlfriend.

☆ **Dislikes:** People who "just bow to the almighty dollar," hypocrisy, prejudice.

☆ **Quote:** "I know a lot of kids who drink and smoke and I figured someone's got to be responsible. I could either do it with them, or clean up after them. I chose to clean up after them. Whoa!" ○

QUOTES FROM TEENS!

"I'm not on a crusade, but I have to do what I want to do. If I do what others want me to do, I'll be cheating myself."

NAT SYNOWIEC, 18

Going along isn't getting ahead

Many high school kids face tough challenges involving pressures to join gangs or activities that could put them in serious trouble. Here's some advice to avoid the pitfalls:

☆ Find ways to keep busy and out of contact with the troublemakers. Get involved in sports or extracurriculars. Get a part-time job. Do volunteer work.

☆ Don't be lured by the idea that you'll be more popular or accepted. Joining a gang won't get you to college or give you a well-paying job. Good grades will.

☆ Expand your horizons. Get to know people of other cultures. Don't set up barriers. You'll have to learn to get along with people from all kinds of backgrounds as you go through life.

☆ Try to find an adult ally — a parent, a teacher or a family friend, someone you can trust and whose opinion you respect. Seek them out when you're being pressured and talk about it. They've been there, too. ○

College was Ivan Samano's goal "since forever." Getting there while avoiding a clash of cultures was the hardest work.

Many of Ivan's Chaldean friends at Sterling Heights High School were gang members. And Ivan spent his four years in school balancing loyalties, his Chaldean heritage and his grades.

"Some of my Chaldean friends — they'd ask, 'Why do you want to hang with white guys?' Or, 'Come on and help us take care of some of the whites.'

"All these guys were my friends, brothers. But I wouldn't affiliate with them that way," Ivan says.

He avoided some of the pressure by staying too busy to go gang-banging. He worked jobs at a Big Boy and a neighborhood coney and volunteered in the Beaumont Hospital emergency room.

His father, a high school math teacher, helped by accepting nothing less than good grades and "grilling everyone I was ever with that he didn't know … you can't get anything by the man."

"Not that I liked it all the time," Ivan says. "Sometimes I really resented it. But in the end you realize it's for your own good. I mean, I'm going to Wayne and lots of those other guys are just going to spend the rest of their lives working at a fast-food place."

Ivan will attend Wayne State University on a presidential scholarship.

In high school, he felt the most intense pressure as a freshman, when strong rivalries among ethnic teens spilled into the halls of Sterling Heights High.

The situation was an outgrowth of a natural ethnic pride that had grown, strengthened "and quite frankly, gotten out of hand," says Assistant Principal James Tropea.

Tropea created the American Club to help ease tensions in a school where 12 percent of students were born in another country and more than half speak a language other than English at home.

"We are one of the most culturally diverse communities in the state," says Tropea. "We have something like 30 identifiable cultural groups. So it was a natural thing for a lot of these kids to associate with others of their culture."

The American Club brought students of those different cultures together in a variety of social settings. Dinner at an Italian restaurant. A Chaldean Christmas celebration.

Ivan believes the club — and some serious and early intervention by his father — helped him avoid fights and stay fixed on the goal of college.

STRATEGIES FOR SUCCESS

IVAN SAMANO

Ivan *resisted the pressure to join gang activities.*

☆ **Age:** 18

☆ **High School:** Sterling Heights High School, Class of 1994

☆ **Educational goal:** To complete medical school and become a dermatologist.

☆ **Likes:** Shooting pool and playing basketball.

☆ **Dislikes:** People who drink and drive.

☆ **Quote:** "Parents just don't understand school and kids take advantage of that. Parents need to get more involved." ○

> "**I'm going to Wayne (State) and lots of those other guys are just going to spend the rest of their lives working at a fast-food place.**"
>
> IVAN SAMANO, 18

"Basically it's true — if you talk to someone and get to know them, you're probably not going to get into a fight or an argument when they bump into you at school," he says.

His father, Mark Samano, is a math teacher at Hazel Park High School and Oakland Community College "and the one person I most want to be like," Ivan says.

Ivan will be a premed student at Wayne, working toward another long-time goal — to become a dermatologist and "get a job where I can wear a tie."

"I just like the way it feels to dress up for work," he says.

A door creaks open and a light goes on

Blooming late is better than not blooming at all. Sometimes it's difficult to imagine resurrecting an iffy high school career in just a year or two. But pulling up your grades and participating in school activities for even a short time shows colleges and employers that you have potential. Here's some advice for late bloomers:

☆ Think about what you want out of life and talk to counselors, parents and teachers about what it will take to achieve your goals. If you want something badly enough, chances are just knowing what you have to do will inspire you to get your act together.

☆ If you're bored or don't have many interests, push yourself to sample new activities. Sooner or later you'll find something that excites you. Take a computer class, learn to dance, try student government.

☆ Accept that failure is part of the learning process. Don't let that hold you back. So what

continued ▶

Alittle soft-shoe, a lot of guts and a few girls helped rescue Mike Fletcher's mediocre high school career.

For three years, Mike had played it low key.

He did just enough schoolwork to get by at Walled Lake Central High School. He knew a lot of people but had few meaningful friendships. He didn't participate in school activities. And he got in minor trouble for smoking and leaving school grounds.

He was so uninspired that he tried to find a way to attend night school so he could work more hours at his two jobs.

"It was work, work, work for me," says Mike, 19, of West Bloomfield Township. "That was where I got satisfaction, you know. That was where I felt good about myself."

Then, in October of his senior year, Mike took a big risk. At a friend's urging, he tried out for the school musical, "The Pajama Game."

Beforehand, Mike hadn't even ventured down the hallway where the theater classes were held. But one day he peeked inside the auditorium and the students and teachers inside drew him in.

"They were like, 'Mike, Mike, come on in. We're so glad you're here,' " he says. "They were so welcoming and warm. And there were like 35 girls to six guys, so I thought, 'What the heck.' "

At first Mike got a bit part. Then, when one of the leads quit, Mike was asked to tackle the part. His dancing, singing and acting wowed his classmates, parents and even him.

"Everywhere I went I was paid attention to," Mike says. "It was incredible. It was a real ego boost, like people gravitated to me or something. I had become like a role model."

The acclaim helped Mike gain confidence. And that, he says, made all the difference. Knowing he could succeed inspired him to try harder in class. He went from earning mostly C's to snagging A's and B's. He devoured books like never before in English. And he started dreaming of careers — actor, chef, doctor.

"I used to think my path was set for me and I definitely wasn't going to some Ivy League school," Mike says. "It was more like I was going to do some sort of labor. Now, it's like the sky is the limit."

Jim Fletcher, Mike's father, recognized that his son was a late bloomer but had confidence that he'd blossom sooner or later. He noticed Mike changing during his junior year.

"I could see him starting to get more serious about school then. Really, he just finally matured," Jim Fletcher says. "This should have happened

STRATEGIES FOR SUCCESS

MIKE FLETCHER

continued ▼

if you don't get the lead in the school play. You might learn something along the way and maybe make a friend or two.

☆ Once you start turning your school performance around, don't look back.

☆ Let teachers and counselors know you want to improve and seek suggestions and help from them. Then try some of their advice. ○

Mike's *life changed when he tried out for the school musical.*

☆ **Age:** 19

☆ **School:** Walled Lake Central High School, Class of '94

☆ **Educational goal:** Unsure. Considering becoming a doctor, an actor or a chef. Attending Oakland Community College.

☆ **Likes:** Good friends, good acting, good literature, cooking and working with people.

☆ **Dislikes:** His insecurities.

☆ **Quote:** "If you think you want something, just go for it. What's there really to be a afraid of? It's a learning experience whatever you do, wherever you go." ○

"I used to think my path was set for me and I definitely wasn't going to some Ivy League school. It was more like I was going to do some sort of labor. Now, it's like the sky is the limit."

MIKE FLETCHER, 19

STRATEGIES FOR SUCCESS

three years ago, but hey, it happened."

Mike says he just couldn't focus on school during his first three years at Central, and nothing his parents told him could change that.

Fear of failure, rejection and just plain looking foolish always held him back — from joining the football team, from actively participating in class, from asking certain girls out on dates, even from taking to the stage, a secret longtime dream.

And he was captivated by the money and independence he got from working at a party store and a golf club.

Now, Mike works just one job. He graduated in June and is headed to Oakland Community College to take math, English and political science — and his first acting class. He's not sure where he'll go from there, but he's sure he'll go far.

"The only thing is, I'm a freshman all over again," Mike says with a laugh. "Only this time, I'm going to try everything. It's like the whole world is new and you have to take advantage of everything you can. It's really true. These are the best days, and you won't get them back."

You've got four years to test your wings

TIPS

Abs-solutely necessary

All right.

You're in high school. Your mind is geeked — but what about that bod? You're going to need physical stamina for the challenges ahead.

Except for athletes, however, physical conditioning isn't stressed enough in high schools. You may have to get in shape on your own. As you work on it, keep these fitness tests in mind. High school students should be able to pass them, says Dr. Charles Kuntzleman of the University of Michigan.

Endurance: Males should be able to run a mile in less than nine minutes, females in less than 10 minutes. About 40 percent of male Michigan high school students can't do this; about 60 percent of females can't.

Flexibility: Males and females should be able to sit on the floor with legs extended in front and soles of feet touching a wall and touch toes or wall with fingertips without bending legs. About 40 percent of male Michigan high school students can't do this; about 15 percent of females can't.

Strength: Males should be able to do 30 straight leg push-ups in one minute; females should be able to do 20 bent-leg push-ups in one minute.

Males should be able to do 38 bent-leg curl-ups in a minute; females should be able to do 30 in a minute. About 50 percent of Michigan high school students can't do either of those exercises.

No fear, for sure

You're going to be making a lot of decisions in high school. You need to steel yourself.

"You can't sit around and say, 'What if? What if?' You have to get to a point where you are strong enough to just do it," says Teri Manning, 18, a recent graduate of Walled Lake Central High School.

You need to think about the consequences.

"I don't have any problems making the right choices because I always think about the consequences of my choices. Like, 'Is the three hours I'd spend at this party worth being tired out for eight hours of work the next day?'" Teri says.

And you need to take risks.

"You've got to go out for things, try things. You can't be scared that you won't be the best at it. The potential is always there. Take the risk," says Mike Fletcher, 19, another 1994 Walled Lake Central graduate.

Here's some more advice:

■ Make those decisions head-on. No wimping out. No fear.

■ List your options first. Then analyze what good and bad things would happen with each one. Then, make your decision and stick with it. Don't bounce back and forth and don't look back.

■ For career decisions, ask your counselor how you can tap into the Michigan Occupational Information System (MOIS). You can find out what career options are available, what kind of education and skills they require and if you have the aptitude. Some schools offer the service; most public libraries offer the service for a small fee.

A SURVIVOR'S GUIDE

Stress reducers

Making decisions is stressful. Lots of other things about high school are stressful, too.

Some people wield great powers over themselves. It's almost like stress rolls off them like water off a duck's back.

"I used to whine a lot. And one day I realized that I did not want to be known as a whiner. So I started working on my self-esteem. I have to keep telling myself, 'I'm a good person. I'm not a loser.' I've put up a real shield," says Teri Manning, 18.

Here are some other strategies for lowering stress:

■ Do the things you like to do — within reason. You'll be less anxious and more motivated to work if you pursue classes and, ultimately, a career that interests you than if you do something just because everybody else is doing it or because you think you'll get rich doing it.

■ Often teenagers get stressed out trying to be someone they're not. Some students try to be accepted by the most popular crowd. They'll try to dress like them, steer clear of students who aren't considered cool, etc. Pick your friends and define yourself based on your interests and likes rather than what others have determined is hip.

■ Plan for the future but live in the present. You can't control what will happen, so it's best not to be consumed with worry over it.

■ Try to locate the exact source of the stress. Everything probably isn't going wrong. The real source may be one thing: a poor relationship with a teacher, bad grades in one class, your parents bugging you about something. Once you figure out the source, it will be easier to find a way to resolve it.

■ Talk to a counselor or another adult you trust. Sometimes just airing your troubles makes them seem less overwhelming.

■ Try deep breathing, muscle relaxation or meditation to relax. Such techniques, which can lower blood pressure, help restore feelings of equilibrium and control. Most libraries and bookstores have books on stress-reduction techniques.

■ Exercise. Find an aerobic activity you enjoy and do it.

■ Counteract the negative things you hear throughout the day by thinking about the positive things you know about yourself. You may be a kind or musically talented person, or you may have a great backhand. Emphasize the things you like about yourself while trying to improve the things you don't.

■ Look on mistakes as opportunities. If you've gotten a bad grade or had your driving privileges revoked, it isn't the end of the world. Assess why it happened and see what you can do to turn the situation around.

Fritter not

You've been here before:

You've had weeks to complete a project, but here it is, the night before it's due, and you're just getting started.

What went wrong? Oh, the usual.

You frittered away your time while your project festered in the back of your mind.

It doesn't have to be that way. So next time, think ahead.

170

A SURVIVOR'S GUIDE

■ Set long- and short-term goals. Few people can learn to swim, write a play or fix a car the first time they try. They have to master things one step at a time. Set many short-term goals that will get you to the long-term goal.

■ Re-evaluate goals periodically and don't be afraid to change them.

■ Make lists of things to do and set deadlines. That way, you'll be able see progress as you cross off things. Set priorities, so the most important things get done first.

■ Be realistic. Don't commit yourself to things you can't possibly finish. Dreaming is important, but don't set goals you'll never achieve. On the other hand, don't aim too low.

■ Don't procrastinate. You usually end up with loads of work that must be done in a short time. You sacrifice quality because you're in a rush.

Don't get ground up

No doubt about it — studying can be a grind. It gets in the way of life, doesn't it? On the other hand, high school IS your life for four years. If you don't make the best of it, it'll leave a mark on the *rest* of your life.

You can figure this out. It isn't that tough.

■ Evaluate your study habits. Think about what clicked when you scored well on a test or turned in a great project. Try to keep recreating that. You may be better, for example, at spreading out studying for a big test instead of cramming at the last minute.

■ Separate work time from play time. Do homework all at once, whether in study hall, when you first get home from school or after dinner. That way, you don't drag it out all night. Getting it done early means play time can be more fun because homework isn't hanging over your head.

■ Study with a friend — but don't chatter while you're doing it. The buddy system works for many people who can't motivate themselves to diet or exercise. It also can work for those who need study support. Buddies also can work well if you need tutoring and are embarrassed or lack inspiration to get help. Find someone else who's struggling in the same subject and get tutored together.

■ Get a calendar or planner and use it. Write down when assignments are due and tests are scheduled. Getting in the habit of writing things down and referring to a planner will come in handy in the future.

■ Learn how to use school and public libraries and spend time in them.

■ Review your notes at least a couple of times a week. That's a quick way to keep track of what you're learning and what your teachers are stressing.

■ Reward yourself when you finish an assignment or score well on a test. Go to a movie, take a walk, head to the mall, play a video game — do whatever you enjoy. It'll provide a positive motivation to keep you going.

■ Recognize what you are good at and what subjects you struggle with. Get help where you need it. Study the subject you are having trouble with first. You'll feel better that it's out of the way and you'll enjoy the other stuff more.

■ Write down questions you have so you can ask them in class.

■ Hang out with the smart kids. Try to study with them and compare notes. Find out what works for them and try it for yourself.

■ Learn shorthand or develop a shorthand of your own that makes sense and will help you take notes quicker. Some students eliminate vowels from words or use only the first couple of syllables of words. Others take down every other word and eliminate unnecessary words such as "the" and "at."

■ Rewrite messy class notes. It'll make a better study guide when tests come up, plus you'll be reviewing the lesson by recopying the notes.

Have you derailed?

Jenna Mathias, 17, a graduate of Walled Lake Central High School, is headed to college to study physical therapy. She's rolling down the track now, but it wasn't always that way.

"I always used to think, 'I'm never going to get a good GPA.' and 'It's so hard to keep up good grades,' " she says. "But once I got on the right track, it wasn't hard to stay there. Really, the hard part was making the decision to get on the right track in the first place."

More advice:

■ You may need a new set of friends. Return to the group you hung out with before your grades dropped, your attitude changed or you started drinking or doing drugs. Or make new friends who are the kind of people you want to be like.

Rachel Apostolopoulos, a junior at South Redford High School who dropped out briefly in ninth grade, brought her grade-point average up from 0.8 to 3.2. She started by changing friends.

"Your friends are a big influence on you. If the people you hang out with have no morals or ambitions, they're probably going to bring you down and you're going to be like them."

■ Ditch dates that cause you trouble. Rachel was dating a skinhead; they fought a lot, which upset her and took her mind off school.

■ Realize the only person you're hurting is yourself. Rachel says she realized that if she didn't get a diploma, she'd have more trouble getting a job and making enough money to live on her own. "I just decided I'm going to do it and started motivating myself," she says.

■ Discipline yourself. Even though she hates it, Rachel does her homework immediately after school, before she goes out or to work.

■ If drugs or alcohol are the problem, talk to your parents, a school counselor, a health professional, a minister or someone else you trust. Check in the Yellow Pages under Alcoholism Information and Treatment Centers for local Alcoholics Anonymous groups. These groups also provide support for children of alcoholics. For drug problems, check in the Yellow Pages under Drug Abuse and Addiction Information and Treatment.

Teachers are people, too

Face it — teachers matter a lot. Even the bad ones hold the keys to your future, so it's wise to use strategies to get along and to get what you need out of class. Most teachers have your best interests at heart. If you treat them with courtesy and respect, and come prepared to learn, you won't have a problem.

These tactics help, too:

A SURVIVOR'S GUIDE

■ Can the sarcasm. Participate in class with meaningful questions and contributions. Show you are interested and prepared.

■ Be prepared for class. Read assigned material and even search for supplemental readings. That will broaden your understanding and ensure that you have something unique to offer the class.

■ Complete your assignments. That shows the teacher you're responsible and you care.

■ Come to class with the supplies needed — textbook, notebooks, pens and pencils.

■ Get to know your teachers. Find out what they're interested in, how long they've been teaching, what their likes and dislikes are. They'll try to know and understand you more if you return the courtesy.

■ If you don't like or can't work with a teacher's style, try talking to him or her first. Explain your situation calmly and politely. If the teacher isn't receptive, explain the situation to your counselor.

■ If nothing seems to help, and if you can't take the course from another teacher, get a group of students together and pool your knowledge. One student may have little trouble learning from a teacher that others struggle with. Putting your heads together can help.

■ Approach your classes with a positive attitude. You have to be there, so you may as well get the most out of it.

■ Sit in front. It sounds corny, but it helps tune out distractions and gives a signal that you are interested and willing to learn.

■ Don't distract others. Don't whisper, crack your gum, tap your pencil, crack your knuckles or pass notes. Be respectful of the teacher and the other students.

■ Don't take so many notes that you forget to really listen to what the teacher is saying. Writing down every word can cause you to miss the big picture of the lesson because you're so caught up in note-taking.

This is boring!

Given that not every day can be a Cedar Point ride, what can you do to spice things up?

■ If you're bored in a class, chances are you already know the material. Ask the teacher, your counselor and administrators if you can try to test out of the course. If you can and do, take something more challenging. Try advanced placement classes.

■ Find other students who are bored with school or certain classes and devise constructive, educational ways to improve the situation. For example, if you want to improve a rote science class, propose that the class — or just a team of students — study something special, such as pollution in the Rouge River.

■ Ask to do an independent study project on a topic that interests you.

■ Search the electives your school offers and experiment. If the choices don't thrill you, check out the course offerings at a community college. Community colleges are opening their doors more and more to younger students; many also have cooperative relationships with schools.

■ If you'd like to try a class offered at another high school in your district, ask your counselor if you can sign up.

■ Arrange your schedule so that a fun class such as gym or swimming breaks up the day.

A SURVIVOR'S GUIDE

■ Sometimes boredom can be a sign of mild depression. Lack of enthusiasm to do just about anything is cause for concern. Talk to your parents, a doctor or a counselor if you think your problem may be serious.

■ If you're bored because you don't know what to do or where to start searching for ideas, read something challenging and then write about it. Send a letter to the newspaper. Learn to play a new game.

■ If you're interested in mechanics, go to a garage and watch the mechanics work. Whatever you do, take the initiative. Put out the effort.

■ Do community service volunteer work. Get involved in helping others. There are so many people who need help. This will help you get a handle on the future.

■ Join a sport or club. Sports give many students an incentive to get good grades.

I say, you say

Teachers can lecture about it. Parents can preach about it. But when it comes down to resolving conflicts, it's mostly up to those directly involved.

"It's like if somebody old like a teacher comes up and tells you what to do, you go, 'Yeah, right, whatever.' You're more likely to listen to a peer because they understand you more. We know how our friends think and feel," says T.J. Valente, 18, a recent graduate of Mott High School in Warren.

More and more schools are adopting peer mediation programs, where students are trained to help other students work through differences. Here's what the five-step program at West Bloomfield High School entails:

Step 1: Both sides must stop any arguing or name-calling and talk directly to mediators, who, if requested, can be the same gender and ethnicity of those in dispute. Cases can be handled by more than one mediator. Mediators set a non-judgmental tone and stay neutral. Discussions are confidential.

Step 2: Each student tells his or her side.

Step 3: Each student gains understanding of the other's gripes until they reach a point where they are willing to work on solutions.

Step 4: They work out and agree on solutions.

Step 5: They sign an agreement; some students remain friends, others do not.

Getting out of the gang

Kirk Darby, 17, is a senior at John Glenn High School in Westland. But he used to be a dropout who ran with Detroit gangs.

"I just got sick of getting high and partying all the time. I put the gang-banging behind me and now I don't worry about whether I'm going to live to an old age," he says. "Now, I'm coming to school for me."

A great reason. Here are some more strategies for staying out of gangs and away from violence:

■ Stay in school. Police say most regular offenders are dropouts or kids who often get suspended. You're less likely to tangle with trouble if you're in class.

■ Avoid troublemakers. Says Officer Duane Gregg of the Redford Township Police Department's Gang Intervention Unit: "If you're going to hang around them, act like them, talk and walk like them, you're going to be treated like them. And you're going to pay the consequences that they pay."

174

A SURVIVOR'S GUIDE

■ Find a mentor — someone with experience to guide you through the shark-infested waters. Older people who have gone through the same experiences can offer advice and tell what worked for them. Ask older students, counselors, parents, teachers and even co-workers or bosses you trust.

■ If you're being picked on or recruited for a gang, avoid the usual places those people hang out. Stay after school for clubs or sports or to study, if necessary. If that doesn't work, tell someone at school. They can help arrange alternative scheduling and transportation and ask police to cruise by at certain times.

■ Get a part-time job. If you don't like school or home, work is a good substitute for occupying your time and keeping you away from less productive activities.

■ If you're already hanging out with a gang or problematic friends, and you're afraid to stop for fear of being beaten up or worse, blame your action on something or someone else. "If the kids start getting on your back, say you need to work for money," Gregg says. "Say you need to save for a car. Say your parents are going to ship you to Alabama to live with an aunt and uncle if you don't go back to school, which I've seen happen.

"It's better than winding up in jail. Or dead."

Beating the bullies

One South Redford High School student talks slowly. When he started high school, students would yell that he "talked like a robot." The name-calling and taunts got to him. "I would shut up and not talk. I figured, 'If they can't hear me talk, they can't cut me down.'"

Now, no one makes fun of him, partly because of the way he dealt with them.

■ Walk away from fights; cool off and think about it. "I got in a fight with a girl for calling me names. She had her friends throw things at me, call me names. … It got so bad, I had to get out of a class and threaten a school harassment complaint to get them to stop. It was stupid; it wasn't worth it."

■ "Don't take it so seriously," he says. "If you take it seriously all the time, you beat all down on yourself and you don't know when someone's joking."

Nothing sexy about it

You've probably felt it, a lift of the skirt, a pinch, eyes resting in places where it makes you feel uncomfortable. Or maybe you've seen it. Indeed, high school students across the country say there's more sexual harassment in their schools every year. In one July survey of 1,127 high school students, 55 percent said they had been touched, grabbed or pinched in a sexual way at school. That's up from 34 percent in 1983.

Dealing with sexual harassment can be tough. Many students don't want to get other students or teachers mad at them by reporting. But the tide is turning, and more and more, others are supporting those who report, says Robert Shoop, a professor of educational law at Kansas State University and a national expert on school sexual harassment.

Here are steps Shoop suggests to stop sexual harassment at your school:

■ Find out if your school has a written policy against sexual harassment. If not, find other students and parents who will lobby the school board to put one in place. There's no clearer message to teachers, students and parents that it won't be tolerated.

A SURVIVOR'S GUIDE

■ If they're stalling, let them know that sexual harassment in schools now is against federal law and that many school districts have been sued and lost millions of dollars.

The policy should define what harassment is (any unwanted attention of a sexual mature that interferes with students' education; no one has the right to touch them without their permission, or humiliate or embarrass them) and say every student has a right to a safe environment.

■ If you're harassed, first tell the person who did it that it offends you and to stop. If that doesn't work, report it to the person who handles such complaints, such as the assistant principal or a district harassment officer.

Punishment should range from counseling to expulsion, depending on how serious and threatening the incident was. False reporters, beware: Those who lie may receive the punishment that fits the harassment they made up.

■ If you're scared to report or fear retaliation, tell a trusted teacher, administrator or parent what's happening. "They can stand in the hall and see it happen and then they can report it instead," Shoop says. "That takes the burden off the student; it's not his or her responsibility anymore."

■ If you or someone else reports the harassment and nothing happens, get help from other students, parents and supportive teachers and put pressure on the school board to do something. No school board member likes to infuriate voters, especially when they're right.

Going with the flow

Teri Manning, 18, a the Walled Lake Central graduate, thinks kids use peer pressure as an excuse.

"You put the pressure on yourself because you want to be cool. Like saying in a class, 'He made me laugh.' Nobody can make you do anything unless they're holding a gun to your head. You do it yourself," she says.

That may be true, but it's hard not to go with the flow. First, you have to think things through:

■ Ask yourself what might happen and what you can do to prevent yourself from getting caught up in something you probably shouldn't. What would it cost you not to buckle under the pressure? Are you willing to pay the price if you get caught? How might other people react if word gets out that you've done this?

■ Talk honestly about your feelings. Tell your friends that you don't feel good about doing something or that you think you'll regret trying drugs or shoplifting or whatever. You may be surprised that others in the group agree with or support you.

■ Laugh it off. If you are in a situation in which you don't want to sound like a goody-goody by challenging your friends' schemes, say something like: "Why bother doing that — why don't I just go jump off of a bridge?"

■ Use your parents as an excuse. "My parents would kill me if they caught me."

■ Just say "No!" Sometimes it's the only way out.

■ Practice with a friend how to say "no" to a variety of pressures.

■ Make friends with people who don't get into trouble.

176

A SURVIVOR'S GUIDE

■ Get busy. Join sports, choirs, activities that will fill your time productively. You'll have less time to get in trouble. Remember that phrase, "An idle mind is the devil's workshop." Dumb phrase. Smart idea.

■ Set goals. Career goals, academic goals, social goals. And then ask yourself if having sex, doing drugs or drinking alcohol will get you closer to those goals.

■ Be yourself. Don't get caught up trying to act like someone or something you're not. That's when you get in trouble.

Helping a pal

Form your own peer groups around topics you need to talk about: not getting along with your parents, dropping out of school, gangs and violence, pregnancy, alcoholism and drug abuse at home, etc. Ask your high school's counseling office for help in organizing and letting students know.

Last year at South Redford High School in Redford Township, counselors offered peer assistance groups on alcoholic parents, trauma and loss, and academic problems. So many students wanted to join, there was a waiting list. They're doubling the number of groups and adding one specifically for ninth-graders anxious about starting high school.

"Kids have a need to talk," says Kake Pyrros, a Redford High counselor. "They need to know other kids are going through the same things in their lives, and they're surviving. They support each other."

Some keys to the South Redford groups' success: students refer themselves; they're not chosen or pressured. Each group promises to keep anything said in meetings confidential. And each is lead by a counselor to give an adult's perspective when asked.

Romulus High School has had success with such groups, too. They offer support for everyone from student moms to grandparents raising grandchildren.

Parents can start their own groups. They can learn from each other how better to deal with teens and young adults, Pyrros says. Redford has three groups for parents.

It's about R-E-S-P-E-C-T

■ Give respect and you'll get it back. Treat the adults in your life politely, even if you don't like them. The more restraint and maturity you show, the more adults will get off your back and treat you like the near adult you are.

■ Follow through on projects, homework and promises. If you say you'll do something, do it. Learn not to make promises or agree to deadlines that you can't meet.

■ Respect yourself. Don't let people take advantage of you. Stand up for your rights. How you feel about yourself is how others will treat you. Respect your body and your mind.

It's about S-E-X, too

Talk about peer pressure. Jenna Mathias, a 17-year-old graduate of Walled Lake Central High School, says some of her friends can't believe she hasn't had sex.

"My God, I'm not even 18 yet and they say I've waited so long," Jenna says. "No. I've worked so hard to get to where I can go to college. I'm not going to have sex and risk ending everything I've worked for. I can't see doing that."

A SURVIVOR'S GUIDE

Experts say 50 percent of teen pregnancies occur within six months of beginning sexual activity; 22 percent occur within the first month.

If you're worried about this topic, you need to keep some things in mind:

■ Think twice about having sex if your reason for doing it is:

You think everybody else is doing it.

You've been talked into it.

Your partner says having sex will make you a "real" man or woman.

■ If you have a serious boyfriend or girlfriend, talk over your feelings about having sex. If you decide not to do it, support each other. Don't send mixed messages.

■ If somebody says to you, "If you love me, you'd do it," you know they don't love you. If they loved you, they wouldn't pressure you.

■ Insist on being treated as an equal. If somebody doesn't consider you at least half of the relationship, that person isn't going to listen to what you say about sex and other issues.

■ Saying "no" gets easier after you've done it a few times. You'll feel stronger and more in control of your life.

■ If you don't want to have sex, don't put yourself into situations where it's likely to happen — in your boyfriend or girlfriend's bedroom for extended periods, in the car making out or at a party drunk. Plan activities that will keep you busy with groups of people or in public places.

■ If you've weighed the pros and cons and decide that having sex is the right thing for you, use birth control. Latex condoms are the best form of protection from sexually transmitted diseases (STDs), including AIDS. But they aren't foolproof.

■ Girls should get routine pelvic examinations if they are sexually active. That is crucial for detecting STDs and for overall good health. It may also be necessary for girls who want to use the birth control pill or other forms of prescription birth control.

■ Talk to your parents about birth control. That's difficult, but it's the right thing to do. They may be pleased that you're talking to them about it or they may explode. Either way, it's best to be open because that will show you are taking responsibility for your life and that you care what they think.

■ Before you talk to your parents, plan out what you want to say. Pick a time when you know you won't be in a hurry or disturbed. And try to talk to them before you actually start using birth control. That way you won't be approaching them with anything to hide.

■ Listen to what your parents say about sex and birth control. You may not agree with them, but they may come up with some ideas or alternatives you haven't thought of.

■ If you don't feel you can talk to your parents about birth control and sex, find another adult you trust and discuss the issues with that person.

■ If you can't confide in any adult you know, consult a health professional.

$$$$$ and ¢¢¢¢

You wouldn't believe the people who are well into adulthood and who haven't figured out the money thing. They spend like the U.S. Congress and save like it, too. They are dolts. Don't be a dolt. Do these things instead:

■ Save until you've reached your goal, whether it's for bills or college. Any number of strategies could work. But you've got to be disciplined. One South Redford High student needs $800 a year for car

178

A SURVIVOR'S GUIDE

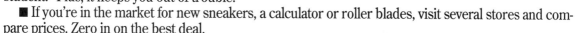

insurance. He works 15-50 hours a week as a busboy at $5.75 an hour. He puts his whole paycheck in the bank until the balance reaches $800. Then he keeps out a few dollars a week for spending money.

■ Volunteer to work weekend nights. "You save money right there because you're not going out and spending it," says the South Redford student. "Plus, it keeps you out of trouble."

■ If you're in the market for new sneakers, a calculator or roller blades, visit several stores and compare prices. Zero in on the best deal.

■ For larger items, such as cars, read consumer-oriented publications. Ask your friends and family if they know people in a business related to the product you want to buy. For example, find a mechanic who can tell you whether a car is problem-plagued, or what it should be worth.

■ Be wary of salespeople who push too hard for a sale. They could be pushing a bad deal.

Parents — you gotta love 'em

Teri Manning's mom is her best friend.

"She's always there for me. I went on my spring break with my mom. And to think, in seventh and eighth grade I was embarrassed by my mom," says Teri, 18, a recent graduate of Walled Lake Central High School.

Corey Stewart, on the other hand, thinks some parents set up barriers.

"Too many parents think their kids' problems are insignificant. It's like, 'What do you have to worry about? You don't have bills or kids to take care of," says the 16-year-old sophomore at John Glenn High School in Westland.

Here are some strategies for bridging the gulf:

■ Talk to your parents. Tell them about your life, your interests, your fears, your goals. Ask them about their lives, too. And really listen. You may be amazed at the good advice you can learn from their experiences.

■ Look at them when they talk to you and don't respond to everything they say with an argument. Tell them when you agree with them. They need some reinforcement, just like you need to know from them when they're proud of you.

■ Parents and teenagers who are having trouble should sit down and work out a contract, monitor it and change it if necessary.

■ If your parents are unsupportive or not present, seek out a caring adult who's willing to listen and advise you. Find someone you like and ask for help.

■ Don't alienate your parents. You are always going to have disagreements. But you can minimize the strain if you put yourselves in their shoes and ask them to do the same with you. Remember, though, if you want your parents to trust you, you have to show them you can be responsible.

■ Help yourself and your family out. If you break your bike, find out how to fix it and do it instead of asking them to do it for you. If your parents think working while you're in school is a good idea, find a part-time job and start paying for some of your clothes or entertainment.

■ If your parents are pressuring you to do or be something — be an all-A student, a lawyer, a pro tennis player — and you don't want to do it or are not capable of it, ask your counselor if you could make an appointment to discuss your goals with your parents present.

A SURVIVOR'S GUIDE

■ Sit down with your parents during a calm time and draw up a blueprint for how you will conduct yourselves during a disagreement or conflict. If you need a time out before you discuss the problem, let your parents know that that's why you may need to walk away for a while. Establishing rules for arguments can prevent hurt feelings and misunderstandings and will likely lead to better communication.

■ Use "I" statements instead of "you" statements. For example, say, "I don't understand why I have to clean my room," instead of, "You're so unreasonable making me clean my room."

■ Paraphrase and repeat to your parents what they've said to you. That way, they know you heard and understood them.

■ If none of this advice works and your parents are unwilling to cooperate, seek a trusted adult and find out if it's possible to bring that person in to mediate. Or ask your parents and your counselor if you can set up a session where all of you can discuss a problem or concern together.

■ Don't forget to take deep breaths and relax. You'll hear and respond better during a conflict if you force yourself to remain calm.

Find a stand-in parent

Lots of teens don't feel comfortable talking to their parents about sex, pregnancy, AIDS, drugs and other controversial issues. But sometimes, a friend just doesn't have the experience or knowledge you need to make decisions about such important things.

If you don't have an older sibling, aunt, uncle or cousin that you feel comfortable talking with, students say the next best place to look for an adult is school. Surprising? Not if you know how to look for them:

■ Try the obvious places first, say students at Romulus High School. The school is one of several in the state with a health clinic, where students can get examinations and counseling on almost any issues and administrators are trained, warm and confidential. If your high school doesn't have such a place, try your counseling office. See if you feel comfortable talking to someone there.

■ Get to know your teachers; talk to them and listen to them, says Deanna Bishop, 17, a senior at Romulus High School. "If they bad-mouth other students and let out their secrets, then don't go to them," says Deanna, who regularly gets advice from a trusted teacher. "Trust your instincts."

■ Give your teachers and administrators a chance to talk to you, to test whether they're interested in your well-being, says Kim Bolus, 16, a Romulus High junior. "If that teacher asks how you are and understands you, then they care a lot more than other people," she says.

■ Be cautious the first few times you talk to the person; "See how much you can trust them and how comfortable you feel," suggests Nathan Lockhart, 18, who graduated in June from Romulus.

■ Ask other students, particularly older ones, about who students can confide in.

A few words for moms and dads

Parents also need a few words of encouragement and tried-and-true tips for surviving high school along with their kids. Here goes:

■ Encourage your son or daughter to try things, to take healthy risks. Then, praise him or her for accomplishments or simply for trying.

A SURVIVOR'S GUIDE

■ Accept that your child probably won't be a carbon copy of you. Self-expression is important for kids — even it means having green hair and a pierced nose. Those basically are harmless ways of searching for identity and establishing independence.

■ Let your child solve his or her own problems. Your child won't learn independence and self-sufficiency if you always intervene. That may mean watching your child make painful mistakes.

■ Don't dish out punishment for making mistakes. Help your child learn from them.

■ Keep up the communication and bring your kids into family decisions. If you're going to establish household rules, let your kids have a voice in what those will be. Let them know their opinions count.

■ Respect your teenager's privacy. Teens need to have a space of their own — usually the bedroom. Tread warily.

■ Develop a support network of your own. When times get tough, talk to friends, other parents and other adult family members. You'd be amazed at how many have gone through the same struggles.

■ Go to school activities and to parent-teacher conferences and open houses. Talk to teachers and know what they expect of your child. Ask about your child's work and discuss it.

■ Don't pressure your child to go to the college of YOUR choice or choose the career YOU want. Offer your opinions and guidance, but let your child make the decision.

■ Encourage your child to get involved in more than one activity. All work and no sports or extracurriculars can be just as limiting as all play and no work. Students need to be well-rounded not only for college and career success, but for personal happiness.

■ Keep a calendar of important dates and deadlines. Remind your teenager what needs to be done by when. Missing a college application deadline can be devastating.

More on surviving

■ "The Teenage Survival Book" by Sol Gordon, Times Books, 1975, $16.

■ "Greetings from High School" by Marian Salzman and Teresa Reisgies, The Peterson's H.S. Series, Princeton Guides, 1991, $7.95.

■ "My Feelings, My Self: Lynda Madaras' Growing Up Guide for Girls," Newmarket Press, 1993, $9.95.

■ "Bringing Up Your Parents: The Teenager's Handbook" by Alex J. Packer, Free Spirit Publishing Inc., 1993, $12.95.

■ "How to Talk So Kids Will Listen and Listen So Kids Will Talk" by Faber and Elaine Mazlish, Avon Books, 1982, $10.

■ "You and School: A Survival Guide for Adolescence," by Gail C. Roberts and Lorraine Guttormson, Free Spirit Publishing Inc., 1990, $8.95.

■ "Growing Up Feeling Good: A Growing Up Handbook Especially for Kids," Ellen Rosenberg, Puffin Books, 1987, $11.99.

■ "The New Our Bodies Ourselves," Boston Women's Health Collective, Simon & Schuster, 1992, $20.

■ "Kids Can Succeed: 51 Tips for Real Life from One Kid to Another," by Daryl Bernstein; Bob Adams Inc., 1993, $5.95.

EXPAND YOUR MIND

Here is a list of books and plays for high school students, compiled from sources that include the American Library Association, Birmingham Groves High School and Berkley High School.

BOOKS

☆ "Things Fall Apart," *Chinua Achebe*

☆ "Watership Down," *Richard Adams*

☆ "Little Women," *Louisa May Alcott*

☆ "Bless Me, Ultima," *Rudolfo Anaya*

☆ "I Know Why the Caged Bird Sings," *Maya Angelou*

☆ "State of Siege," *Eric Ambler*

☆ "Sounder," *William Armstrong*

☆ "The Dollmaker," *Harriet Arnow*

☆ "The Handmaid's Tale" and "Cat's Eye," *Margaret Atwood*

☆ "Pride and Prejudice," *Jane Austen*

☆ "Go Tell It On the Mountain," *James Baldwin*

☆ "Something Wicked This Way Comes," "The Martian Chronicles," and "Fahrenheit 451," *Ray Bradbury*

☆ "The Long, Long Trail," *Max Brand*

☆ "Jane Eyre," *Emily Bronte*

☆ "Wayne Gretzky," *S.H. Burchard*

☆ "The Stranger," *Albert Camus*

☆ "Journey to Ixtlan," *Carlos Casteneda*

☆ "Rainbow Jordan," *Alice Childress*

☆ "Seven Days to a Brand New Me," *Ellen Conford*

☆ "The Party's Over," *Caroline Cooney*

☆ "I Heard the Owl Call My Name," *Margaret Craven*

☆ "The Crazy Horse Electric Game" and "Running Loose," *Chris Crutcher*

☆ "The Cat Ate My Gymsuit," *Paula Danziger*

☆ "On the Devil's Court," *Carl Deuker*

☆ "A Tale of Two Cities," *Charles Dickens*

☆ "Ragtime," *E.L. Doctorow*

☆ "Yellow Raft on Blue Water," *Michael Dorris*

☆ "Sherlock Holmes: Selected Stories," *Arthur Conan Doyle*

☆ "The Count of Monte Cristo," *Alexander Dumas*

☆ "I Know What You Did Last Summer," *Lois Duncan*

☆ "Love and Rivalry," *Doris Faber*

☆ "The Portable Faulkner," *William Faulkner*

☆ "The Great Gatsby," *F. Scott Fitzgerald*

☆ "Madame Bovary," *Gustave Flaubert*

☆ "A Gathering of Old Men," *Ernest Gaines*

☆ "My Side of the Mountain," *Jean Craighead George*

☆ "Lord of the Flies," *William Golding*

☆ "Morning Is a Long Time Coming," *Bette Green*

☆ "I Never Promised You a Rose Garden" and "Of Such Small Differences," *Joanne Greenberg*

☆ "Ordinary People," *Judith Guest*

☆ "Death Be Not Proud," *John Gunther*

☆ "Cowboys Don't Cry," *Marilyn Halvorson*

☆ "The Return of the Native," *Thomas Hardy*

☆ "Stranger in a Strange Land," *Robert Heinlein*

☆ "A Farewell to Arms," *Ernest Hemingway*

☆ "All Creatures Great and Small" and "All Things Bright and Beautiful," *James Herriot*

☆ "Siddhartha," *Herman Hesse*

☆ "A Portrait of the Artist as a Young Man," *James Joyce*

☆ "The Chant of Jimmie Blacksmith," *Thomas Keneally*

☆ "Fell," *M.E. Kerr*

☆ "The Shining," *Stephen King*

☆ "The Bean Trees," *Barbara Kingsolver*

☆ "To Kill a Mockingbird," *Harper Lee*

☆ "Gift from the Sea," *Anne Morrow Lindgergh*

☆ "The Brave" and "The Contender," *Robert Lipsyte*

☆ "The Giver," *Lois Lowry*

EXPAND YOUR MIND

☆ "The Call of the Wild," *Jack London*

☆ "The Fixer," *Bernard Malamud*

☆ "In Country," *Bobbie Anne Mason*

☆ "The Last Mission," *Harry Mazer*

☆ "Member of the Wedding" and "The Heart is a Lonely Hunter," *Carson McCullers*

☆ "The Truth Trap," *Frances Miller*

☆ "Gone With the Wind," *Margaret Mitchell*

☆ "Beloved," *Toni Morrison*

☆ "Somewhere in the Darkness" and "Fallen Angels," *Walter Myers*

☆ "Edgar Allen," *John Neufeld*

☆ "Everything That Rises Must Converge," *Flannery O'Connor*

☆ "Cry, the Beloved Country," *Alan Paton*

☆ "The Island," *Gary Paulsen*

☆ "Remembering the Good Times," *Richard Peck*

☆ "How Can You Hijack a Cave?" *P.J. Petersen*

☆ "The Chosen," *Chaim Potok*

☆ "The King Must Die," *Mary Renault*

☆ "The Catcher in the Rye," *J.D. Salinger*

☆ "On the Beach," *Neville Shute*

☆ "A Tree Grows in Brooklyn," *Betty Smith*

☆ "Red Star Over China," *Edgar Snow*

☆ "One Day in the Life of Ivan Denisovich," *Alexander Solzhenitsyn*

☆ "East of Eden," *John Steinbeck*

☆ "The Crystal Cave," *Mary Stewart*

☆ "Paint Your Wagon," *George Suilein*

☆ "Gulliver's Travels," *Jonathan Swift*

☆ "The Joy Luck Club," *Amy Tan*

☆ "The Queen's Gambit," *Walter Tevis*

☆ "The Lord of the Rings" and "The Hobbit," *J.R.R. Tolkien*

☆ "The Adventures of Huckleberry Finn" and "The Prince and the Pauper," *Mark Twain*

☆ "The Accidental Tourist," *Anne Tyler*

☆ "Lincoln: A Novel," *Gore Vidal*

☆ "The Inheritance," *Claudia Von Canon*

☆ "The Color Purple," *Alice Walter*

☆ "The Time Machine," *H.G. Wells*

☆ "The Once and Future King," *T.H. White*

☆ "The Caine Mutiny," *Herman Wouk*

☆ "Black Boy," *Richard Wright*

☆ "Dragonwings," *Laurence Yep* ○

PLAYS

☆ "Agamemnon," *Aeschylus*

☆ "Lysistrata," *Aristophans*

☆ "Oedipus the King," *Sophocles*

☆ "King Lear," *Shakespeare*

☆ "The Sheep Well," *Lope de Vega*

☆ "The Misanthrope," *Moliere*

☆ "The School for Scandal," *Richard Sheridan*

☆ "A Doll's House," *Henrik Ibsen*

☆ "Miss Julie," *August Strindberg*

☆ "The Importance of Being Earnest," *Oscar Wilde*

☆ "Cyrano de Bergerac," *Edmond Rostand*

☆ "Riders to the Sea," *John Millington Synge*

☆ "The Cherry Orchard," *Anton Checkov*

☆ "Pygmalion" and "Saint Joan," *George Bernard Shaw*

☆ "Blood Wedding," *Federico Garcia Lorca*

☆ "The Children's Hour," *Lillian Hellman*

☆ "Blithe Spirit," *Noel Coward*

☆ "Mother Courage and Her Children," *Bertolt Brecht*

☆ "No Exit," *Jean-Paul Sartre*

☆ "Glass Menagerie," *Tennessee Williams*

☆ "Antigone" and "The Lark," *Jean Anouilh*

☆ "The Madwoman of Chaillot," *Jean Giraudoux*

☆ "Waiting for Godot, *Samuel Beckett*

☆ "The Crucible," *Arthur Miller*

☆ "The Matchmaker," *Thornton Wilder* ○

What comes after high school

OK, so you're getting a high school education. What else do you need to get a good job?

The answer, increasingly, is more education and training.

The key to earning a good paycheck in America's changing economy — and not getting stuck in the millions of lower-paying jobs out there — is to learn the right skills.

You will almost always need something to offer beyond that high school diploma. The days when high school graduates could walk into well-paying factory or technical jobs are ending. Even blue-collar jobs increasingly require more and more skills.

While there are jobs you can get without spending years in a university, college remains the path to the best jobs. Either two- or four-year degrees after high school generally ensure more money and security, says David Small, assistant vice president for student services at the University of Houston.

"I wouldn't say it's essential, but it's very desirable," Small says. "Generally, someone without college peaks early in earnings and their income doesn't change or starts to go down before they retire."

The bottom line: Like a ticket to a hot concert, your ticket to a comfortable lifestyle is getting harder to find.

The need for higher skills and education is clear when you look at the better-paying occupations in America that are expected to grow the most jobs over the next 10 years:

■ Fourteen of the 30 top jobs on the list accompanying this article require a basic four-year college degree for success.

■ In 13 other occupations, a four-year degree would help, while a two-year degree often is necessary.

■ At least four jobs (doctors, lawyers, college faculty, top executives) require advanced degrees, with several other professions — especially teaching — demanding them for the best pay.

Only five of these better-paying boom jobs don't seem to call for degrees to get started: Truck drivers, corrections officers, auto mechanics, insurance adjusters and the entertainment industry.

Yet a closer examination shows that even in those fields, special training ensures the most success.

In the entertainment area, for instance, many actors and filmmakers have degrees in film, business, acting or related fields. Directing and producing movies, plays or TV films are highly competitive and skilled professions.

In fact, the field would easily make the college-degree list if it weren't for the few actors and entertainers who make it with little or no formal training.

Auto mechanics get better pay as they acquire more training and experience, and the complicated electronics and computers in modern vehicles need mechanics who know math and how to use sophisticated equipment.

Prison guards and insurance adjusters can start without degrees, but training by agencies or companies is required and two-year degrees sometimes are needed.

Truck driving, while it can demand relatively few skills in lower-paying jobs, requires advanced training or experience to move on to larger vehicles and better pay.

Heading the list of the well-paying boom jobs is the field of nursing.

WHERE THE BUCKS ARE:
30 Better-Paying Jobs That Will Grow By 2005

JOB	JOB GROWTH (IN 1,000s OF JOBS)	EDUCATION/ SKILLS SUGGESTED	MEDIAN PAY ($/WEEK)
Registered nurses	765	4-yr college	662
Truck drivers	648	high sch/special training	418
Systems analysts (computers)	**501**	**4-yr college**	**810**
Teachers, secondary	462	4-yr college	610
Marketing/sales supervisors	407	2/4-yr college	479
General managers/top executives	380	4/6-yr college	NA
Teachers, elementary	311	4-yr college	567
Accountants/auditors	304	4-yr college, exam	600
Clerical supervisors/managers	301	2/4-yr college	523
Teachers, special education	**267**	**4-yr college**	**550**
Licensed practical nurses	261	2-yr college	413
Human services workers	**256**	**2/4-yr college**	**479**
Computer scientists/engineers	**236**	**4-yr college**	**810**
College/university faculty	214	6/8-yr college	799
Corrections officers	197	high sch/spec training	470
Physicians	195	4-yr college/4-yr+ med sch	1,007
Lawyers	195	4-yr college/3-yr law	1,085
Social workers	191	4/6-yr college	489
Financial managers	174	4-yr college	764
Computer programmers	169	2/4-yr college	685
Automotive mechanics	168	special/industry training	408
Radiologic technicians	102	2-yr college	543
Personnel/labor relations	102	4/6-yr college	610
Police/detectives	92	some college/spec. training	529
Electrical/electronic engineers	90	4-yr college	892
Paralegals	81	spec training or 2-yr coll	489
Physical therapists	79	4/6-yr college	682
Insurance adjusters/examiners	72	high sch/spec training	430
Producers/directors/actors	69	spec training/coll possible	673
Psychologists	69	6-yr college	665
National Median Wage, 1992			**445**

Note: Select jobs may pay more or less.
IN BOLD: America's hottest jobs, with high percentage increases and more new jobs than replacements.

In numbers, registered nursing is expected to create more jobs by the year 2005 than any other occupation in the United States. Indeed, the 765,000 extra registered nursing jobs and 261,000 practical nursing jobs predicted by 2005 are only the tip of a coming boom in health care employment.

Six of the 30 top growth fields involve health care, with good opportunities in everything from X-ray technology to physical therapy.

Other hot fields:
MANAGEMENT: Three of the top 10 job-growth areas involve managing or supervising people in the complex workplaces of the future. But you often need business degrees or even MBAs to become marketing and sales supervisors, general busi-

HOT **JOBS!**

ness managers or clerical supervisors. **TEACHING:** With another trio in the top 10, this field will increasingly need special education teachers and vocational teachers who train people for the changing workplace. Other boomlets are expected for elementary and secondary school teachers. **COMPUTERS:** You could have guessed this one. The key jobs are programming, repair and, especially, using computers to analyze business or scientific information. The job of systems analysis is the nation's third-highest job growth area by 2005, with an extra 501,000 jobs expected.

The growth in lawyers will promote a need for paralegals to help them. The economy also will

WHERE THE BUCKS AREN'T:
25 Lower-Paying Occupations That Will Grow

JOB	JOB GROWTH 1992-2005		MEDIAN PAY ($/WEEK)
	(IN 1,000s)	(IN PERCENT)	
Retail salespersons	786	21	270
Cashiers	670	24	219
General office clerks	654	24	356
Waiters/waitresses	637	36	222
Nursing aides/orderlies	594	45	266
Janitors/cleaners/maids	548	19	291
Food preparation workers	524	43	216
Home health aides	479	138	309
Child care workers	450	66	NA
Guards	408	51	315
Teacher aides/assistants	381	43	265
Maintenance workers	319	28	NA
Gardeners/groundskeepers	311	35	276
Food counter workers	308	20	204
Receptionists/information clerks	305	34	319
Cooks, restaurant	276	46	245
Cooks, fast food/short order	257	36	NA
Hairdressers/stylists/cosmotologists	218	35	260
Medical assistants	128	71	309
Freight/stock/material movers (hand)	111	13	308
Amusement/recreation attendants	96	46	292
Sales counter/rental clerks	88	36	252
Hand packers/packagers	85	12	268
Recreation workers	78	38	287
Food services workers	77	36	216
National Median Wage, 1992			**445**

Note: Select jobs may pay more or less.

186

GOING DOWNHILL:

30 Occupations with the Largest Job Decline, 1992-2005

JOB	JOB LOSS EXPECTED (1,000s)
Farmers	231
Sewing machine operators, garment industry	162
Private household cleaners, servants	157
Farm workers	133
Typists, word processors	125
Private household child care workers	123
Computer operators, except peripheral	104
Packaging/filling machine operators	71
Precision inspectors/testers	65
Switchboard operators	51
Telephone/cable TV line installers, repairers	40
Textile drawout/winding machine operators	35
Metal and plastic forming machine operators	32
Bartenders	32
Butchers, meatcutters	31
Billing, posting and calculating machine operators	28
Central office/PBX installers, repairers	25
Central office operators	24
Bank tellers	24
Electrical/electronic assemblers	23
Cutting/slicing machine operators	21
Precision electrical/electronic assemblers	21
Telephone station installers, repairers	20
Metal/plastic machine tool cutting operators	19
Peripheral EDP equipment operators	18
Welding machine operators	17
Crushing/mixing machine operators	16
Industrial machinery mechanics	15
Directory assistance operators	14
Sawers/sawing machine operators	13

need thousands of new insurance adjusters and examiners, because baby boomers are learning they need insurance. And the continuing wave of cost-cutting and cost-efficiency in business will provide work for more accountants and auditors.

The nation also will need more human service workers and psychologists to handle our social problems — and more cops and prison guards to handle crime.

One tip when you're considering a career: Try an internship.

Small, of the University of Houston, says not only does an intern learn more about a job, but companies are increasingly hiring only people they have seen in action.

If you lack the training or education for America's good jobs, you're likely to wind up in one of the low-paying jobs that are also expected to grow in the United States.

These jobs are concentrated in stores, restaurants, hotels and offices: Sales workers, cashiers, office clerks, waiters and waitresses, food preparers and counter workers, receptionists and cooks. Other bottom-end boom jobs include janitors, security guards and gardeners.

You should be careful when using lists to select a career. Some of the good jobs on lists can be lower-paying if a worker doesn't have the proper skills. And some of the lower-paying jobs can lead to comfortable paychecks.

YOUR FUTURE

Hospital technicians, for instance, might start out as orderlies. Hotel desk clerks might move up to hotel managers. And waiters can become cooks, who can become chefs.

You also shouldn't limit your career options to jobs on lists.

Andrew Dubrin, a management professor and author at the Rochester Institute of Technology in New York, suggests these additional fields for consideration: court reporters, bank loan officers, financial planners and salespeople.

"There is always room for competent salespeople," Dubrin says. "They can make money in a range of industries."

Terry Mullins, business dean at the University of Evansville in Indiana, believes quality in personal services can be the path to economic security.

"In areas where people normally give low levels of service, if you give high levels of service, then you will succeed," he says.

These areas include home remodeling, catering, tailoring and software instruction, although Mullins says workers in those fields can earn more money with their own businesses instead of working for others.

Even occupations expected to lose jobs will provide paychecks to hundreds of thousands of Americans.

"If you're set on a certain career, then you might want to try it," says George Silvestri, a labor economist with the federal government. "A person should not be discouraged. I would go more with my instincts. Look for personal happiness and satisfaction. That's what's important in the long run."

Small agrees: "A person spends half their waking hours in their career, and a lot more time than that thinking about it, so it's imperative that a person obtains personal satisfaction in what they do."

Getting into college takes hard work

For weeks, handwritten notes scribbled on white index cards kept Ernest Adams on track as he searched for the right college.

Each day, he'd check the cards to figure out what he had to do next for every college on his list. Then he'd do it.

"It was like a job," says Ernest, who devoted numerous hours every week for more than a year to finding and getting himself into the college that he thought would fit his personality and interests.

Ernest was guided by a full-time college counselor at Cranbrook Kingswood Upper School, one of the state's most prestigious private schools.

Since Cranbrook expects all of its students to go to college, planning for college is a major undertaking there. Every year, at least two counselors do nothing but help students learn about and apply to colleges.

Your high school may not provide that kind of support. But, with a few twists, the Cranbrook plan is something you can easily adapt to your own college search.

Cranbrook's top counselor, William McIlrath, encourages students to get deeply involved in researching potential colleges. The more involved the student, the happier he or she is with the final decision, he says. That doesn't mean parents shouldn't get involved. But the student should take the lead.

"Once they become invested in the decision, more often than not, it works out. It makes them better college students," McIlrath says.

The first step is setting a price range, keeping in mind how much financial aid might be available. After that, McIlrath says, adjusting for academic program and social life on campus are the two crucial components.

The Cranbrook plan helps students do both.

Cranbrook students begin their college searches at the beginning of their junior year, and that's when Ernest started his.

Although Cranbrook stresses that students need to take charge of their college searches, the school also knows parents still have lots of influence in the decision. So, one of the first steps is talking to parents about financial and location considerations as well as whether there are colleges they want their son or daughter to consider.

Ernest's mother let him — and Cranbrook — know early that there was little money to spare for college. Her only requirement was that Ernest consider at least one public university in Ohio, his home state, for financial reasons.

Cranbrook juniors fill out a long self-report, listing independent study

---

Here's what you should take in high school if you plan to attend a four-year college or university:

English: 4 years
Science: 2-4 years, including biology, chemistry, physics
Math: 2-4 years, including algebra, geometry, trigonometry, calculus
History: 2-4 years
Foreign Language: 2-4 years of the same language
Other: Music and art.

Here's what you should take in high school if you're planning a career in the arts:

English: 4 years
Science: 1-3 years
Math: 2-4 years
History: 2-4 years
Foreign Language: Not essential
Other: Music, art, drama and dance.

Here's what you should take in high school if you're planning to pursue a vocational or technical career such as auto mechanics or heating and cooling work:

English: 4 years
Science: 1-3 years
Math: 2-4 years

continued ▶

continued ▼

History: 2-4 years
Foreign Language:
Not essential
Other: Shop and
technical skills courses,
such as electronics

*Here's what you should
take in high school if you
want a career in a
business field, such as a
bank teller, word
processor operator or
travel agent.*

English: 4 years
Science: 1-3 years
Math: 2-4 years
History: 2-4 years
Foreign Language:
Not essential
Other: Shorthand,
bookkeeping, typing

**Computer literacy
is helpful in all
careers.** ○

YOUR FUTURE

projects, unassigned books they've read and enjoyed, musical instruments they play, participation in athletics, student government and clubs and summer jobs or activities.

They answer questions about the location, size, environment (urban vs. rural, dormitory living vs. Greek system) and the amount of academic pressure they want in college.

By the time Ernest sat down in his first 45-minute meeting with counselor Charlene Rencher, he already knew a great deal about what he did and didn't want in a college.

"I knew I didn't want to go to the Ivy League. I'm into academics. I'm not afraid of a challenge. I'm not afraid of doing the work. But I didn't want to get wrapped up in that whole Ivy League mentality that a lot of people get caught up in," he says.

So, with Rencher's help, Ernest came up with a list of 20 colleges to examine further.

All were top academic schools with strong science or engineering programs. All were medium-size schools in the eastern United States. Most had a decent percentage of black students.

During his junior year, Ernest wrote all 20 schools, telling them he had played athletics, was interested in biomedical engineering and asking for brochures, catalogs and videotapes.

"That helped a lot. It made the schools aware that I was searching and they were on my list," he says.

That summer, Ernest read everything he could on the 20 schools.

By the end of the summer, he had narrowed the list to about a dozen schools: Virginia, Chicago, Northwestern, Syracuse, Tufts, Carnegie-Mellon, Emory, Ohio State, Duke and Georgetown universities and Boston and Hope colleges.

All are east of the Mississippi River and primarily in the northeast quarter of the country.

"I didn't want to be too far away from home. I don't want to spend too much money on travel expenses," says Ernest, who lives in Canton, Ohio.

Ernest, who attended Cranbrook on a scholarship program for disadvantaged students, chose to apply to only six schools. With a typical application fee of $50, that still meant spending $300.

In the weeks when he was preparing his applications, Ernest kept track of the details by paper-clipping white index cards to each application. Each card held a list of the pieces of information he had to collect for each application and the deadlines for submitting the applications.

That meant he only needed to glance at the applications to figure out what to do next for any college. It kept him on track and on time, with every application out the door well ahead of deadline.

Ernest's careful effort paid off. He was accepted at each of the six colleges: Syracuse, Northwestern, Carnegie-Mellon, Emory, Ohio State and

CRANBROOK'S COLLEGE COUNSELING PLAN

JUNIOR YEAR

FALL

☆ Attend the college night at your school. Talk to as many college representatives as possible. If your school does not have a college night, check with neighboring schools.

☆ Talk seriously with your parents about general guidelines for college: how much they can afford to spend, how far away from home you want to be.

☆ Set a budget for your college search — some colleges charge as much as $50 to apply.

☆ You will need a Social Security number for application forms.

☆ Register for the PSAT in October.

WINTER

☆ Check the exam schedule for the ACT and SAT exams. Make sure you meet the registration deadlines for the exam you plan to take. Here's the spring 1995 exam schedule:

	Registration date	Test date
ACT		
Cost: $17	Jan. 6	Feb. 4
	March 10	April 8
	May 12	June 10
SAT		
Cost:	Feb. 24	April 1
$13-$21	March 31	May 8
	April 28	June 3
Advanced Placement tests		
Cost:	April 1	May 8-12
$72 each		May 15-19

SPRING

☆ Take the SAT or ACT exams.
☆ Develop a preliminary list of college choices.

☆ Start thinking about essays you must write for your application. Set aside two or three pages in a notebook and jot down ideas about yourself. Make notes on anecdotes that would help tell the story of the "real you."

SUMMER

☆ Read about possible college choices. You'll find catalogs and other materials in public libraries.

☆ Write to colleges for more information and, if you're able, visit several schools. If you're taking a summer vacation, try to work a college visit into the trip.

☆ After you've read brochures, catalogs and visited campuses, refine your list of possible college choices.

☆ Write for applications.

☆ Review your experiences to decide which might make suitable topics for college essays. Be honest with yourself!

SENIOR YEAR

FALL

☆ Make copies of all college application materials.

☆ Even though you're a senior, you can still meet with college representatives when they visit your high school. Remember that by now, you're doing some serious selling — and so are they.

☆ Do you need to take the SAT or ACT again? Check the fall exam schedule and make sure you register in time.

☆ If possible, make weekend visits to colleges you're considering.

☆ Decide which teachers will write evaluations for you.

☆ Plan a schedule for completing your applications and keep a separate calendar of deadlines. Make

sure you allow adequate time to avoid unnecessary pressure.

WINTER

☆ Financial aid forms generally arrive at high schools in December. Get a copy early, complete and mail it off in January. (In some cases, your high school counselor may ask to review the form before you mail it in.)

SPRING

☆ If you're placed on a "wait list," discuss that with your adviser.

☆ Accept or reject offers of admission no later than May 1 — unless the college requires an answer sooner.

☆ Notify all colleges to which you've applied of your final decision. Do this in writing and thank the admissions committee for their consideration.

☆ Tell your counselor of your final choice.

Good luck! ○

Many educators insist you can't study for the Scholastic Assessment Test or the American College Test. You can't cram 11 years of schooling into a semester, they say. You've either learned the material or you haven't.

But books and courses can help you learn test-taking tips and some of the secrets of the college entrance exams.

☆ Ask your counselor if your school will be offering tutoring or SAT or ACT preparation courses.

☆ Check your library or local bookstore for special study guides geared to the tests. Some of the most popular are produced by Kaplan Sourcebooks. Kaplan also has test preparation centers around the country. Call 1-800-KAP-TEST for the center near you.

☆ The Princeton Review, which has an Ann Arbor office, also offers test preparation courses. For more information, call 1-313-663-2163, weekdays 9:30 a.m. to 6 p.m. ○

TIPS

Michigan high school students can turn to a computerized service to help them find scholarships and loans for college.

MI-CASHE is being offered by the Michigan Department of Education for a $15 fee. The service will direct students to financial aid sources that match the student's interests, career objectives, backgrounds and academic standing.

Students can best take advantage of the service during their junior year in high school or early in their senior year.

Applications for MI-CASHE should be available in high school counseling offices throughout the state. Or you can obtain an application by writing: MI-CASHE, c/o Michigan Department of Education, Office of Student Financial Assistance, P.O. Box 30428, Lansing 48909. ○

YOUR FUTURE

Hope.

Then came the hard work of whittling that list to one school. He visited several campuses and relied on Rencher to flesh out his feelings about each school.

Even though it was close to home, Ohio State was too big.

The city of Syracuse didn't offer much besides Syracuse University. Scratch Syracuse.

Michigan's Hope College in the small town of Holland was, well, too small and too white. "Everything's really slow around there," Ernest says.

In the end, he chose Northwestern University, the smallest of the Big Ten universities with 7,500 students. High-quality academic program. Close to Chicago. Enough black students for him to feel a sense of community.

And, not the least, a full-ride scholarship because of his financial need.

"It kind of got scary. It got really overwhelming for a while," says Ernest of the two-year search.

"I wasn't even going to apply to Northwestern, but Mrs. Rencher talked me into it. I can't believe I really got in."

Ernest *Adams said choosing the right college was "like a job."*

Mastering computers is all about attitude

"**P**lay around with it."

That's what the kids at Mumford High School's technical center advise each other when first meeting a new computer or computer program.

Don't bother with the manual. Well, maybe give it a quick look. The important thing is to jump into the program right away and start wandering around.

Sitting at a computer terminal in Mumford's technical center, Lakeisha Thues, 16, wanders all the way to South Africa the first time she tries out Internet's Gopher program.

"I'm just playing around with it … seeing what works," Lakeisha says.

Internet is the world-circling collection of computer databases often referred to as the "information superhighway." Gopher is a program that allows users to navigate from one database to another simply by highlighting an entry on a menu and hitting the "enter" button.

By hitting one button after another, Lakeisha hops from screen to screen, from state to state and, finally, to a computer at Rhodes University in Grahamstown, South Africa.

Something goes wrong. She tries to call up one of the South African files and it doesn't work.

No problem. Lakeisha tries something else, and a few minutes later she's hooked into a database of movie reviews in another part of the world.

Attitude counts for a lot in this kind of learning. Lakeisha is treating it all like a game, but it's a game driven by curiosity. Computer teachers say that may be the best way to acquire skills in new technologies, and many Mumford students agree.

"The people who do best want to find out everything they can about that computer, everything about how it works," says Kelly Simon, 17, who graduated in June from Mumford. "You can get jobs anywhere with it … if you know how to figure stuff out."

Some of Mumford's more computer literate students don't even bother with manuals when they first try a machine or program.

"I've never read the directions for anything. … That's just a way to get confused," confides Damon Hutchinson, 17, who graduated in June.

That's not an idle boast, says Claudia Burton, manager of the technical center. When teachers don't have time to wade through the documentation of a new computer program, they give the software to Burton, and she often asks one of her students to have a try.

TIPS

Computers and the programs they run are often baffling and intimidating, especially when someone doesn't have a lot of experience with them. Here are some tips for beginners from high school students who still get baffled occasionally but are no longer intimidated.

☆ Think of the computer as a friend. It may be an obstinate, hard-to-understand friend, but it's not out to get you.

☆ Don't worry about doing something wrong. There's almost always an "undo" or "undelete" button that can save you from disaster. If all else fails and you're completely stuck, just turn the computer off and start again. It won't hold a grudge.

☆ Something always will go wrong, so always remember to save your work. If you are writing a report, or even playing an adventure game, saving every 10 to 15 minutes is a good idea. Then if you do have to turn off the machine, you won't have to start over at the beginning.

continued ▶

continued ▼

☆ Don't worry if you feel intimidated by a computer or a program. That's normal.

☆ Be patient. When something doesn't work, try something else, and then something else.

☆ Computers are good at remembering and are incredibly fast, but they are also stupid. Always remember, you are smarter than any computer.

☆ If you don't have a computer and your school doesn't have a lot of them, find friends who do and ask if you can learn some things on their machines.

☆ But don't ask for help every time you get stuck. Figuring things out for yourself is the best way to learn.

☆ Libraries are good places to learn about computers and how to use them to search through databases for information. Find out what your local library offers.

☆ Play computer games. It helps develop keyboard skills that can be important in using more serious programs. ○

YOUR FUTURE

"I know that in a week or so, sometimes in a couple of hours, they will figure it out," Burton says. "This is their world."

Getting information, making sense of it and learning how to use it is what computer technology is all about. Skill in using the technology is already essential in many jobs and will become more important in the future, educators say.

Every public school in the state has some kind of computer technology training capability, though the extent of the training varies quite a bit from school to school because some districts don't have the money to devote to it, says Tim Staal, president of the Michigan Association for Computer Related Technology in Grand Rapids.

"It has been getting better," Staal says. "Ten years ago we had to pay $2,500 to $3,000 for a basic computer. Now we can get one for about $1,000."

Mumford students are lucky because the school's technical center, built with a grant from Ameritech, is one of the most modern and best-equipped in Michigan.

Just as important, the center is completely integrated into the school curriculum. About 350 of the school's 2,000 students use the center daily for everything from algebra to putting together the school yearbook.

Students who use Pagemaker, a desktop publishing program, for the yearbook pick up a wealth of basic computer skills when they learn how to download, crop and paste photographs and drag pictures and stories around a screen to design a page.

Even more important than knowing how to operate a computer is how to solve problems. Working with computers helps people develop critical thinking skills, Burton says.

"It makes them look at what's happening right now. They are in a program and it's not doing what they want it to do, so they have to figure out how to make it work," she says.

The lucky ones have been using computers since they were little kids, but you don't have to start young to be at home with spreadsheets, databases, and interactive learning programs. Burton recalls meeting a top official with a technology company who went all the way through high school without touching a computer.

"He didn't start until the first year of college ... but he had an open mind," Burton says.

A patient teacher or friend, a computer to fiddle with and time to do the fiddling — that's the prescription for success, Mumford students say.

It helps to have the right attitude, too, says Brandi Pearson, 15.

"A lot of kids come in and just start asking questions without trying to figure it out for themselves," she says. "That's not the best way to learn."

Schools should teach about cultural differences

"Our ability to reach unity in diversity will be the beauty and the test of our civilization." — *Mahatma Gandhi*

Nothing about the performance of the Carman-Ainsworth High School choir class hinted at the differences among the young performers.

No one sang sharp. No one flat. No one was out of sync.

The black, white, Hispanic, Asian and Arabic students blended as one as they sang Michael Jackson hits and songs from the musical "The Secret Garden."

But outside of class, in the hustle of the halls and chaos of the cafeteria, their differences are much more apparent.

"It's not like we go out of our way to avoid one another," says Renee Nassif, 17, a June graduate of the Flint Township school. "But there's tension. It's like you can get along fine with individuals, but dealing with groups … is another story. But everything here is so politically correct, you don't dare say anything."

Students come from Flint and Mundy townships and the cities of Flint and Burton. At first glance, the racially and ethnically diverse high school, with a minority enrollment of 25 percent, seems to be a model of

"Stereotypes *are always there," says Maysan Haydar, a senior at Carman-Ainsworth High School in Flint Township.*

TIPS

☆ If your school is not dealing with issues of diversity or teaching tolerance, ask teachers, administrators and even the school board to consider curriculum changes. There are many resources and community organizations that can help schools teach such lessons.

☆ Read books and watch movies that will help you learn about other cultures, their history, struggles, contributions and customs.

☆ Don't personalize issues. Tensions between races and ethnic groups often are heightened when people feel that they, as individuals, are being blamed for oppression or racism. On the other hand, don't blame individuals; try to talk about issues, history, politics and solutions.

☆ Challenge adults and peers when they use inappropriate language. Even if black students are calling other black students derogatory names or Arab students

continued ▶

continued ▼

are doing the same to other Arab students. Terms that come out of a history of oppression are always inappropriate when used against another person, no matter who is using them.

☆ Test stereotypes. Don't just buy into them. Do the stereotypes you've learned about whites, blacks, Arabs, Asians, etc. match with people you know?

☆ Talk to all kinds of people, especially those who are different than you — different in religion, culture, color. Try to determine what you have in common. Most likely, you'll find that all people want to be safe, productive, happy — just like you.

☆ If you don't know the answer to something about a different culture, ask — don't assume an answer or accept a stereotype.

☆ Ask teachers and other adults about contradictions that you

continued ▶

YOUR WORLD

multicultural harmony.

Few fights at the 1,100-student school have been racially or ethnically motivated. There have been no public protests over offensive programs or lessons.

But students at Carman-Ainsworth, like those in other increasingly mixed schools, may be just surviving rather than thriving on their diversity. And many experts say that's not good enough.

"Today, teenagers are not getting enough help in taking the next step in terms of learning to appreciate their differences," says Dick Lobenthal, executive director of the Anti-Defamation League in Michigan. "Until differences become something that is positive, relationships are tentative, limited and suspicious. That may enable us to coexist, but it will not enable us to thrive collectively."

Lobenthal says schools, parents and students need to do a better job of stressing the similarities among groups of people. Then, he says, differences won't seem to create such a gap.

Failing to build bridges, the experts say, could continue to erode the nation's economic competitiveness. It also could continue to spark the kind of rebellion that erupted in Los Angeles after the 1992 acquittal of white police officers charged with beating a black motorist.

Today's students must learn to celebrate and learn from differences to make it in the next century, experts say, when an estimated 75 percent of those entering the workforce in the United States will be minorities and women.

Isolating oneself will be difficult if not impossible as more communities and companies become more racially and ethnically mixed and interdependent. Americans most likely will work with, supervise, teach and live with people who are different from themselves. International travel and commerce will increase.

Right now, many students learn how to get along on their own — if they learn at all. Too many schools avoid or give only token attention to teaching students how to break down barriers.

Some schools have begun teaching about cultural differences and allowing students to make presentations about their culture; others participate in student exchanges with schools from other communities. But some schools tackle the issues only after a verbal or physical clash.

"One of the reasons it's so important for our kids to get a grip on this issue is that the adults around them haven't done it," says Donald Barr, professor of human service studies at Cornell University. "They look at the world and they see that we are asking much more of them than we are asking of ourselves."

Knowing the history and contributions of blacks, Latinos, Native Americans and other minority groups and their historical relationships with white people can help students understand the rationale for such

Choir *class at Carman-Ainsworth High School.*

things as affirmative action and the movement to compensate black people for their enslavement. And getting to know people of other cultures and experiencing their customs and beliefs can help students see similarities as well as differences.

But few teenagers are inspired to seek such interaction on their own. Learning about others and about tolerance is a struggle, and it often doesn't seem necessary until a problem arises.

"Stereotypes are there always," says Maysan Haydar, 16, a Carman-Ainsworth senior. "They come out for me during things like the Gulf War."

Maysan, whose family is from Saudi Arabia, remembers a student saying about Iraqi leader Saddam Hussein, "Is that your uncle?" after a news report on the Gulf War was shown in class. And Maysan, a Muslim who covers her hair and wears traditional dress, felt all eyes on her during a trip to the small, neighboring town of Clio.

"I was so scared some farmer with a pitchfork was going to get me," she says. "But I guess I'd be scared of someone like me if I didn't know better."

Maysan and other Carman-Ainsworth students have lobbied administrators to allow them to do presentations on their cultures and bring in guest speakers. Administrators usually approve the requests and students run their own shows.

That, students say, helps them feel proud of their heritage and provides an opportunity for other students to ask questions.

"You have to take it on yourself to learn about your own culture and

continued ▼

see in school lessons and in the world around you. Ask about poverty, racism, sexism and how those problems can exist in a democracy, where all people are supposed to be considered equal.

☆ Take advantage of exchange programs or opportunities to visit communities and schools unlike yours. See what it's like in richer communities and poorer ones; experience communities that are not racially integrated as well as ones that are.

☆ If your parents are bigoted, challenge them to look at things differently. But remember, they are the parent and you are the child. Sometimes it's better to just keep quiet while you still live at home. ○

STATS

☆ In Michigan, 77.4 percent of the 340,544 public high school students in 1992-93 were white, 17.3 percent were black, 2.4 percent were Hispanic, 1.4 percent were Asian and 1.3 percent were American Indian.

☆ For the first time in this country's history, white males are a minority in the workplace — 46 percent. They're expected to drop to 45 percent of the workforce by the year 2000.

☆ By 2000 about one in four Americans will be Hispanic, black, Asian or Middle Eastern.

☆ Three-fifths of all working-age women will be in the labor force by 2000.

☆ By 2000, 75 percent of those entering the workforce will be minorities and women. ○

share with others," says Kristina Byrd, 17, who is black and a June graduate. "You can't leave it up to the schools."

Principal Ralph Baldini urges students to take the initiative. He also encourages them to attend events sponsored by groups such as the Muslim Club.

"I don't know that you can legislate or force people to get along with one another," he says. "And we don't try to do that. We spend a lot of time here trying to send the right messages and teach kids to test stereotypes."

Baldini also meets regularly with parents and community members from various racial and ethnic groups. And the school system has begun teaching more about tolerance and diversity in elementary and middle schools.

"Each ethnic group has an avenue of communication," Baldini says. "And one thing we know for sure is that everybody wants to get along."

Barr says students must demand that their schools do more.

"That puts an awful lot of responsibility on the students," he says. "But taking responsibility is a part of living in a democracy."

Anna Diener, 17, a Carman-Ainsworth senior, agrees and sees a lot of hope.

"Already I see that our generation really wants to get along together."

Compassion starts with a little push

Angella Gralewski has always believed helping people in need is the right thing to do. But she thought making it a graduation requirement was ridiculous.

Not only was it totally irrelevant to anything in her life, it was sure to interfere with all the other things Angella wanted to do — get a job, go to Florida with the marching band, hang out with friends.

"I thought, 'Why, why, why? This is so unfair. This is so stupid. I have better things to do with my time.'"

Then Angella, 15, met Ernie Kernick, a 95-year-old resident of the Clinton-Aire Nursing Care Center in Clinton Township. After spending just a few hours with him, Angella didn't think the school's community service program was so dumb anymore.

"I really learned from him. And I really felt good spending time with him," says Angella, a sophomore at L'Anse Creuse High School in Harrison Township. "He just wanted someone to talk to and someone to listen to him. I learned that we all — kids, old people, everybody — want the same things in life — love, attention, compassion."

Teenagers also want to get into college, find a job and get a car.

Angella *Gralewski thought requiring students to perform community service was "stupid." Then she met Ernie Kernick, 95, her friend.*

Community service can be more than another high school chore. It can offer valuable insights into the world of work — and the world in general. Here are some ways to make the most of the experience:

☆ Determine what social issues, problems or community needs interest you and then volunteer to spend time with agencies or programs that address those things. If you don't like children, don't volunteer at a day camp. If you are squeamish about being around sick people, don't volunteer at a hospital or nursing home.

☆ Use community service as a way to explore a career that interests you. If you're interested in law or police work, call the local police station and ask if volunteers are needed for youth or antidrug programs. If you're interested in becoming a veterinarian, volunteer at the local animal shelter or Paws With a Cause, a nonprofit organization that trains dogs to assist people with disabilities.

continued ▶

continued ▼

☆ Make community service a resume builder. Get to your site on time, do more than is expected of you and ask lots of questions. You could walk away with a good job reference and a lot of knowledge.

☆ Observe everything. Watch how workers interact and how organizations work. See how effective your organization is at solving problems. If you're working for the Muscular Dystrophy Association, for example, ask how much money it raises in a year and what it has accomplished. ○

YOUR NEIGHBOR

Community service can be just the ticket.

It doesn't pay, isn't graded and doesn't usually teach quadratic equations, the causes of the Civil War or the meaning of William Faulkner's novels. But community service is designed to instill traits sorely needed in the world and on the job today — respect for others, social responsibility, tolerance and empathy.

In addition, experiences gained in the program can boost performance in school, sharpen understanding of social problems and give students job references and a better sense of what they want to do for a living. Some colleges are beginning to offer scholarships based on community service.

"Just like a picture is worth 1,000 words, an experience can be worth 1,000 pictures," says Jeffrey Howard, director of the Office of Community Service Learning at the University of Michigan. "A student can see many, many pictures of homeless people in the newspaper, but actually going to a soup kitchen will affect them much more. They'll become much more sensitive to the issue and they'll never lose that image in their heads."

Many of those who are being served by the students also learn a lot. In particular, they learn that today's teenagers have a lot to offer.

"For us, the link between the young students and the elderly has been a magical thing," says Nancy Spilski, activities director at the Clinton-Aire Nursing Care Center. "The young people bring innocence and the lighter side of life to our elderly. … The elderly always look forward to the young faces that come here."

Angella helped Ernie roll a bowling ball from his wheelchair and maneuver around the nursing home. Ernie in turn told Angella stories about how his father raised champion beagles and talked about the importance of family.

"I told her to go home and tell her mother that she loves her, because one day she won't be there," Ernie says. "Angie did and she came back and told me her mother felt wonderful."

Beginning with the class of 1996, the 8,000-student L'Anse Creuse Public Schools will require high school students to complete at least 40 hours of community service.

Bloomfield Hills requires at least 100 hours of community service; many other districts, including Romulus Community Schools, the Fitzgerald Public Schools in southwest Warren and the Southfield Public Schools have optional programs.

Some students come up with their own community service ideas or get credit for activities they are already involved in, such as coaching sports teams or helping an elderly neighbor clean house.

The schools post volunteer opportunities on bulletin boards, announce them over the PA and offer special counseling for students who can't figure out what they want to do.

YOUR NEIGHBOR

Nationally, 20 percent of U.S. school districts have or are developing community service requirements. So far, Maryland is the only state that makes it mandatory for all high schools.

The concept of community service isn't new. It's been around since the 1960s when educators started pushing students to get out of the classroom and get involved in — and learn from — their communities.

But the idea of urging and even requiring students to do volunteer work became popular again in the mid-1980s when politicians preached — and Americans bought into — the idea that government couldn't solve all problems. Individuals had to take responsibility for one another.

Community service isn't always greeted with open arms. Many parents and students resent it, at least at first, and call it forced voluntarism.

"Students come to me all the time and ask, 'What did I do wrong? Why do I have to do community service?'" says Dennis Burgio, community service coordinator at L'Anse Creuse High School. "I have to keep explaining that this isn't a punishment. This is a learning experience."

Community service isn't about supplying free labor or imposing values on students. It's about getting a well-rounded education. Research shows that students involved in community service actually get more out of school than those who aren't.

A 1993 U-M study of 90 undergraduates in a political science course, for example, showed that students who were given a community service project got an average of one grade higher and said they learned more from the course than students who were assigned a library research project.

In 1993, President Bill Clinton pushed through the National and Community Service Act, which created a network of community service agencies through which school-age youths may do volunteer work for college credit and tuition money.

Jeff Halpin, 16, a junior at L'Anse Creuse High School, says he was changed by his experience serving meals at a Mt. Clemens homeless shelter.

"Usually you see homeless people all scrubby and living out on the street and you want to stay away from them. I wanted to stay away from them," Jeff says. "But I spent time with homeless people, and I know that they're just like me, only they've had some bad luck."

Sometimes the benefits of community service aren't so obvious, says Emma DeAngelis, a community service coordinator at L'Anse Creuse High School-North in Macomb Township.

"I don't know that you can always measure good citizenship and compassion and responsibility or the kinds of changes the kids experience," DeAngelis says. "They are really survival skills and we'll have to see what the world looks like in a few years to see if community service has made a difference. … But it seems to me that we have no choice. We have to help one another."

"I learned that we all — kids, old people, everybody — want the same things in life — love, attention, compassion."

ANGELLA GRALEWSKI, 15

Students who get involved in activities do better in school than those who don't, experts say. Here are some things to keep in mind about joining clubs and groups:

☆ Participating in activities gives you a chance to meet other kids, learn new things and build your confidence.

☆ Good grades always count for more on college applications than the number of activities you're in.

☆ It's what you do in each activity — not how many clubs you're in — that counts.

☆ Pick activities that showcase your abilities or that you're interested in.

☆ Be organized and budget your time; it's a skill you'll need as an adult.

☆ Don't get involved in too many things — you'll be spread too thin.

☆ Make wise choices about how you spend your time. ○

202

EXTRACURRICULARS

Quality's what matters in club participation

Like millions of kids before them, Andwele Lewis and Andrea Gage were faced with a smorgasbord of activities and organizations to choose from when they came to high school four years ago.

Sports. The French club. Band and choir. Student council. The newspaper. School plays. So many choices.

Andwele, 18, of Detroit, chose the activities such as student senate that would showcase the leadership skills that stand out on college applications.

Andrea, 18, of Ypsilanti, looked for new things that interested her — and continued doing things she liked, including playing her cello.

Both approaches are fine, say the experts who should know — the kids themselves, high school counselors and college admissions officers who wade through the applications of thousands of hopeful high schoolers each year.

The important thing is not how many activities students participate in, but what they do in the extracurricular activities they choose, says Ted Spencer, admissions director at the University of Michigan.

Working hard and becoming a leader in a school group counts for more than just showing up for meetings, he says.

"If you had two equal students with equal grades who were both members of the National Honor Society, you'd probably give the one with the leadership position the nod," Spencer says.

"You could have two athletic students who lettered for four years and were equal, but if one was the team captain, he or she would get the nod."

Study after study shows that students involved in extracurricular activities in high school do better than those who aren't in clubs, organizations and on teams, he says.

Dolan Evanovich agrees. He's the admissions director at Eastern Michigan University.

"We're looking for students who will come here and be leaders on our campus, in our organizations, our fraternities and sororities," Evanovich says.

There are other reasons to get involved, says Gene Collins, the activities director at Stevenson High School in Sterling Heights for 26 years.

"Activities give you a chance to meet other kids and to know them," he says. And learning something new or working hard at an activity is a good confidence builder.

"Even if it's just being good at checkers, you'll feel good about yourself," he says.

EXTRACURRICULARS

At University of Detroit Jesuit High School, Andwele got involved in debate, the black awareness society, the school paper and the basketball team.

The last activity led to a big discovery of his high school years — you can't do it all. In his sophomore year, he realized how much time the practices took away from his studies and another goal — becoming class valedictorian.

"I had to make a decision about what was the most important to me," Andwele says. At season's end, he left the team.

While he still feels honored to have been on the basketball squad, his choice worked out.

In his four years at U-D, he earned a 4.0 grade point, became valedictorian and was accepted to the engineering program at Harvard University.

At Greenhills School in Ann Arbor, Andrea was faced with a similar decision. She had run track in ninth grade but in the 10th grade, she decided to focus more on her studies.

That's the most important thing students should keep in mind, Spencer says.

Activities are fine but what really counts is the grade point and the scores on the ACT or the SAT. Those categories make up about 85 percent of what admissions officers at U-M look for, Spencer says.

"I don't want kids reading that they have to be president of student government and letter four years in athletics. They're much better off when it comes to college if they do well academically," he says.

What happens too often is that kids get involved in activities and their grades suffer.

"A lot of kids feel their activities will offset their deficiencies in the classroom and that's just not the case," Spencer says.

Andrea found that dropping track gave her more time for studies and other interests. She took a dance course "even though I decided I was never going to be a dancer, it was a chance to learn something I wouldn't have otherwise."

She says students shouldn't just get involved in activities that look good on a resume or a college application.

"Don't just go for things you think will help, but do the things that you love," Andrea says. "I know I'm not going to play the cello in an orchestra when I grow up but I think it enriches you, especially things in the arts."

Andrea also took on roles in her school plays — "Music Man" and "Othello" — and became editor of her school paper.

She also kept her grades up and, as an honor roll student, was accepted to study communications at Boston University. But keeping it all balanced was hard.

"In my junior year, it was almost too much," she says. "It was really tough. I didn't get enough sleep — ever."

QUOTES FROM TEENS!

"Don't just go for things you think will help, but do the things that you love."

ANDREA GAGE, 18

"I got an appoint- ment book and I would write down everything I had to do. Sometimes there were conflicts and then I just had to make a decision — what was more impor- tant."

ANDWELE LEWIS, 18

EXTRA CURRICULARS

Getting a different part-time job with fewer hours during the week helped, she says. Instead of long hours at a candy store, she shelved books in the library after school and answered phones at a real estate office on Saturday mornings.

"Then I found I had time for homework," she says.

For some students, taking on extra interests helped them become more organized, not less. That's the way it worked at Grosse Pointe South High School for Rachel O'Bryne, an all-state cross-country runner and student government secretary in her senior year.

Andwele *quit his school's basketball team to help reach his most important goal – class valedictorian.*

"Instead of coming home, wasting time, hanging out and procrastinat- ing, it helped me budget my time," says Rachel, 18, who plans to study biology at U-M.

Andwele says he was able to keep straight the demands on his time with a trick from the business world. "I got an appointment book and I would write down everything I had to do. Sometimes there were con- flicts and then I just had to make a decision — what was more impor- tant."

At L'Anse Creuse High School, Libby Kluka did the same juggling act with track, volleyball, tennis, the honor society, student council and the French club.

When it comes to keeping grades up and participating at school, it all comes down to choices, she says. "You just have to be willing to make sacrifices — like not going out all the time when you want to or talking on the phone all night," says Libby, 18, who was accepted at the University of Virginia.

And there's one last piece of advice for the busy high school student:

"Do not get sucked into the TV," says Rachel, who limited herself to one program a week ("Northern Exposure") during school. "You'll come home and start flipping through those dumb programs and you'll waste hours."

Work — in moderation — doesn't hurt

The evening movie is about to begin as Candace Marquis squirts buttery oil on top of fluffy white popcorn, fills cups with Pepsi and plucks boxes of Skittles from under the glass counter at Beacon East Movie Theatre in Harper Woods.

It's almost 7:30 p.m., and Candace is well into her second job of the day. Her first and full-time job is being a student at Harper Woods High School.

"Work teaches you a lot of responsibility. And I don't like depending on my mom for a lot of things. This gives me a sense of doing something for myself," says Candace, who earns about $68 a week.

In Harper Woods, Candace is in the majority: 59 percent of last year's graduating seniors worked part-time while going to school. Nationally, 28 percent of all teens work, and they work an average of 15 hours a week.

Candace works for the same reason most teenagers work: money.

Candace Marquis, at her second job, working the candy counter at Beacon East Movie Theatre in Harper Woods. She's also a senior at Harper Woods High School. "I'm always tired, basically."

WORK RULES!

Michigan has several rules that govern employment of teenagers.

☆ Minors must have a work permit for all jobs except corn detasseling. (Seriously.) Permits are issued by the school district. Check with the central office to learn where to get yours.

☆ Students may not work hours in which they attend school.

☆ The combined number of hours spent at school and work cannot exceed 48 a week. Since most students are in school 24 hours a week, that leaves a maximum of 24 hours of work a week.

☆ Teenagers cannot work later than 9 p.m. if they're 14 or 15 years old or past 10:30 p.m. if they're 16 or 17 years old. Waivers can be granted to extend the hours for 16- and 17-year-olds but no waivers are available for 14- and 15-year-olds.

☆ Minors cannot work more than 10 hours in a day or a weekly average

continued ▶

WORK RULES!

of 8 hours a day.

☆ Teens cannot work more than six days in a week.

☆ Minors must receive an uninterrupted meal or rest period of at least 30 minutes. They cannot work more than 5 hours at a time without such a break.

☆ The minimum wage is $3.35 an hour unless a business is covered by federal wage laws. If it is, then the minimum wage is $4.25. A business is covered by federal law if it is doing at least $500,000 worth of business in a year — that means most fast-food franchises are covered by federal law. ○

SCHOOL AND WORK

The key to being successful as a working teenager is moderation. Candace and other students say they manage school, work and their social life best when they limit the hours they work. Research shows that students who work 15 to 20 hours a week do as well as and sometimes better than their nonworking peers.

The same studies indicate that students who work more than 20 hours a week take fewer math and science classes, miss school more often, spend less time on homework and do poorly on standardized tests.

In order to work, minors must have a work permit. The state prohibits minors from spending more than 48 hours a week in school and work combined, says Michael Dankert, chief of the wage and hour division of the Michigan Department of Labor.

But working students say some employers have figured out an easy way around that: They simply write the kids a check for the legal hours worked and pay them in cash for the hours over the limit.

If a teen's high school, which issues the work permit, believes a student is working excessive hours, the school can revoke the permit, Dankert says.

"They're in the best situation to monitor whether a student should be working and whether working is in the best interest of the child," he says.

Candace Miller got her work permit as soon as she was 16 and went to work at Wendy's.

"I got a job because I really need the money," she said. "But when I got my first paycheck, I just went like *ugggghhhh* because there wasn't very much there."

Candace says all of her take-home pay every other week gets spent on clothes, going out with friends and gas and insurance for her car. She has saved nothing.

"I don't make enough money to save money. I have so many things I have to pay for," she says.

Classes at Harper Woods High School start at 8:30 a.m., so Candace is up at 7 a.m. on school days to get ready. When school ends at 3 p.m., she runs off to an hour or two of cheerleading or softball practice.

If she's working that day, she's at the movie theater by 5 or 6 p.m. and works until about 11 p.m.

Then, she heads home and does homework until about 2 a.m.

"I'm always tired, basically," she admits.

But Candace says the grueling schedule hasn't hurt her grades. She has a 3.8 cumulative grade-point average, making her second in her class at Harper Woods.

"I'm the kind of person who knows what I have to get done. My mom wouldn't have let me keep working if I hadn't kept my grades up," she says.

But she admits to feeling stressed.

206

SCHOOL AND WORK

"I get everything done that needs to be done. But I get stressed because of all the things I know I have to get done," she says.

Her friend, Jeff Miller, 17, says his part-time job also has made him more conscientious about getting assignments done on time.

"I think it's actually improved my grades. I make sure that I do my homework. Before, I would put it off. I might just sit around and go play basketball. Now, I know I'm short on time so I'm more conscious of what I do," says Jeff, a senior who also has a 3.8 GPA at Harper Woods. He works 20 to 25 hours a week as a cook at Eastpointe Cafe in Eastpointe.

Although Candace and Jeff are top students, Paul Rasmussen, their high school counselor, says the benefits of working often are greatest for the marginal student who sees little reason to be interested in school or anything else.

"I often suggest employment to students who are seriously underachieving. It seems to help them get their life in focus. Often, they suddenly find the time to do what they needed to do in the first place," the counselor says.

Part of the inspiration may be the reality of seeing the kinds of jobs they could end up with if they aren't serious about getting a good education.

Jeff, who eventually hopes to earn a law degree, says minimum wage jobs are not for him.

"I want something easier. This is hard work. It's fun but I wouldn't want to be doing this when I'm in my 30s."

*"**I don't** make enough money to save money," Candace says.*

"Work teaches you a lot of responsibility. And I don't like depending on my mom for things. This gives me a sense of doing something for myself."

CANDACE MARQUIS, 17